PAINFUL JOURNEY

a Story of Escape and Survival

JERRY GBARDY

Copyright © 2014 by Jerry Gbardy
First Edition – August 2014

ISBN
978-1-4602-4152-3 (Hardcover)
978-1-4602-4153-0 (Paperback)
978-1-4602-4154-7 (eBook)

All rights reserved.

No part of this publication may be reproduced in any form, or by any means, electronic or mechanical, including photocopying, recording, or any information browsing, storage, or retrieval system, without permission in writing from the publisher.

Produced by:

FriesenPress
Suite 300 – 852 Fort Street
Victoria, BC, Canada V8W 1H8

www.friesenpress.com

Distributed to the trade by The Ingram Book Company

Cover Image: The Babangida Highway leading west to the Sierra Leonean Border
Courtesy: Jerry Gbardy

In Memory of:

My siblings, Cecelia and Beto, Uncles J Norman Bantoe & Thomas Giah, all my relatives, friends, and the thousands of innocent Liberians killed in the senseless war.

Table of Contents

Acknowledgement I

Introduction III

Chapter One 1
Growing Up In Tappita

Chapter Two 31
Build-Up To The Civil War: 1979-1989

Chapter Three 49
Making The Run

Chapter Four 65
Beginning Of Refugee Life

Chapter Five 79
Seventy-Two Hour Trek To Safety

Chapter Six 93
Waterloo Refugee Center Chairman

Chapter Seven 129
The Cairo Adventure

Chapter Eight 143
The Third And Final Run

Chapter Nine 161
Emotional Return Home

Chapter Ten 183
Coming Full Circle

Chapter Eleven 199
Rebuilding The 'House Of Cards'

Epilogue 211
References 213

ACKNOWLEDGEMENT

Finding the time to write this book was not an easy endeavor. All the time that I spent as a refugee, I thought – casually too – that I might one day catalog what I was experiencing for future reference. It was a prospect that I did not give serious thought, even after I left the refugee camps in Sierra Leone and immigrated to Vancouver, British Columbia, Canada.

Then it finally dawned on me. I could not have written this book if I did not get the support from my family. Joanna, for giving me the latitude to do what I love doing best, writing. I am thankful to Gerald for helping to organize the chapters and particularly to Jeryna for her proficiency in typing most of the work in this book despite having her personal school work to do also. I am extremely grateful for that and dedicate this book to them. I am also grateful to my nephew Kulah A. Parker for his regular phone calls from Brooklyn Park, MN reminding me to finish the book. Those calls energized me and indeed made a huge difference.

Juliana Kromah, tenki as they say in Sierra Leonean Creole for writing the *Creole* sentences in this book. Her contribution was helpful and invaluable. I would like to recognize the contribution of Justus Mirembe who made the initial cover design and laid out the pictures in this book. I am also thankful to my co-workers at the Coast Mountain Bus Company (formerly BC Transit), especially Said Brahma for translating the Arabic sentences into English and others who in no small way, had motivated me to complete the book including everyone who saw me writing while in the cafeteria and who urged me to hurry up and finish so that they could read my story. Similarly, my friends Leiman

Cooper and Bobson Sesay at the African Canadian Soccer and Cultural Association who had shown tremendous support and encouragement.

I would also like to thank Veronica Fynn, Adjunct Professor at the University of British Columbia for her critique but helpful comments. I owe my deepest gratitude to Dr. Isaac Bartuah Roland who was also a Liberian refugee and professor at the Milton Margai Teachers' College in Freetown, Sierra Leone. Dr Roland served as my *de facto* academic advisor. His contribution towards my academic pursuit when I was a refugee in Sierra Leone cannot be overemphasized. My long time University of Liberia schoolmate and friend, now a doctor of philosophy and author, Emmanuel Dolo; thanks for his scholarly advice and input. One person who has had tremendous impact in my academic life is Mr. William G Voahn, my English and Literature teacher in junior and senior high school. His teaching helped shape my love for reading and writing. Without the knowledge he imparted, I could not have been adequately prepared to write this book. I therefore owe him a humongous debt of gratitude.

Finally I thank everyone whose name unmentioned but in one way or the other, made writing this book possible.

INTRODUCTION

Liberia as a nation was embroiled in an orgy of civil violence for fourteen years. During that period, every Liberian: young and old; rich and poor; combatant and non-combatant; I mean just everyone experienced the effects of the war. All were affected including those who thought from the beginning that their tribes were not involved and did not consider the severity of the war while constantly making dismissive and divisive comments such as: "I am not going anywhere." "The war will not reach here." Or better yet, "The rebels know who they are coming for," many could be heard saying. And so everyone has a story of the war that is compelling and worth telling. But some stories are more compelling than others. Nevertheless all these stories need to be told. Telling one's story about the traumas of the war is in a huge way, another form of therapy.

Even though, I fled the country two days before the carnage erupted in Monrovia where I was residing, which spared me the horrors of being directly positioned in the line of fire, I lost family members and loved ones. My brother, Beto; Sister Cecelia; Uncle Bantoe and Uncle T; nephew, Darling Boy; and several other relatives were killed. Additionally, in Sierra Leone where I fled to, I faced a lot of adversities on a daily basis. A civil war broke out in that country also. What I experienced in Sierra Leone, to certain extent, was no different from what would have befallen me in terms of death or physical trauma, had I remained in Liberia. In the morning of the invasion of Sierra Leone, I came close to being killed. I even had to conceal my Liberian identity and Liberian accent to save myself from mob action.

In Liberia, many persecuted tribal members had to deny their ethnicity and families in order to stay alive. Others watched as their loved ones were butchered before their eyes. Some were caught up in the crossfire and still have the physical scars to show, while others may even have the mental scar that they will endure for prolonged period. If I had remained in the country, I cannot at this time say what would have become of me. Perhaps, as member of one of the persecuted tribes, I could have been forced to deny my tribal identity, just like the others, in order to survive or I could have been killed. Imagine at the University of Liberia Fendall campus, where thousands of internally displaced people were, my cousin told me a story that she was put under gunpoint and threatened to be killed if she did not disclose information about my whereabouts. The person who made the threat was one whom I had considered a friend while we were living in Monrovia..

Liberians are generally good-natured, cheerful, neighborly and fun-loving people. In terms of land area and population, the country is relatively small to the extent that it boasts of high levels of inter-connectedness. Thus it is fair to argue that in Liberia's contemporary history, tribal animosity did not exist then not until General Thomas Quiwonkpa, a Gio from Nimba County, fell out with his closest friend, Head of State Samuel Doe of the Krahn tribe from Grand Gedeh County in 1983. One may not know his compatriot he or she is having a conversation with, but deep into the conversation, it may soon be revealed that the person knows somebody or something that they both know and can relate to. But all that changed over a period of time when the entire nation descended into the chronic level of insanity culminating into organized barbarism. Author David Lamb puts it quite succinctly in the book, *The Africans*: "...very nice people doing terrible things to one another," (Lamb: 1987, xi). What makes it more disturbing and incredibly ironic is that the barbarism was committed by people who styled themselves freedom fighters, liberators, peace councilors, and defenders.

Consequently, over a period of time between 1979 and 1989, the country practically transformed from one which was characterized by peaceful co-existence to one imbued with anger, hatred, vengeance and score-settling. Comment such as the one below by Dr. Alfred Kulah a notable Liberian who hails from Nimba County, is demonstrative of the deep-seated anger and hatred that had consumed a large segment of the society and developed into one of the most horrific civil wars ever fought in modern times: "I am afraid that if they allow this man (Doe) to be killed, it will be recorded in history that there was once a tribe called Krahn in Liberia" (Berkeley, 2002:43).

Historically Liberia being a class society from the time of its founding where the minority group known as Americo-Liberians controlled the social, economic and political helms of power, and subjected the majority population known as the indigenous people to many forms of social and political injustices, anger simply seethed, awaiting explosion. However, it is not the intention of this book to delve extensively into political events that occured before the 1979 Rice Riots. Instead this book will briefly examine the political events of Liberia's recent past, from 1979 to 1989, which partially precipitated the war. For example, in 1979 during the Rice Riots when more than forty unarmed demonstrators were killed by the Liberian police and their bodies were not turned over to their families for burial, (Liebenow, 1987), the people became angry and that paved the way for the 1980 military coup. There was deep-seated anger developed when 13 officials of the ousted Tolbert government were summarily executed in the wake of the military coup and their bodies were not turned over to their families either. A year later in 1981, the military regime executed five top level military junta members including the vice-head of state. Then in 1983 there was the Nimba Raid followed by the 1985 November 12 Invasion of the country. And then when the Doe government used excessive force to put down the raid and the invasion, many Liberians felt the direct impact of the excesses. That engendered more and more anger ultimately leading to the war.

The war itself has caused considerable agony, grief, and anger. Am I angry too? You bet I am but not vengeful. The fact that a group of Liberians, (former soldiers, former officials of the Tolbert and Doe governments, academics, and professionals) would conspire and undergo training in guerilla warfare in Libya to launch a brutal civil war on the basis of ethnicity which forced me into refugee camps at the prime of my life, is the source of my anger. However that does not in any way provide me with the justification to buy the biggest Kalashnikov from

Eastern Europe, even if I can afford it, to go to Liberia and begin shooting everyone that was directly or indirectly responsible for the war.

Painful Journey: A Story of Escape and Survival is part contemporary Liberian history and part my life story. Thus I will attempt to do so with a great deal of objectivity. Why was I forced to leave this beautiful paradise that I had lived in from birth? In Chapter One, I have added a narrative on my growing up in Tappita, Nimba County. In Chapter Two, I will attempt to delve briefly into the historical events of the founding of the nation and into the period from 1979 leading up to the 1989 war. Chapters Three to Eight are devoted to detailing how I made the run and survived the turbulent years as a refugee in foreign countries and finally resettled in Canada. Moving forward, a detailed narrative of my experience during my visit to Liberia after seventeen years is in Chapter Nine. Chapter Ten will also discuss my second visit to Liberia that took me to Sierra Leone to visit the place where my refugee life began. Finally, Chapter Eleven will attempt to advance some suggestions on how to achieve reconciliation, economic development and improve the judicial system.

Consequently, I will invite everyone, be it Liberian, or non-Liberian, who may experience the traumas of war or ethnic violence, to use this book as an inspiration to tell their story also. Even if their story is deemed to be less compelling or insignificant, one thing is certain: it is grossly unique in its own way. Therefore I strongly believe that by telling one's individual stories, this is one best way to bring a closure to the tragedy in one's mind and contribute to the national healing process. Judging from the magnitude of the national tragedy, there is no doubt that a comprehensive approach is required in gauging and participating in the debate to solving Liberia's chronic political problems; albeit, we have to begin from somewhere. Every petty step germane toward rebuilding the nation is a step in the right direction. It is my fervent hope that this book will be one of those small but significant steps.

CHAPTER ONE
Growing Up In Tappita

There is an old adage which states: "School days are the best." For me, my days at the Tappeh Memorial High School were the best. I had good times at the University of Liberia. I had lots of friends that I hung up with. We had fun. But the difference between my high school days and the university days is that at the university, it was time for making decision for life. I worked full-time at the National Housing Authority and I had a family to take care of after my readmission at the university in 1986. I had dropped from the university at the end of the first year (1982) owing to lack of funding. In short, my university life was definitely a time to balance the art of taking care of family, going to school, working full time, and having fun with friends.

Comparatively, my life in high school was considered somehow carefree. I did not have to worry about what to eat, what to wear, and where to sleep. My parents, my paternal uncle, J Norman Bantoe, and other relatives were always there to take care of those basic necessities of life for me. My duty was to go to school, do my share of the chores at home and play football (soccer). I enjoyed every moment of those years.

I went to live in Tappita in the early 1970s after my father was honorably retired from the Liberian army. My dad, Joe Gbardy Sarwolor was a member of the Armed Forces of Liberia. He was enlisted in 1931 when it was then called the Liberian Frontier Force which was established in 1908. Its primary responsibility was to patrol the borders in the hinterland against the British and the French who were expanding their colonies of Sierra Leone, Guinea and Cote d'Ivoire. The Force would later become the Armed Forces of Liberia in 1962 (Carey, 2008). Later, its other responsibility was to collect hut tax from the indigenous population. My father joined the army probably between the ages of fifteen and twenty. Given the fact that his parents were illiterate, they only counted the number of farms cultivated and harvested after his birth. So as times faded away, so did the memory of number of farms. That was why he did not know the exact year he was born, but I will put it between 1905 and 1910. Albeit, he clearly remembered the year he was enlisted because his Americo-Liberian recruiting officers marked the year, which was during the era of Liberia's seventeenth president, Edwin J. Barclay. Sarwolor was not his family name. It was the name of the village from which he and his cousins had come to seek enlistment (the village no longer exists). His Americo-Liberian recruiting officers called him Joe Sarwolor (as in Joe from Sarwolor Town), his cousins, Johnny Sarwolor, and Willie Sarwolor. They had escaped the porter system in the hinterland in which indigenous men were forced to carry Americo-Liberian government officials in hammocks to villages and towns with no motor roads. Likewise, Zeaty Beah my father's younger brother, fleeing the same slave labor, crossed the border and settled among the Krahns in the Ivory Coast, otherwise referred to as Guere, got married and raised his own family. One of his sons, Beah Norbert, went on to be training commandant of the Ivorian national police. I have not seen him but our mother and the rest of my surviving siblings did. They stayed with him in Abidjan for some time during the Liberian war.

    When my father was honorably retired in 1973 after 42 years of dedicated service, we went home east to Grand Gedeh County and settled in B'hai, a very small town located on the Tappita-Zwedru Highway. It was my first time going there. Adjusting to a new life up country where there were no electricity and pipe borne water facilities unlike Monrovia and Kakata, proved a bit challenging for me for a little while. To complicate my adjustment process, I could not speak a full sentence in Krahn without adding several wards of English, which as a matter of fact, made the boys and girls in the town - most of whom spoke only Krahn - to poke fun at me all the time. Additionally, my Krahn accent was weird, which made it terribly embarrassing for me also. I had grown up in my father's large household speaking only English among my siblings. He had two wives: Ma Zawee, his first, who all the children referred to as mother because she raised all my mother's children including her own. Ma Zawee had two, Sayee and Sarah. My mother, who was dowried very young, by far younger than my father and Ma Zawee, birthed Payennon, Cecelia, me, Lacy, Beto; followed by my twin siblings, Zlay and Pajibo (Zaire). All of us - except Beto who was born in Kakata and the twins, born in Tappita - were born in Cape Palmas (Maryland County). Our eldest sisters, Sayee and Sarah were already married years back before I was old enough to recognize things around me. My father was transferred to Monrovia in the mid sixties and subsequently to Kakata, about 35 miles east of Monrovia.

In Kakata, I began primary education at a Catholic school, St. Christopher's in 1968. I dreaded walking six miles to and from school every day. Additionally, I hated going to that school because my classmates, majority of whom were children of Americo-Liberian families, made fun of my last name, Sarwolor, in the first week of school. Therefore, most mornings my father, with a piece of rattan in hand, would follow me all the way to school. He would use the rattan to whip me if I refused to go. He finally met with Father David, the Parish Priest to change my last name to my father's first. Thus my name became Jerry Joe. I would later change my name to my father's real surname when I left Kakata in 1973.

When in B'hai, where to live and go to school was a major nagging problem my parents faced. After considering various options, they sent me to Tappita in Nimba County, a city 35 miles west of B'hai which was much closer than Zwedru the county capital. In Tappita, I lived in the east end Gibson Town suburb of the city. It was from that location that I used to walk six miles to and from school. Coming from St Christopher's, a Catholic school in Kakata, my desire was to attend St. Francis, another Catholic school in Tappita, but my dad being a retiree, could no longer afford to pay my tuition. His retirement income of $22.00 per month was not enough to take care of the family and pay my tuition at the same time in a private school. (Before retirement it was $33 per month). In fact, it would take about three to four months before he would receive one month's pension check which was sent by the Ministry of Finance to Zwedru about three hours drive away.

3

Sometimes after five months, he would send me to Zwedru to get his checks, only to be told that, "Only one check arrived," or "No check here for your father." It continued like that for a few years. Finally, the last time I went there was in 1981 before I went to live in Monrovia. That time the officer in charge told me, "The Ministry of Finance has stopped issuing check to your father. They said he has 'died.'" I did not have the time to stick around in Zwedru to verify the man's statement because I was returning to B'hai to go to Monrovia for school. Besides, I knew no one in Zwedru to help me pursue the case. Well that was the end of it. I suspected that the disbursing officer was illegally taking my father's checks for himself. (In a developing country such as Liberia, that was highly possible). My father finally passed away on September 30, 1986.

Consequently, I enrolled in a public school, the Tappita Memorial High in 1974, the year it was elevated to high school status by the Ministry of Education with Ansumana Kromah as its first principal. Before elevation to high school status, it was a junior high school called Tappita Public School. The school is located at the north entrance of the city occupying about fifteen to twenty acres of beautiful landscape up on a hill with beautiful mango and palm trees waving their branches to visitors entering the city from the north side. Memorial High is the largest public school in Tappita and one of the best in Nimba County in terms of the qualified instructors and the high standard of knowledge they impart.

The rural city of Tappita is located approximately 153 miles northeast of Monrovia. It was the largest city in Lower Nimba County approximately 76 miles south of Sanniquellie city, the county capital. The 2010 population census puts the estimates of the entire Tappita District to 122687 people, according to the County Development Agenda (CDA) (www.emansion.gov.lr). It is located at a point where three highways meet: one going further south through the Gbi Forest to the port city of Buchanan, another stretching east to Zwedru, and the other heading north to Ganta. A rural airstrip owned and operated by the Mid-Baptist Mission, sits atop the hill to the west. The church also operated a health post and the Christian High School. We will get to that later in this chapter. The economy of the area was basically subsistence agriculture boosted by commercial logging and commercial transportation. A logging company, MIM Timber, operated from Tappita where it hired many residents of the city and surrounding towns and villages. Five major tribes lived together in peace and harmony in the city: majority Gio, followed by Mandingo, Mano, Gbi, and Krahn. Growing up in Tappita, I did not know what ethnic difference was. My friendship with my peers was based on a natural bond that developed and on nothing else.

While in Tappita, I became friends with two extremely smart guys who had had a tremendous impact on my life. First it was Robert Yarsuo Lormia and later Patrick Gonkarnue Lurlay. My friendship with Lormia started from Grade Six in 1974. We lived in the Gibson Town suburb of Tappita; he with his mother, while I was with some distant relatives living in the area surrounded by fruit trees: orange, avocado, guava, tangerine, grape fruit, mango, and many more. We attended the Tappeh Memorial High School (elementary, junior high and high school in one). The elementary was later separated from Memorial High. From school, we would find some change to go watch Karate movies at the T Musa Cinema, the only one in town showing movies weekly, bi-weekly or monthly. That ultimately was dependent on when Mr. T Musa would have the time to travel 153 miles southwest to Monrovia for movies. Those days, we watched Karate movies with actors such as, Bruce Lee, Wang Yu, Bolo, Fung Shih Yu, and Yasuaki Kurata (Liberian-given screen name, 14-10). Other actors with Liberian-given screen names that we watched also included: Bloody Fist, Kojama, Waterfong, etc. As soon as we came from the movies around midnight, it was time for cooking some rice with chicken from his mother's poultry. In the morning we were at it again, walking on the three-mile dusty highway to school. By the time we got to school, our white uniform shirts were partly red from dust induced by passing vehicles. During week-ends, we would walk several miles to his mother's farm to do some farm work and cut palm nuts. Those were the good old days that we relish.

From Grade Six till our graduation from high school, we were close friends (and still are) and academic arch-rivals. Robert and I always worked harder in class to out-score each other. As a matter of fact, he was my source of inspiration and motivation. During those days, when a teacher was distributing our marked test papers, I would be curious to know what his test score was and vice versa. If he scored higher than I, I would study harder the next time to beat him also. I remember at the end of the first semester, we were both slated to be promoted to Grade 7. He got the promotion. I did not simply because I had missed a science test with Teacher Dahn Borh (Mr. Dahn Borh was appointed Agriculture Attaché to the Liberian Embassy in Italy in 1982).

I needed to clear the incomplete in order to tally my grade point average but I did not. That cost me the promotion. When Robert left, I was utterly disappointed but only had myself to blame. Had I done the test, things would have been different. In those days, Tappeh Memorial High had a policy of granting double promotions to students with exceptional performances. Anyway at the end of the year, I was promoted to Grade 7 and of course, Lormia moved on to the next class. He was a step ahead of me now. I took it as a serious challenge. By the end of the first semester in 1975, I got promoted to Grade 8, and bingo, there Lormia was! In 1980 we were the only two to pass the University of Liberia entrance examination among students from all the high schools in Lower Nimba County who sat the exam.

In 1976, Uncle J Norman Bantoe got a job with the Liberia National Police and was transferred to Tappita. I relocated from Gibson Town to live with him and his wife, Aunt Esther in Mano Camp, west of the city. Later in the year, Aunt Esther's nephew Justin Pour and cousin, Edwin Pour joined me in the Bantoe household. At the close of 1976, my friendship with Patrick began. I cannot point to a specific incident on how it began, but it just happened. Patrick Lurlay lived with his parents in the central part of town about four blocks from my house. He was from a very large family by African standard. We became very close. Nothing or nobody could come between us. His dad, Mr. George Lurlay, had a lot of children. Many people seeing Patrick and me together everyday thought I was one of his dad's children. Mr. Lurlay was a medical practitioner assigned to a health post in Diala, a small town east of Tappita on the highway to Grand Gedeh County. Because of that, they referred to him as "Dr" George.

Patrick was in his early teens as I was but he was more mature for his age. He was a daredevil adventurer, never afraid to take risk. He would make a way where there seemed to be none. He had an air of dynamism and exuberance about him. Socially at that age, he knew many things that I did not know. He taught me how to play the guitar, the piano, and cards or hang out in the club. He used to play the guitar while we sang at many indoor programs organized by the school. We also performed at the 1977 inter-school Flag Day program. He was street smarter than I. But we complemented each others in many ways. We protected each other in every aspect. But Patrick was always overly protective of me.

During most soccer practices, we would be on the same team. That meant we would have each other's back during the entire practice sessions. That also meant that our side was unbeatable. This day other players protested. They wanted Patrick and me to play on opposite teams. We agreed. But that arrangement did not preclude Patrick from protecting me. A player on Patrick's team had inadvertently fouled me and play stopped momentarily. The guy came to me to offer his apology. While that was going on, Patrick barged into the guy and hit him twice before he could know it. I, on whose behalf Patrick was fighting, became the peacemaker. I held my man and pleaded with him from further hitting the guy. I was bigger in body size than the guy. I was capable of dealing with the situation myself but I was waiting for the time – as I always did - when the guy would be on the ball or around the ball. In the game of football, that is the right way to do it lest you risk being sent off. Patrick wanted none of that. His was a "hot stove reaction" decision-making style.

"No one fouls my Kibu and goes free," Patrick threatened. Kibu was a funny nickname we called each other. "Jerry if it had not been because of you I was going to fight Patrick back," the guy said.

In all fairness he could not fight Patrick one on one. In fact I was there and the guy and others around knew what that meant. If any other person got involved, it would have been a brawl. The guy's comment was only a face-saving measure because Patrick hit him twice without reply.

"Ok my man, forget it," I tried to calm the guy. Patrick went back to his position and so did the guy. Play resumed and ended without further incidents.

Patrick did not become part of the school team until late 1978. I enjoyed the sporting field trips. It was in 1975, the principal of the school, Ansumana Kromah who was also coach of the school soccer team, used to personally lead the team out of town. Besides the school team, the principal also coached the city team, Torwah. He would later be appointed as Assistant Superintendent for Development in Nimba County. Under Coach Kromah, both teams achieved record successes. He brought together students from all walks of life, irrespective of ethnicity and trained them to be better students and players. I gradually eased my way into the city team also from constant practising. Those trips took us to play Gboveh High in Gbarnga, central Liberia; Sanniquellie Central High, in Sanniquellie to the north; and Tubman Wilson Institute in Zwedru, to the east; and many other schools. Field trips for the city team took us to Toulepleu and Danane in Cote d'Ivoire. For the trip to Gbarnga, I was too young to play but I made the trip. I did not even wear a substitute jersey. But another teenager, William Barshall, was a regular on both the school and city teams. He was very skillful at ball handling, dribbling and making incisive passes. When we returned from Gbarnga, I began to show up for practice regularly to earn my way into the team. The coach recognized that and decided to give me a chance when we went to Sanniquellie in the latter part of 1975 even though I was still in the mid-teens. At that time, I was still timid playing among older and bigger guys. Central High was a fully fledged high school with high profile players such as Tokpa Kekpeh, Isaac Goodluck, Abdulai "Four-Wheel" Konneh (for his stamina, agility, physique, and strong tackles) and many others. Those were star soccer players who had been playing at county and national levels. As for my school, it was just rising to full high school status. By 1975 the highest grade was Grade 11. Memorial High graduated its first students in 1976. Anyway we were going to play soccer and not to participate in academic competition.

We arrived in Sanniquellie around 2 o'clock p.m., couple of hours before the game. It was my first time in that part of the county. After finding some food to eat and doing a little bit of sightseeing, the principal took us to a place to dress. I was not scheduled to play. There were other players who were better than I at that time. The game was hyped up. The more I thought about the many spectators in the city, who were going to the field on Central High campus, the more I got afraid to play. Imagine I had not played on the school team at home before, so I did not expect to play now. But Principal-Coach Kromah had other plans for me. He believed in me.

"Stick around, I might use you in this game if necessary," he said.

"Ok Mr. Kromah," I responded with little hesitation.

After dressing, we boarded the pickup truck to the field singing. Approaching the campus from a distance, we could not see the playing pitch owing to the large number of spectators who had enveloped it. We arrived to loud cheers. But when Sanniquellie Central High players arrived, the noise was more deafening than the one that greeted us. The game started without me. In the first half, Tokpa got a goal for the home side from a distance. He was a long range specialist with powerful shots. He would kick a football like a rocket fired from a projectile. By the second half we were down by two. During the course of the second half, our player nicknamed Arkran for his sliding tackles, got injured and the coach signaled for me to get dressed. I hurriedly prepared myself on the touchline. When I was ready, the referee waved me on to the field. Meanwhile Barshall, William Debleh, and others were controlling things for us but we could not get a goal. Play went on for a while until I had an opportunity to make name for myself and the school when a loose ball rolled between the goalie and me a few yards outside of the 18-yard box. Central High defender, Four-Wheel was my marker. He was one of the best in Nimba County. Four-Wheel came galloping at me like a hyena after a deer while the ball was still rolling on the left side of the goalpost. I panicked and shot the ball agonizingly wide over the bar. The spectators roared! I could not believe the miss. I had just missed a glorious opportunity to bring our team back into the game. On the way back to Tappita, that miss was the talk of my teammates.

By 1977 I had grown in the art of the game and had become a regular on the team. My position at that time was in the mid-field. In June of that year the school travelled to Zwedru. The city was the capital of my home county, Grand Gedeh. It was my first time going there. I played the full ninety minutes of the game. It was one of my best performances but in the end we lost miserably (4-1) to the Tubman Wilson Institute. What a run-of-the-mill way to be welcomed in my home!

At the close of 1977, I travelled with our sister school, Christian High to participate in the Ricks mini-Olympic. The sporting events were an annual affair hosted by Ricks Institute, a Baptist Church-run boarding school situated a few miles north of Monrovia. The sports director of Christian High selected the following students to beef up the team: Wuo Zarwolo and I from Tappeh Memorial High and Barshall, who had already transferred to Sanniquellie Central High and schoolmate, Obi Quoi. We arrived Thursday night and returned to Tappita Sunday. The trip was memorable. Our team reached the grand finale of the competition. On the way to the finale, we defeated the hosts on Friday, dispatched Elizabeth Tubman Memorial Institute of Caldwell, and dumped Bassa High of Buchanan in the semi-final on Saturday. We had a very powerful battle cry before, during, and after games. One person would chant, "When chicken white" the rest would respond, "It's white." The chants made us very popular and appear invincible on Ricks campus. It succeeded in instilling fear in our opponents who believed that our soccer prowess was propelled by some invisible hands of the gods. My teammates included, Prince Myers, Barshall, Goalie Obi Quoi, John Yehee, Augustus Jarry, Wuo Zarwolo, to name a few. The team was great and that final game was the game of our lives. Our opponents were the Charlotte Tolbert Memorial High of Monrovia. At that time Charlotte Tolbert boasted of Liberian national team players such as Waka Herron, Kofi Bruce, Teah Toe, etc. The game was broadcast live nation-wide on the ELWA Radio. In the end we lost to the better side. They were tactically better prepared than we were.

Upon my return from Ricks, around December of that year, Patrick suggested if we could change our school. He wanted us to go to Sanniquellie to attend Central High. Sanniquellie, situated in the north is the capital of Nimba County. In 1959 a meeting held in that city between Presidents William VS Tubman of Liberia, Ahmed Sekou Toure of Guinea, and Kwame Nkrumah of Ghana started talks that led to the formation of the Organization of African Unity (OAU) now African Union (AU). "It will be better for our exposure. And two, Mr. Kromah and Barshall are already in Sanniquellie Central High. We will not have problem adjusting," Patrick pointed out.

At that time Sanniquellie was tough to live in as students. It was not an easy place to adjust. It was widely rumored that students there were selfish and would never want to share. I wanted to try a new environment also. Given the fact that I was also good at playing soccer, the environment would be ideal for my exposure. So I bought into the idea.

"Ok, but I will have to talk to my uncle first."

At home, I met with my uncle that evening when he came from work.

"Uncle, I want to attend the Sanniquellie Central High with Patrick."

"Who will you be staying with?" he asked.

"We will be renting."

"They say Sanniquellie is a tough place to live. Do you think it will be a good idea?"

"Yes Uncle. It will be part of my growing up."

"Have you told your aunt yet?" Uncle Bantoe added.

"No, but I will," I said.

"You get my blessing and support. Tomorrow I will give you some money for transportation and entrance exam fees. If life starts getting tough for you, come back." When I told his wife Aunt Esther that evening, she was supportive as well. I ran to Patrick the next day and relayed the good news. Both of us began to celebrate. Two days later, Uncle Bantoe gave me all the money I had asked for. Patrick and I boarded a vehicle for Ganta and then north to Sanniquellie. Barshall hosted us. He was happy that his friends from Tappita were going to join him and he accompanied us to Central High campus where we signed up for the entrance exam and waited for the next few days to take the exam. Four days later, Patrick and I returned to Tappita after taking the exam. Around that same time Christian High School authorities were in hot pursuit of me. They approached my uncle on several occasions for him to prevail on me to attend their school. They had granted me a scholarship owing to my outstanding performance on the soccer field at Ricks. Meanwhile the results from Central High came out and we passed. But I started having second thoughts about going to Sanniquellie. I let Patrick know my change of mind. I argued that on second thought it did not make sense for us to leave the environment where we had the proper support network and go to a place of tremendous uncertainties. He agreed for us to remain in Tappita. And so the decision to remain was finally agreed upon by both of us.

However, I decided to take the offer from Christian High School. The school was a private Mid-Baptist Church-run school. Patrick joined me at Christian High also. My decision to go to Christian High School surprised everyone. All my instructors especially Principal Justin Wehjlah who had succeeded Mr. Kromah, academic mentor William Voahn, plus my teammates at Tappeh Memorial High felt betrayed. I was a soccer superstar. Both schools wanted me but Memorial High wanted me the most. They had groomed me from ground up. Uncle Bantoe, who was also highly respected in the community, got inundated with visits from my school authorities for me to reconsider my decision. His response always was, "The man is free to attend whichever school he chooses. My duty is to provide the support." I went to Christian High but I missed my school dearly. But I had Patrick with me.

Interestingly, I was surprised to find out that the academic standard in Christian High at that time, in 1978 was substandard compared to Memorial High. The school did not have a university graduate as instructor unlike Memorial High which boasted of having in its ranks, Mr. William Voahn, Mr. Arthur Kernean, Principal Wehjlah, (all University of Liberia graduates), some interns from University of Liberia Teachers College, graduates of Rural Teachers Training Institutes (KRTTI & ZRTTI), and some instructors from the United States of America under the Peace Corps Volunteer Program. The Principal of Christian High was only a high school graduate which I found out later when I entered the school.

One day in the English Grammar class, the instructor gave some words for us to form the "doer/agent". Among them was a word "gang." At the board, the teacher wrote "ganger" and tended to defend his decision. Coming from the tutelage of English and Literature instructors such as Mr. Voahn and Mr. Kernean, I disagreed with the teacher. I told him the correct answer was "gangster." The teacher did not like that. He told me that I thought I knew better than he. His reaction frightened me. It was also the *coup de grace*. At that point I decided to go back to my old school.

"Uncle, I want to go back to my old school," I revealed to Uncle Bantoe.

"Why?"

"I do not think they teach well. The teaching is substandard in my opinion."

"Why did you say that?" my uncle probed further.

"In our English grammar class today, the teacher gave an incorrect answer for a word he had written on the board and went on to defend his position. And when I challenged him and gave the right one, he got mad at me."

"It is not for playing football that you go to school. Your main reason is to get an education. If you are not getting proper teaching in that school and want to leave, I cannot blame you."

When the news hit Memorial High that I was returning, everyone was in celebratory mood. That evening, when we met on the soccer field for a match between the old and new students, I was swarmed by my teammates. Patrick stayed at Christian High until the end of the semester. His dad had paid his school fees which were non-refundable. Therefore he chose to stay until the school fee ran its course. Meanwhile, the sports director at Christian High kept on talking to Uncle Bantoe for me to go back to the school but I refused.

Back at Tappeh Memorial High, Principal Ansumana Kromah was reassigned to Sanniquellie by the Ministry of Education and was succeeded by Mr Justin C. Wehjlah. That transfer happened circa late 1977 after our trip to Zwedru. His departure created a huge vacuum in the soccer team. He was an inspiration, a mentor, and a very great soccer coach also. As coach he made me to believe in myself as a person and as a player. I fully retained his coaching philosophy, techniques, knowledge of the game, tactics, strategy, and manner of discipline which he imparted. By 1978 I practically took over the school team as coach-player. I was in Grade 11 now. Patrick rejoined me in Memorial High after the first semester of 1978. Prior to his coming back to Memorial High, our friendship was going through some strains. We were never together the whole day as before. We would only meet after school and stay together till bed time when we would part ways. But if it was campus clean-up day, I would hurriedly complete my work and go up to Christian High campus. He did likewise.

In Grade 11, two incidents occurred that helped shape my academic life and political beliefs. Math had been one of my favorable subjects leading up to Grade 11. At some point before Grade 11, I had planned on becoming a civil engineer. My uncle agreed. He had brought home many materials on civil engineering that I read regularly. I remember in

Grade 10 in 1977, I was so good at Algebra that the teacher, a US Peace Corps Volunteer, Miss Jan Radke used to allow me to tutor my peers in class. But Grade 11 was different. I was struggling to understand the geometry being taught by another US Peace Corps Volunteer. Under the teacher, I had scored only 80% as my term average for the third period of the first semester. My woe deepened when Patrick came all the way from his campus to visit me while our class was still in session. The math class was the last before recess. Patrick stood by the window and made eye contact with me. After that, he proceeded to hand me the guitar through the window. I got up from my seat and received it. The Peace Corps teacher did not like that. He immediately reached for his roll book and opened the page where he had recorded our grades.

"Mr. Jerry Gbardy, you are not far from getting a minus from your term average," the teacher warned.

"Why?" I asked

"Minus five," he responded.

"But Mr." –

"Minus five," the teacher added.

I zipped my lips and so did the entire class. At that moment the teacher held the roll book in his left hand and a lead pencil in the right while walking from side to side in front of the class.

"Is anybody here to help Mr. Gbardy?" There was complete silence that one could hear a sound of a pin drop. Toward that end, he continued, "Nobody to help Mr. Gbardy? Thank you for your cooperation." He closed the roll book, put it back on the table, and resumed teaching like nothing had happened. I was incensed but could not say or do anything. Because of the 10 points deducted from my grade, it rattled my overall semester grade point average considerably. Owing to that, I have come to lose lifetime interest in math.

Interestingly, the Peace Corps volunteer did not end that semester in Memorial High. But his damage to me had already been done. His departure was under some mysterious circumstances. It was rumored that he was allegedly declared *persona non grata* by the Liberian government. The math teacher was on campus when a vehicle from the Peace Corps Office in Monrovia came to pick him up. I was glad that he left; otherwise I would have failed in math that year.

Painful Journey: a Story of Escape and Survival

Looking back today at what happened, there is no doubt in my mind that the Peace Corps Volunteer abused his power and over-extended his authority. The degree of punishment he dished out on me did not commensurate with the offense that I had committed – far from that. He could have simply told me to get out of his class or given me another punishment that should not have brought reduction of my grade into the equation. Could he have done that to a student in the United States? Quite unlikely.

I am sincerely looking forward to the time when there will be a great many politicians and individuals in the Liberian political landscape, in our communities who live by principle; ones who believe in what they say and say what they believe. I believe that there are many principled individuals around but are perhaps shielded behind the multitude of gravy-seeking demagogues, who would stand in the open to castigate others, especially government officials. But when given the opportunity to make a difference, they soon get mired in what Liberian politician Gabriel Bacchus Matthews once referred to as the "politics of bread and belly."

From Grade 11, I have learned to follow a political belief or politician on a basis of my conviction - on the basis of it being the right thing to do and not what someone else says we should do. I examine a situation carefully before getting into it. At that point, I become unwavering unless it is necessary that I disengage at some point when things appear to run contrary to the objectives, principles, and core values of what I stand for.

One sunny day in Grade 11, we were in class during the third period. Everyone was looking forward to the bell ringing in order for us to go out for recess when the French Teacher sought permission from his colleague to allow him make an announcement. When given the opportunity, he told the class that we should be prepared to take a quiz during his class time, the period immediately after recess. The questions were to be drawn from a lesson in the book, *Pierre et Seydou 2*. We had not reached to that chapter in the book but he was going to test us from it anyway. When he left, everyone converged on me to solicit my view on whether we should take the test or not. I mastered all the lessons in *Pierre et Seydou* 1&2 from cover to cover. So taking the test was not going to be a problem. That same teacher had taught me French in Grade Six, Grade Seven, and Grade 10 and I was one of his best students along with Lormia, Arthur Wehyee, and another student Peter Fouah (who went on to be French announcer on national radio, ELBC in the 1980s). Majority of my classmates wanted the teacher to first teach the chapter before giving the quiz at another date. After much discussion, we reached a consensus not to take the test. In that light, I told my classmates that I wanted to take the quiz. But as long as everyone said they were not prepared to take the quiz, I was not going to take it also. I was going to do so in solidarity with them. I would not betray them. At that point they made me the spokesperson to tell the teacher our decision.

During the fourth period, the French teacher arrived and began to request everyone to "grab a pen and paper, put all books away, and prepare for the French quiz."

I raised my hand, asked for permission to speak and the teacher gave me the go ahead.

"Teacher, we have not reached to that lesson in the book yet."

"And so?" he asked sarcastically.

"And so we have decided not to take the test. We want you to teach the chapter first."

"So Mr. Gbardy you are the spokesman for the people?" he asked angrily.

"Not so much about being spokesman. We just want the right thing to be done since this is a foreign language," I tried to clarify my position.

"Ok Mr. Spokesman, if you do not want to take the quiz, don't. Class, whoever does not want to take the quiz you are welcome." "But," he continued, "from now to the end of the year, you will receive 50% throughout. You already know your grade. So if you want to sit in my class from now on, it is up to you," the teacher shouted.

As soon as he said that, everyone began to rush for their pen and paper to take the quiz. I was stunned. But I had uttered the words and I was not going to go back on them. So I did not take the test. My classmates betrayed me. They left me hanging dry.

"Mr. Gbardy, please get out of my class."

Painful Journey: a Story of Escape and Survival

As I was getting out, he added, "From now to the end of the year, you score 50%." I walked out without a comment.

The 1978 school year progressed. The Peace Corps Volunteer math teacher was gone. On the other hand my math grade point average took a heavy beating. I was also receiving periodic failing grades from the French teacher. My buddy Patrick was back with me in Memorial High and that meant a whole lot to me. So life went on. It thus became business as usual again doing regular soccer practices, going on field trips, and above all just having fun. In our attempts to have fun on campus sometimes landed us in trouble with senior students. As seniors, Grade 12 students were given power and authority by the school authorities to help enforce rules and regulations on campus. The seniors were responsible to book and punish students for the following minor offences: uniform shirt tail not tucked in, not wearing the proper color of uniform, shoes, making noise during general assembly, coming to school late, etc, etc. The punishments took the form of cutting grass or picking up garbage around campus. Most times Kibu and I would get booked for not tucking in our shirt tails or for making noise during general assembly. The seniors would give us assignments that we would not want to do. Every other morning during devotion, Principal Wehjlah would stand up on stage with the following announcement:

"Jerry Gbardy and Patrick Lurlay, report to my office after here."

The next day, "Patrick Lurlay and Jerry Gbardy report to my office." We took great pleasure and delight in hearing those announcements because they popularized us indeed.

At the end of the school year, my A+ grades in the first three periods and the midterm exam added to three 50s dropped my final average to failing mark. That meant I was supposed to spend my summer vacation in French class. The teacher submitted his grades and left for Lome, Togo. When the Grade 11 Class Sponsor, Mr. J Howard Matadi received all my second semester French grades in red, he called me to a meeting and inquired what had happened that resulted into my failing. Did I have family problem? If I did, why didn't I notify the school? After all the questioning borne out of speculation, I told him what had transpired between the French Teacher and me. Mr. Matadi was convinced that I had told him the truth. Other students had filed similar complaints against the French Teacher also. The man was in the habit of failing students for the rest of the year even if the incident occurred in the beginning of the year. He got away with that unprofessional behavior for a long time. He was untouchable. But that year the French Teacher's grades were rejected by the faculty committee. From the overwhelming evidence they got from many students, every student who "failed in French" and was supposed to go to Summer School, got a pass. Since that time, I have learned a valuable lesson not to ever follow group action without being convinced that it is the right thing to do.

The French Teacher returned the following year and also taught Grade 12 French. Interestingly he never bothered to ask me for the summer school certificate. He only resorted to endless insinuations and taking indirect swipe at me that, "some people are untouchable in this class."

Back to the soccer field: In the latter part of 1978, the school had several sporting engagements in soccer, basketball, volleyball, and girls-kickball with visiting high schools. There was one particular game scheduled for some time in August against the Kwendin Vocational Training Center (KVTC, a Baptist Church-run boarding school that President Tolbert visited regularly) that we gave much attention. The school, located about 7 miles south of Tappita, had a lot of good players. A prolific striker by the nickname of VC-10 played for that school. Therefore we had to tactically plan how to contain him. Our team scheduled two practices in the day: one before class and the other, after school. As coach-player I sought permission from Principal Wehjlah to have morning soccer practices before classes began. The principal approved. The morning sessions went on well. We loved those sessions. It was an opportunity for us to bond together well as players and as a team.

I used to love - and still do today - teasing and giving nicknames, sometimes funning nicknames to teammates and friends alike which would become the subject for poking fun at a person. There was one Barjolo who played goalie for us. His performance at goal-keeping was below average, miniscule at best. In Liberian English, the adjective is *fee-cee*. Barjolo was notoriously *fee-cee*. So I used to spend extra time coaching him. The guy was stocky, burly looking with an average height of 5 feet 5 inches or something like that. I called him "False Giant." It became his name for a while but he did not like it. My man Patrick seized up on that and started picking on the guy all the time whether during practice, on or off campus. That infuriated Barjolo to the extent that he began to incessantly complain to me all the time to tell Patrick to desist. The funning thing was that little did Barjolo know that the person to whom he was always complaining was the inventor of the name. But as leader of the team I would hypocritically reassure him that the teasing would stop.

During one of our morning sessions, I deliberately made Patrick a member of Barjolo's team. I had thought that by being on the same team, Patrick would refrain from calling Barjolo his unwanted name. I was wrong. For Patrick it did not matter whether on the same team or opposing team.

"False Giant, pass the ball," Patrick called out to his goalie.

"Patrick, my name is Barjolo. Stop calling me False Giant," Barjolo responded.

Everybody on the field began to laugh. We carried on for few minutes when Patrick forgot and called Barjolo the name again. This time Barjolo left the goalpost and walked to the center of the field to complain to me. He threatened to fight Patrick if the name-calling did not stop. I stopped play and quietly advised Patrick that his continuous provocation of Barjolo was making my job difficult. Because once everyone started laughing, it was difficult for me as coach-player to contain myself also.

"Ok Kibu, I will stop," Patrick promised.

A few minutes later when I looked from the other end of the field, I saw Patrick running toward me. Everyone including myself started laughing. Patrick ran as fast as he could and stood behind me.

"Kibu False Giant is coming to beat me. Stop him! Stop him!"

Barjolo came toward me while Patrick was standing behind me running his mouth and moving from left to right. I was between two huge guys and was trying to stop Barjolo from attempting to throw punches at Patrick. Of course I was making sure that Barjolo's punches did not land. Meanwhile Patrick would not stop running his mouth while swaying from side to side and using my body as a shield.

"Kibu, don't let False Giant beat me," Patrick continued shouting.

"Barjolo, please no fighting," I blurted out.

"But Jerry, he is still calling me False Giant."

"Patrick, just stop calling the guy that name."

"Ok Kibu I will. Tell the guy to leave." He was laughing while saying that, which only angered Barjolo the more. In the end with the help of other teammates, the situation was brought under control. That was the end of practice for that morning. On our way home, it was fun and laughter all the way.

During the game with Kwendin, I scored two goals. Peterson Marbiah scored one and another teammate, the diminutive Cummings Diakpo, scored the other. KVTC abandoned the game in the middle of the second half when Peterson scored his second and the team's fifth. KVTC players claimed the goal was scored from an off side position after a corner kick. We agreed for the goal to be disallowed and let play resume. They refused and left the field. They were terribly embarrassed by the score line as was suspected.

Late in 1978 Christian High was invited to participate in the Ricks mini-Olympic again. In spite of the disappointment that I did not attend the school, they still took me with them. In fact, they had no choice. They needed me more than I did. The trip started and ended on a bad note. On the way to Ricks, some students were involved in heated verbal exchanges with their principal in the parking lot in Ganta City. The students became so disrespectful to the Principal that they began calling him names. They were heard openly saying that he was only a high school graduate who did not deserve the position. One of the students came close to physically assaulting the Principal.

After Ganta, Bouu-mehn, the driver who took us on the trip, was an up country driver who was scared as hell to drive in a big city such as Monrovia, we suspected. He devised a scheme to say his vehicle had "mechanical problem" which could only be fixed in Tappita. So he left us on the highway in Caresburg, a city about 30 miles from Monrovia and returned to Tappita more than 123 miles away. How bizarre! We had to look for another vehicle while waiting on the highway. The next mishap was that during the Beauty Pageant hosted by Ricks on Thursday night, Christian High queen performed so dismally that she became a laughing stock for the duration of the sporting events. On Friday morning during a kickball[1] match, Ricks girls embarrassed Christian High girls 66 home runs to six. Yes, 66 to six, no exaggeration here!

During the field of play, we got kicked out of the tournament in our first game. Our prolific goal-scorer, Prince Myers missed his post-match penalty kick that kicked us out of the tournament. Prince Myers would later become Commissioner of the Bureau of Immigration and Naturalization of Liberia. On the way back to Tappita, we almost got killed by a train in the middle of the bridge. At that time, the bridge spanning over the St. Paul River outside Monrovia was used by both vehicles and freight trains. Our vehicle was in the middle of the bridge heading east when we sighted the train heading west toward us. The driver stepped on the gas in order to get out of the way. The train missed us by a whisker. I think nobody would have survived had our vehicle collided head-on with the fast-moving train. We were extremely lucky to be alive. On the highway while reaching Gbarnga City, three students got involved in physical altercation in the vehicle while it was moving. The vehicle almost flipped over. It was just one disaster after another.

At the close of 1978 national politics got in full swing. The Progressive Alliance of Liberia (PAL) and the Movement of Justice in Africa (MOJA) began making inroads in Nimba County and our city was no exception. There were several MOJA militants living in Tappita, among them were James Kpawo Zarway, Bobby Nimley, H Napoleon Nayou, Isaac Paye, etc. PAL did not have a real go-to guy in the city. However, many students, including myself subscribed to the teachings of Chairman Baccus Mathews and PAL. At that time it was unheard of or unthinkable to form a political organization to challenge the True Whig Party oligarchy. Liberia at that time was a one-part state. But PAL and MOJA did. PAL Secretary General Oscar Quiah visited Tappita and called a mass meeting in the market square that I also attended. At that meeting I signed up to be member. Quiah promised to head another delegation back to Tappita to set up a proper leadership

---

[1] In Liberia, kickball is like the American baseball. The diamond-shaped field and rules are the same but with reduced number of innings. The game is only played by girls and the ball, the size of a soccer ball, is kicked not hit with bat.

structure in the city. That did not happen again until the April 14, 1979 Rice Riots occurred.

At certain point between the closing stages of 1978 and the opening school year of 1979, one Mewaseh Paybaye joined the teaching staff of Tappeh Memorial High School. Paybaye, a gifted mathematician, was an intern from the University of Liberia Teachers' College. In the classroom, he succeeded Mr. Dingwall Paye who had temporarily taken over the departed Peace Corps Volunteer's math class. Paybaye was also an avid football (soccer) enthusiast. He knew and loved the beautiful game. Therefore he took over the team as coach. Like Principal Kromah before him, Paybaye commanded tremendous respect from the students on the team. We bonded well with him. Under his coaching, our team was also successful in winning several games. The team that suffered the most humiliation from us was the Johnny Voker High in Saclepea City. The score against them during the course of the game was 5-0 when their school principal negotiated with Coach Paybaye to end the game in order to avoid more crumbling embarrassments. I had got a brace and was on my way to getting a hat trick when their principal called his players on the sideline to abandon the game. The crowd roared in utter disappointment.

We entered 1979 with high hopes of graduating from high school and going on to university. Our extra curriculum activities, which were much source of fun and physical development continued. By then political developments in the country, particularly Nimba County, were on the rise. Nimba County became the center of political activism in the country. The wind of change blew in the county more than others. On Saturday April 14, the rice riots occurred in Monrovia. Even though I was not at the epicenter of the demonstrations, I, like other students and instructors of my school, was directly affected. The trouble started on Monday April 16, 1979 when Nimba County Superintendent Fulton Dunbar, who was a descendant of the Americo-Liberia ruling class, led an array of county officials to Tappita and ordered the principals of all the junior and senior high schools in the city to assemble the students in the Mid-Liberia Baptist Church situated in the center of town. During the meeting, every county official who spoke, admonished the students not to "join PAL and 'MOJO.'" James Kpou Zarway, a MOJA militant and classroom instructor posed a strongly worded political question that all the platform guests individually wrestled with but could not answer. It has been a very long time now so I cannot quote the question here but the question certainly stirred things up. Maybe the platform guests did not understand the question because of extensive vocabulary in the sentence. The failure of the officials to answer the question correctly exposed them to more ridicule, embarrassment, and public humiliation as evidenced by the relentless booing and jeering by the students. The superintendent had had enough! He ordered the meeting closed and advised all the PAL and MOJA members to assemble at the commissioner compound at the north end of town where massive arrests of students and instructors ensued, followed by more house to house arrests.

Superintendent Dunbar, who was already a law unto himself before the rice riots, became increasingly heavy-handed during that period after the Tolbert government imposed a state of emergency. He ruled Nimba County like a fiefdom. Before the rice riots, the superintendent would sometimes pull over motorists on the highway for traffic violation such as speeding, overloading, broken taillights, etc, and literally flog them. If he did not dispense jungle justice himself, he would order the "carboy" (conductor) to flog the driver and vise versa. Consequently during the period of the state of emergency, he placed the entire Nimba County under siege as there were massive waves of arrests of suspected PAL and MOJA members across the county. My high school principal, Justin Wehjlah, Registrar Pewee Sumo, and some of my schoolmates were among the group incarcerated at the South Beach Prison Compound in far away Monrovia. As an active member of PAL, I went underground for several weeks to escape the powerful Superintendent. About two weeks later, all those incarcerated in the South Beach Prison were released and brought back to Tappita. But I still remained underground. It would be another two weeks before I came from hiding after being assured by Patrick and another friend, Sam Okai that all was well. However, my return coincided with all the "Where is Dr. Taryor?" or "Bring Back Dr. Taryor" campaigns.

Dr. Nya Kwiawon Taryor had fled the country in the aftermath of the April 14 Rice Riots. He was an executive of MOJA and pastor of the United Methodist Church in Tappita. The Pastor resided in his home town of Gbahn, a few miles east of Ganta. Every Sunday he commuted from there to preach in the church in Tappita. He was extremely popular in the county and country. The Methodist Church attracted a lot of members every time the Pastor was in town to preach. An elementary school run by the Methodist Church with H. Napoleon Nayou as principal, was named in Dr. Taryor's honor. Dr. Taryor's flight in the wake of the riots, created more political tensions in the county. The county was up in arms signing petitions here and there to force the Tolbert government to produce him. I was one of those taking the petition around for signatures. Most of us in Tappita had no clue about his whereabouts. It was widely speculated that Taryor was kidnapped and murdered by government security personnel. Finally, couple of months later, he returned to Liberia. Tappita was one of the very first places that he visited. I attended a mass rally that he spoke at in the market square. He looked physically drained and had lost a considerable amount of weight. During the speech, the Pastor told the crowd of the ordeal he went through at the hands of Guinean security personnel before being taken to President Sekou Toure. We were all glad to see him back.

Meanwhile, Tappeh Memorial High authorities moved repeatedly to advise students against participating in national political activities on campus. Their incarceration in the wake of the Rice Riots was a major factor that gave impetus to the decision. As students who were conscious of political happenings around us, we could not divorce ourselves completely from politics. The country had awakened and there was no turning back. But we only participated in those activities off campus.

Like all Grade 12 students across the country, we at Memorial High began looking forward to sitting the West African Examinations Council (WAEC) exams with high hopes and expectations. Successful passing of the exams was a gateway to participating in the commencement convocation and entering any post secondary institution of learning in Liberia. Wearing the graduation gown during commencement while surrounded by family members and friends, particularly in rural Liberia was the greatest achievement every parent looked for in their child. Therefore the exams were not to be taken lightly by any stretch of the imagination. They were administered by examiners from the Council from far away Monrovia. While Patrick and I were busy having fun, playing soccer, and poking fun at our peers here and there, we were also preparing for the national exams. We would read any academic material that was deemed to have been relevant to our success. We organized on-campus after school study classes which were sometimes conducted by one Samuel Zuu, a member of our class. The nation-wide WAEC exams were scheduled for some time in October of 1979.

Two days before the main day, the exam papers arrived and were taken to a local government administrator's official residence (the commissioner compound). On the day of the exams, when all the students from the various high schools assembled on Memorial High campus fully prepared, news broke that there would be no exams after all. The examiners discovered that one of the boxes containing the exam papers had been tampered with. Upon investigation, it was authentically revealed that a member of our class who was also a member of the District Education Officer (DEO), Jerry Toemehn's household was the main suspect. The DEO moved quickly after consultations with the Chief Education Officer (CEO) in Sanniquellie, the county capital to cancel the WAEC exams. There was commotion all over the place. The cancellation was a major blow and a setback. When would we take the WAEC exams again? How would I enter the University of Liberia which entrance exams would be administered at the end of the year, if I did not have a WAEC exam certificate? Meanwhile, our classmate who allegedly stole the test was expelled from the school with immediate effect.

The school year came to an end in November 1979 without any fanfare. I left town to visit Sister Sarah somewhere in another part of the county. I returned two weeks later to find out that the WAEC exams would be re-administered in mid-December. On exam day once again, we assembled in the auditorium of Tappeh Memorial High. This time the invigilators were more stringent and vigilant than ever. We were seated according to our ID numbers. So Patrick sat across the auditorium far away from me. I sat with another brilliant classmate of ours, Nathan G. Sandwiched between us was a female friend of ours from Christian High School. She bothered Nathan and me constantly to help her with some of the answers. Of course we did. In the process, one invigilator saw us. He walked over to our bench and wrote down the ID numbers of three of us. Good thing he did not dismiss us from the exam hall. After the exams, Patrick and I left for Monrovia. He went to live with his brother George in the Gardnersville area and I, with my elder sister, Payennon in the Sinkor suburb. Early 1980, the results came out while we were away. The surprise of the year: Nathan G and Jerry Gbardy, two of the brilliant students of the class had failed. My friends Patrick and Lormia passed. Of course, the girl from Christian High who we were caught helping, passed. Wow! Anyway there was still an opportunity for us to redeem ourselves. The school would allow us to return as special students to sit with the present Grade 12 only for the subject we had the deficiency in if we chose to.

I returned to Tappita on Thursday April 10, 1980 to prepare for re-sitting the WAEC exams. I had planned to report to the school campus on Monday for registration but unfortunately, on Saturday April 12, 1980, the military seized power in Monrovia.

The next day while many of us gathered near the local telecommunication station monitoring the news, we heard excessive celebratory gunfire coming from a Mercedes Benz with its flashers on and racing at breakneck speed, approaching the town from the north. It stopped when it reached our gathering. One Samuel Dahn and Cpl Reeves Buoye stepped out. Buoye was member of the Liberian army and was clutching an M-16 rifle in his hand. They introduced themselves and asked for Nimba County Representative, Hon Sammy Kpahn's residence. Someone directed them to the residence and they proceeded there without delay. Everyone in the gathering ran there also to witness the spectacle. The mission of Dahn and Buoye on that Sunday afternoon was to arrest Hon. Kpahn. He was sought out because, as member of the House of Representatives, he was part of the legislative body that had passed a Joint Resolution that gave President Tolbert emergency powers to ban the Progressive People's Party in the wake of the party's call for his resignation.

Prior to that morning, I had attended a political meeting in Sanniquellie in December in which Dahn was one of the speakers. So I knew who he was. At that time, he was an executive of PAL, a national political organization that would later register as a political party. The meeting, held on the Dokie Elementary School Campus, was chaired by PAL county leader Samuel Dokie. A night prior, Dahn was released from the military Post Stockade in Monrovia along with PAL national leader Gabriel Baccus Matthews, Samuel Dokie, and other party executives.

In January 1980, four months before the military coup, Samuel Dahn, Samuel Dokie, and a host of opposition politicians in Nimba County, were arrested and incarcerated in Monrovia. According to James Kpou Zarway, a local MOJA executive in Tappita who spoke to us upon hearing the news of the arrests, informed us that the opposition politicians' incarceration stemmed from the fact that under Dokie's leadership, the opposition politicians had allegedly called on residents of the Nimba County not to pay taxes to the national government since their taxes were being used by the Americo-Liberian power-elite to enrich themselves.

Samuel Dokie was hard-nosed, hot-headed Liberian politician from Nimba County. He had worked in the Tolbert government as assistant superintendent, a position he would later resign in 1979. In the wake of his resignation, Dokie donated his private residence to PAL for use as headquarters. After the 1980 coup, freed from jail, the military junta appointed him as deputy minister of internal affairs and was dismissed two years later. He spearheaded the Nimba Raid in 1983 and fled Liberia. He would later join Taylor's NPFL that trained in Libya and launched the civil war. Finally Dokie fell out with Taylor in 1994 and was murdered in November 1997 along with his family while en route to a wedding in Nimba County.

At Hon Kpahn's residence that fateful Sunday afternoon, they also found Counselor Isaac Nyenplu who was President Tolbert's ministerial investigator sent to Tappita to investigate corruption in public offices (Nyenplu would become justice minister in the Doe military regime in the 1980s). Both former government officials were brought to the police station in the center of town and publicly flogged. In order to justify the flogging as payback, Samuel Dahn displayed his both hands that were severely tortured while in jail. It was not a pretty sight to see. After the public flogging, the captured former government officials were thrown in the back seat of the car and driven to the campus of KVTC in Kwendin, a town seven miles south of Tappita.

As students who were joyously celebrating the coup, we boarded a large open back truck and followed Dahn and Buoye to Kwendin. At the boarding school, the mood was somber. Some of the students who were children of prominent Americo-Liberian families in Monrovia were seen openly weeping in their dormitories. After chatting with Principal Faliku Kromah regarding the safety of the students, Dahn and Buoye left the campus and returned to Monrovia with the former officials of the ousted Tolbert government. Dahn would be later appointed assistant minister of agriculture while Cpl Buoye was promoted to the rank of colonel and appointed commandant of the Post Stockade. Months later, Hon Kpahn was among groups of detained former Tolbert government officials to be released by the military junta. According to reliable sources, Hon Kpahn threw a party in Graie, a small town 18 miles north of Tappita in honor of Assistant Minister Dahn. On his way back to Monrovia, Minster Dahn's Chevy Blazer Sports Utility Vehicle flipped over and burst into flames, killing him and others in it. It was reported that they had a few jerricans full of gasoline in the vehicle that had ignited the fire.

Couple of weeks after the military takeover, school reopened. I returned to the Tappeh Memorial High campus to report myself to school authorities. When I arrived, I bumped into my English and Literature instructor, Mr. Voahn at the south entrance of the building. He was so surprised when he saw me.

"Jerry, why and how did it happen?"

"I do not know Mr. Voahn."

"That's life. Just accept it and do your best on the exams next time," he advised.

"Ok," I said.

Between the two of us, Nathan was more distraught and more disappointed than I. He confided to me that life was not fair. Why did we have to fail after all the good work we had done in school for the entire year? Had we not been caught helping that girl, would our results have come out differently? Accordingly he vowed not to return as special student. But I did.

About a month after the coup, Uncle Bantoe got a job in Monrovia and relocated with his family. I stayed behind to redo the exams. At that point, I moved in with another friend, Sam Okai, who was attending

Christian High School. He was a very friendly, sociable, and personable person and was very good at playing soccer also.

On the school team, I resumed my duties as coach-player after Mr. Paybaye returned to the University of Liberia to complete his studies. I played my last game for the school against St Samuel High School located in the beautiful iron-ore mining city of LAMCO-Yekepa near the northern border with Guinea. I left something special with all the soccer enthusiasts of the school and the city to remember. The game was my last for the school. As Special Student, I was not required to sit in all the classes except the two that I was deficient in during the national exams. Therefore I had too much time on my hands to do extra soccer drills before the rest of the team reported for practices. I would run about 5 to 10 miles every day while preparing for the game. When gameday arrived, I was unbelievably fitter than one could imagine. I took the game to the visitors. I orchestrated proceedings from the middle. In the first half, we scored a beautiful goal that the referee inadvertently disallowed. I was standing on the top of the opponents' 18-yard box. A through pass was threaded to me by teammate Sebastian Smith with my back toward my opponents' goalpost. Without breaking the ball, I let it roll between my feet and with a flick of the inside of my right foot, I back-heeled the ball to my left. From twenty-five yards, teammate Peter Gleekiah latched on to the ball so powerfully to the left of the post that the goalie did not see it. The spectators roared in excitement! We began celebrating but rather prematurely. The referee had sounded the whistle for "offside." He would later tell me after the game that due to excitement, he blew the whistle by accident. The first half ended zero all.

We resumed the second half with more determination. For us the game was a must win because we were playing on home soil. Midway into the second half, a major opportunity came our way again. We were outside the opponents' 18-yard box when Peter Gleekiah, after seeing off a few of our opponents, made a diagonal pass from my left. Peterson Marbiah dummied the ball to create a decoy that carried two defenders with him in the process. I was left unmarked with the ball rolling two feet away. From about twenty yards, I did a flick kick with the outside of my right foot. It was my signature shot. The ball had so much spin on it that it sailed menacingly over the goalie in the top left corner. Goal!

It was riveting! It was absolutely stunning. It was the one and only goal that broke the deadlock and was certainly my parting gift for Tappeh Memorial High School. The goal set off scenes of unbridled joy and celebrations as many spectators ran on the field and carried me shoulder high. Scenes of the game were photographed and posted in the school's 1980 Yearbook.

Off the soccer pitch, I re-sat the exams in July. In August I also took the University of Liberia entrance exam. I stayed in Tappita until the results came. Fortunately I passed both exams. Christian High had planned to participate in the Ricks mini-Olympic in November of that year and I was selected to be part of the team again. Unfortunately during the night before our departure, Principal Justin Wehjlah of Tappeh Memorial High was killed by lightning strike. The trip was cancelled. I left Tappita after his burial. In March 1981, I finally moved to Monrovia to live with Sister Payennon to attend the University of Liberia. By then, Patrick had already gone to the southeastern county of Maryland to attend the William VS Tubman Technical College. At the end of the First Semester, he came back to Monrovia and moved with me at my sister's residence on 16th Street, Sinkor. Okai completed high school at the end of 1981 and joined us also, bringing with him another friend, BB. I entered the University of Liberia in 1982. Patrick also did. By 1983 Patrick left for the United States of America. BB returned to Tappita in the middle of 1982. Unfortunately Okai stayed in Liberia throughout the war. He passed away in 2001. Patrick now resides in Washington State and works for Boeing, a leading world aircraft manufacturer as Manager, Boeing Information Technology. Every time our both families meet, the two of us will stay up for the rest of the night reminiscing on the good old days. Lormia is in Liberia and works for the government of Liberia as Ambassador-at-Large in the Ministry of Foreign Affairs. He is one of the first persons I call and visit anytime I arrive in Liberia.

CHAPTER TWO

Build-Up to the Civil War: 1979-1989

Although historically there were many socio-economic and political events of Liberia's past that had significantly contributed to Liberia's contemporary grief for which a plethora of books and other academic materials had been written, this chapter will endeavor to confine itself to the political events of recent history that occurred before the 1989 civil war. I refer to the April 14, 1979 Rice Riots, the April 12, 1980 military coup d'état, the 1983 Nimba Raid, and the abortive invasion of November 12, 1985. Undoubtedly the advent of these events, one precipitating the other, culminated into the brutal civil war that was fought for 14 years. Therefore, there is little wonder about the most horrendous way in which the war was fought. There were massive summary executions, gross human rights violations, ethnic cleansings, and forced exiles. All these horrible events in the nation's history can be chronicled as engendering anger, ethnic hatred, and inspiring cascades of vengeance among large segments of the country, which ultimately brewed the civil war. I will attempt to briefly deal with these events in the order that they occurred.

Brief Historical Background

The Preamble of the 1847 Constitution of Liberia reads:
We the people of the Republic of Liberia were originally the inhabitants of the United States of North America. In some parts of that country, we were debarred by law from all the rights and privileges of men--in other

parts, public sentiment, more powerful than law, frowned us down. We were everywhere shut out from all civil office. We were excluded from all participation in the government. We were taxed without our consent. We were compelled to contribute to the resources of a country, which gave us no protection. We were made a separate and distinct class, and against us every avenue to improvement was effectually closed. Strangers from all lands of a color different from ours were preferred before us. We uttered our complaints, but they were unattended to, or only met by alleging the peculiar institutions of the country. All hope of a favorable change in our country was thus wholly extinguished in our bosoms, and we looked with anxiety abroad for some asylum from the deep degradation[2].

Liberia as a nation has a unique political history that is replete with far too many striking anomalies. For several generations, the Americo-Liberians cried for freedom and liberty on slave plantations as is evidenced in the Preamble above. Every Liberian national symbol or document such as the Seal, the National Anthem, and the Ode: the *Lone Star Forever* has the words "freedom" and "liberty" inscribed in or on it. However once they established themselves in Liberia, the Americo Liberians imposed on the natives, the very injustices they experienced on slave plantations in America. From the country's founding, the Americo-Liberians immediately planted a seed of division not only between themselves and the indigenous people they met on the land but between themselves: the light-skinned and the dark-skinned returnees. The light-skinned (Mulattos) former slaves discriminated against their dark-skinned brothers and sisters. Then at the lowest rung of the discrimination ladder were the aboriginal people who were only granted citizenship on their own land in 1904, 57 years after independence. They were considered backward and uncivilized. Because of that Liberia, which means "land of the free" squandered every conceivable opportunity available to symbolize a beacon of freedom and hope for all oppressed peoples in the world.

---

[2]Preamble of the 1847 Constitution of the Republic of Liberia which was suspended immediately after the 1980 military coup. A new Constitution which came into force in 1986 was written by the Amos Sawyer Commission.

Painful Journey: a Story of Escape and Survival

Politically, Liberia was a one-party state ruled by the True Whig Party (TWP). Joseph Jenkins Roberts, who was born and raised in Norfolk, Virginia, USA, was the country's first President. In theory the style of government and constitution is fashioned on that of the United States but differs in many ways, in practice and application – the *Liberian Way* (see chapter 11). The Americo-Liberian elites monopolized political power and created a class system akin to the master-servant relationship they left in America.

Liberia is a tiny country situated on the west coast of Africa bounded by the Republic of Guinea to the north, Cote d'Ivoire to the east, and Sierra Leone to the west. It has a land area of 43, 000 square miles and is strategically perched above a long stretch of natural sandy beaches on the coast of the Atlantic Ocean from Maryland County in the southeast, to Grand Cape Mount County in the west. It was founded in 1822 by freed American slaves and captured slaves repatriated to Africa with assistance provided by a philanthropic organization called the American Colonization Society (ACS) and the United States government. The nation declared independence on July 26, 1847 making it the oldest independent republic in Africa. Until the military coup of 1980, the nation had been dominated by a group of former slaves historically referred to as Americo-Liberians who comprise about 5% of the population. The rest of the 95% encompasses a population of the indigenous people consisting of several tribal groups that had inhabited the land prior to the arrival of the free slaves. The tribal groups are: Vai, Gola, Dey, Mende, Lorma, Kissi, Belle, Gbandi, Kpelle, Bassa, Mandingo, Gio, and Mano. Others are Krahn, Gbi, Grebo and Kru. At present, the population is a little over 3 million people. Administratively there are 15 political subdivisions, otherwise known as counties that are headed by superintendents who are appointed by the President of the Republic. The counties are: Monsterrado, Bong, Grand Gedeh, Nimba, Bomi and Maryland. Others are Grand Kru, Margibi, Gbarpolu, Cape Mount, Lofa, River Cess, Grand Bassa, River Gee and Bong.

The Rice Riots

Liberia is endowed with a huge repository of natural resources: fertile soil, large bodies of water, and a tropical rain forest which is 45% of West Africa's total rain forest *(www.forestmonitor.org)*. Two hundred and fifty thousand species of marketable hardwood, cash crops, and food crops are produced from Liberia's fertile soil (Sirleaf, 2009). The main staple of the Liberian diet is rice. The commodity which is imported is consumed in majority of Liberian households three times a day – breakfast, lunch and dinner. There are other primary nutritious consumer products grown in Liberia such as cassava, yam, eddoes, and potatoes that are supplementary to rice. A Liberian will consume either one of these supplemental food items during the day but will still complain of having not yet eaten. Unless he or she adds rice, there will be no end to his whining of being hungry. In a political context, rice is seen as crucial to maintaining political and economic stability to the national body politic. In 1979 the Tolbert government miscalculated this critical issue and paid a very heavy price for it.

Thus in 1979, when the Tolbert government, through Agriculture Minister Florence Chenoweth[3] proposed the increase in the price of rice, there was trouble. The masses rose "up in arms". The proposed increase and the event that followed led to what has come to be referred to as the April 14, 1979 Rice Riots which eventually laid the groundwork for the 1980 military coup. The minister's rationale for the proposed increase was that it would have served as an incentive for the farmers to produce more. In spite of all the reform-minded President Tolbert's national slogan of "self-reliance" and "self-sufficiency" in food production, there was inadequate incentive given to farmers to grow food. The importation of rice accounted for 25 percent of the 200,000 tons consumed. Urban Liberians at that time received an average monthly salary of $80 while the price of a 100 pound bag of rice would have been increased from $22 to $27. Tolbert himself owned large farms (Sirleaf, 2009). The price increase would have stretched the family budget to breaking point (Liebenow, 1987).

---

[3] Florence Chenoweth is the present Agriculture Minister in the Ellen Johnson-Sirleaf administration

Undoubtedly, the income gap between the Americo-Liberian power elites and the masses had widened to astronomical proportions: 4 percent of the population owned 60 percent of the national wealth (ibid). Given the socio-economic and political imbalance coupled with the slow pace of change Tolbert had promised to implement, the Progressive Alliance of Liberia (PAL) of Baccus Matthews not only organized the demonstrations to protest the increase in the price of the main staple but also exposed the widespread injustices and inequality perpetrated by the Americo-Liberian oligarchy against the masses.

The Progressive Alliance of Liberia (PAL) was founded in the United States of America in 1975 by young Liberian students who had become so dissatisfied with the continued domination of Liberian politics by the Americo-Liberian oligarchy. It was President Tolbert himself who had invited leaders of PAL to return to Liberia and register as a political party (Sirleaf, 2009). President Tolbert who had served as vice president for 19 years under Liberia's cult President Tubman, promised change but the pace of the change was slow in the eyes of the students. The group chose Gabriel Baccus Matthews as their chairman. Matthews, a graduate of City University of New York, is regarded by many as the "father" of multi-party democracy in contemporary Liberian politics. Sirleaf refers to him as the "Godfather of Liberian Democracy" (ibid, 82). Under his chairmanship, PAL introduced a special kind of African socialism modeled after Tanzanian President Julius Nyerere's *Ujamaa-ism*[4]. Accordingly, PAL was to operate in keeping with African principles and values (Liebenow, 1987). The main recruiting targets of the organization were students, low-income and unemployed workers, and rural peasants. Leaders of PAL advocated the processing in Liberia of primary products such as iron ore and rubber produced in Liberia and exported by foreign concessionaires namely: Bong Mines, LAMCO, and Firestone. PAL published a periodical in Monrovia entitled *Voice of the Revolution* through which it articulated its core beliefs and policies.

---

[4] Ujamaa-ism was the concept that formed the basis of President Julius Nyerere's social and economic development policies in Tanzania. In 1967 he published his development blueprint titled, the Arusha Declaration in which he demonstrated the need for an African model of development that formed the basis of African Socialism. Ujamaa originates from a Swahili word for extended familyhood.

Another political organization that participated in the planned demonstrations was the Movement for Justice in Africa (MOJA). Some of its leaders were also arrested during the Rice Riots. MOJA was founded in 1973 by groups of professors and students of the University of Liberia. The movement's main leader was Dr Togba Nah Tipoteh, former professor of Economics at the University of Liberia. Two other leaders were both professors of the Political Science Department of the University of Liberia: Dr Amos Sawyer and Dr. H Boima Fahnbulleh Jr., whose father Ambassador Henry Fahnbulleh Sr., had been imprisoned in 1968 by President Tubman based on a trumped up charge of conspiracy to overthrow the Liberian government. Dr Sawyer would later write the Liberian Constitution of 1986 and would later serve as Interim President of Liberia from 1990-1994. At present he is Chairman of the Good Governance Commission in the Johnson Sirleaf administration. Unlike the policies of PAL in which they directly engaged the government and called for socioeconomic and political reforms, MOJA avoided direct confrontations with the Tolbert government. Like the policies of the Tolbert government: increase in food production and a self-reliant economy, MOJA set up a rural development organization known as *Susukuu*[5], an agricultural cooperative through which they worked with rural farmers in Grand Gedeh to increase their farming and production capacities (Liebenow, 1987).

During the demonstrations, the Tolbert government deployed police, soldiers and armored personnel carriers. The soldiers for their part did not actively participate in the use of brute force to quell the demonstrations. It was the police who were ordered by the government through Police Commissioner Varney Dempster to shoot indiscriminately into the crowd of about 2000 people. At the end of the day, it was reported that more than forty people were killed but the Tolbert government refused to turn the bodies over to their families for burial (ibid). There were widespread looting and destruction of public and

---

[5]Susukuu is a combination of two Liberian institutions. Susu is a form of savings bank in which committed members contribute money in a pool and give it to members on a rotational basis. The process is continued until the last member in the circle receives their share. Kuu is a communal farming method in which a group of farmers take turn in working on individual member's farms.

private properties. "More than 160 stores had been ransacked, many of them owned by Lebanese, resulting in $35 million worth of property damage and theft (Sirleaf, 2009). President Tolbert, in a nation-wide radio address, accused PAL leader Gabriel Baccus Matthews and his collaborators of "engaging in rampant vandalism, looting and hooliganism." Matthews fled to a foreign embassy near Monrovia and was later turned over to the government by a Liberian clergyman, Bishop Brown. At that time, I was in high school in Tappita, Nimba County about 153 miles northeast of Monrovia.

Meanwhile, the Tolbert government solicited help from President Sekou Toure of neighboring Guinea in restoring law and order. President Toure responded by dispatching 700 Guinean military personnel who spent about three weeks in Monrovia before returning home. The government suspended the writ of *habeas corpus* (an order which requires a person under arrest to be brought to court), imposed a state of emergency, and closed the University of Liberia. They carried out massive arrests of citizens including the leaders of PAL and MOJA. All those arrested were charged with sedition and treason, and jailed. Before the Organization of African Unity (OAU) scheduled conference in June 1979, of which President Tolbert was the incoming chairman, by virtue of the fact of being the host; the government granted executive clemency to all the detainees. The conference passed off successfully in Liberia without any political incidents. The Rice Riots virtually exposed the vulnerability of the Tolbert government which eventually marked the beginning of its fall.

In late 1979, PAL filed legal documents with the Probate Court of Monrovia to register as a political party. After much legal hurdles that the government placed in the way to block PAL's registration, the organization finally registered on January 8, 1980 as the Progressive People's Party (PPP). In the evening hours of March 3, 1980 at the party headquarters, the leadership of the party requested all the assembled members to march to the Executive Mansion (presidential palace) to have a meeting with the President. At the entrance of Mansion, the security forces denied them access to the main grounds. In fact, President Tolbert was out of town. About four days later, PPP issued a Declaration of Intent. In the Declaration, Chairman Matthews called for a nation-wide strike to force the president to resign. The Party's decision infuriated President Tolbert, who in a radio address to the nation, vowed to be "mean and tough." Once again as was predicted, he ordered the arrest of Matthews and other party executives and subsequently banned the PPP after being given emergency powers by the Legislature.

The April 12 1980 Coup

I had been in Monrovia since mid-December 1979 and had attended many gatherings at the PPP headquarters on Gurley Street. Between December 1979 and late March 1980 when the party leaders were arrested, there was an increasingly menacing atmosphere looming in the city. Strange things began to happen, one of which was a report of an explosion in the Topoe Village area of Gardnersville, the northern suburb of Monrovia that killed one person believed to be a PPP member. There were rumors of demonstrations everywhere in Monrovia that added more fuel to the menacing atmosphere. In the Waterside business district of Monrovia, someone would say that PAL was gathering to demonstrate, and the whole area would run amok. On April 12, 1980 two days before the anniversary of the rice riots, the government of Dr. William R Tolbert Jr, Liberia's 19th President was overthrown in a bloody coup by 17 non-commissioned officers of the army, all of them indigenous Liberians. The Americo-Liberian oligarchy that had ruled Liberian for 133 years had been violently dethroned.

Meanwhile in Monrovia and around the entire nation, the coup was received with wild jubilations. The junta moved swiftly to assert control. They constituted a military council under the rubric of the People's Redemption Council with Master Sergeant Samuel Doe as Chairman and Head of State; Staff Sergeant Thomas Weh Syen, Vice Chairman/Vice Head of State; Corporal J Nicholas Podier, Speaker; Corporal Fallah Varney, Secretary General who later died in a tragic motor vehicle accident early 1981; and Thomas Quiwonkpa, "Strongman of the Revolution" as Commanding General of the Armed Forces of Liberia. Doe became the first indigenous Liberian to head the government after 133 years of independence. Civilians appointed to high level positions included: Gabriel Baccus Matthews and

Painful Journey: a Story of Escape and Survival

Oscar Quiah[6] of the banned PPP, Minister of Foreign Affairs and Minister of Internal Affairs minister respectively; Dr. Togba Nah Tipoteh and Dr. H. Boima Fahnbulleh of MOJA were named Ministers of Planning & Economic Affairs and Education respectively. At present Tipoteh is still President of Susukuu, an NGO founded in 1973 (Sirleaf, 2009). Fahnbulleh was later appointed Foreign Minister succeeding Matthews. He is the present National Security Advisor to President Johnson-Sirleaf after having been her harshest critic for long time (ibid). The military council commissioned a tribunal that was chaired by General Frank Senkpeni to try former officials of the ousted Tolbert government. At the end of the trials, 13 former officials mostly of Americo-Liberian stock, were found guilty of rampant corruption, abuse of public office, and condemned to death by firing squad. Ten days later (April 22, 1980), the executions were carried out in a gruesome fashion on the beach behind the military barracks. The convicted were tied to poles and shot. There were widespread cases of rape, looting of homes and businesses, and wanton destruction of properties owned by Americo-Liberians which literally uncovered what uncontrolled military rule signified (Schwab, 2001). The coup and its corresponding reprisals against the Americo-Liberians served as a central propellant for mass exodus into exile (Sirleaf, 2009).

The Nimba Raid

The events of late October, 1983 which infamously came to be referred to as the Nimba Raid did indeed add more fuel to the conspiracy to remove Doe from power. It was the first open sign that there was a deep-seated Krahn-Gio/Mano tribal animosity within the military junta. Prior to the raid, on August 14, 1981 the junta executed five members of its own including vice head of state Maj-General Thomas Weh Sehn. Others were, Col. Harry Johnson, Col. Henry Zuo, Col. Robert Sumo, and Col. Nelson Toe, which created some level of division within the junta, but not deeply ethnically based and as open as the

---

[6] Internal Affairs Minister Oscar Quiah and Planning and Economic Affair Minister Togba Nah Tipoteh were implicated in the coup plot of 1981 in which Vice Head of State Weh Sehn and other top junta members were executed. Quiah was acquitted by the military tribunal. Tipoteh who was out of the country at the time of his implication resigned his position and did not return to the country.

one that developed between Doe and Quiwonkpa, which destroyed the foundation of the junta. In fact, Col Nelson Toe and Col Harry Johnson were also members of Doe's Krahn tribe. General Thomas Quiwonkpa was a Gio from Nimba County while Head of State Samuel Doe belonged to the Krahn ethnic group from Grand Gedeh County.

In a statement to the Truth and Reconciliation Commission, Alhaji Kromah indicated that Head of State Doe had several key areas in the military strategically manned by members of his tribe. While on the other hand, from the days of the coup, General Quiwonkpa had burst on the scene as a national hero, popular among the "masses" and the soldiers of whom he was their commanding general. It was expected by the general public that a split between the two top coup makers, would create chaos. "People knew the chaos a split between Doe and Quiwonkpa was likely to cause," Kromah testified (Kromah, 2008).

Under pressure from the international community for a return to civilian rule, Doe appointed a Constitution Drafting Commission headed by Dr. Amos Sawyer. When it was apparent that the pathway to civilian rule was getting paved, Doe began to hint at heading the constitutional government himself. Quiwonkpa, sensing that his power base would be diminished if Doe became civilian president, advised Doe against any intention of running, stating that it would be "a betrayal of the revolution and he was not going to encourage it," as was revealed by Alhaji Kromah[7]. The Commanding General (CG) wanted Doe to stick to their promise of handing over power to the civilians. But Doe had made up his mind and was poised to follow through with his plan.

The Commanding General's opposition to Doe's ambition created a serious rift between the two top brass of the military junta. In that light, Doe appointed Quiwonkpa to the position of Secretary-General of the military council which was deemed to be lower in stature. General Quiwonkpa refused to accept the position. The head of state considered the General's refusal an affront to his authority. In a press release, which was broadcast on national radio, Doe indicated that as career soldiers,

---

[7] Statement by Kromah, Alhaji, former information minister of Liberia during the military regime, to the Truth and Reconciliation Commission; Monrovia, August 11, 2008. Kromah also headed the ULIMO-K armed faction in the 1990s. At present he is Ambassador-at-Large, Ministry of Foreign Affairs.

a subordinate officer should never refuse to execute an order from a superior officer. Such disobedience was subject to stiffer punishment in keeping with the Uniform Code of Military Justice. He therefore had no other choice but to dismiss the General, strip him of all his entitlements, and subsequently order him out of the military barracks (Kromah, 2008).

The Commanding General relocated to a temporary private residence on Carey Street in downtown Monrovia where a group of his supporters and friends, mostly from Nimba County, frequented to demonstrate their support as well as allegedly instigate him for action against Doe. The constant visits were alleged to have fueled the flames of ethnic tensions between Doe and Quiwonkpa. The Liberian public was informed of this when several of the General's associates were arrested and paraded before national TV. One of the accused, Major Kalonko Luo, who engaged in a ferocious process of confessing the alleged conspiracy on national TV, implicated several of the General's associates including: former Labour Minister Moses Duopu and former Managing Director of the Liberian Electricity Corporation, Harry Yuahn. Others were: Col John Nuahn, Lt Paul Toweh, Cooper Teah, and many more. Fearing for his life, General Quiwonkpa eventually fled Monrovia north to his farm in Nimba County close to the border with Guinea and the Ivory Coast.

Some supporters who converged on the farm with him included former Deputy Minister of Internal Affairs, Samuel Dokie and former Inspector General of the Armed Forces of Liberia, General Robert Saye. Robert Saye attended the Tappeh Memorial High School in 1974, the same year I enrolled in the school. I was not his crowd by any measure: age wise, social leaning, academic, or otherwise. He did not know me, aside from probably seeing my name on the Honor Roll, four classes below his, every term. He was in Grade 10 while I, Grade 6. I had voted for him in an election in which he voted for President of the Students Council government and won by a landslide. Bob Saye, as we referred to him during his days at Tappeh Memorial High, was eloquent, a man of tremendous qualities, and above all, book smart.

He probably might not have returned as student to Tappeh Memorial High School beyond 1974, except occasional appearances when he would be dressed in military uniform to teach students military drills, especially during period leading up to August 24, the day set aside by the Liberian government to commemorate National Flag Day. He was Captain in the militia, a paramilitary organization established by the Liberian government for ceremonial drill purposes.

One day circa 1977, President Tolbert made a stopover on Tappeh Memorial High Campus en route to the Kwendin Vocational Training Center, about seven miles south of Tappita. That meant students had to assemble to receive the President as usual. During the official ceremony, Captain Robert Saye, smartly dressed in appropriate military uniform, led the President on an "inspection of the guards" tour. He had put on a remarkable performance which did not go unnoticed by the President. After the inspection, the President shook Captain Saye's hand and would not let go. They chatted for some time while the rest of us still standing in formation, looked on. When it was all done, a jubilant Bob Saye came running to the students with good news: President Tolbert had requested that he join him upon his return to Monrovia. When the President returned to Monrovia, as was advised, Bob Saye followed, spent several weeks in Monrovia, but was unsuccessful in meeting with the President. The disappointed Bob Saye however, returned to Nimba.

A year later, President Tolbert visited Kwendin again with the usual stopover on Tappeh Memorial High Campus. Having been through that situation a year earlier, it was déjà vu all over again. This time when President Tolbert held Bob Saye's hand, I guess he must have probably said, "I thought I had told you before to meet me in Monrovia?" At that point, the President ordered a member of his entourage to take Bob Saye along with them to Kwendin. The next time President Tolbert visited Tappita, which certainly was his last, Robert Saye was in full Armed Forces of Liberia military regalia and assigned with the President. He wore the insignia of the rank of lieutenant. Lieutenant Saye was on duty at the Executive Mansion on April 12, 1980 when the military coup occurred and he was incarcerated by the coup makers. Two days later he was released by the military and appointed Superintendent of Nimba County. From there, the military junta appointed him Deputy Minister of Internal Affairs. Between 1982 and 1983, he was again promoted to the rank of General and appointed Inspector General of the Armed Forces of Liberia, a position he would be relieved of later that year.

Painful Journey: a Story of Escape and Survival

One night at General Quiwonkpa's farm, something went terribly awry when a sentry, Galakpai mistakenly shot and killed General Robert Saye. Sadly that night, Nimba County as well as Liberia lost one of its finest. Albeit from the farm, Samuel Dokie led the raid on government offices and on facilities of the iron-ore mining company, LAMCO in Yekepa that killed a number of people (Ellis, 1999). They further attacked the residence of Plant Protection Force Director, Charles Julu and killed his son in the process. Julu was a Krahn man and joint security chief exercising great deal of power and authority among the Gios and the linguistically related Manos in Nimba. Due to that, he became the focal point for all the anti-Doe sentiments that brewed in the county. Majority of the main actors in the raid hailed from Nimba County.

The government responded by perpetrating massive reprisals against the people in the county. There were stories of mass arrests, detentions, harassments, rape and intimidation of some residents of Yekepa, Sanniquellie, Ganta and other towns and villages for alleged complicity in the raid. Quiwonkpa fled along with Dokie, Prince Johnson and others. Months later the government freed Major Kalonko Luo and the Monrovia-based group after a relentless appeal from the public. Minister Duopu, Yuahn and others, fled into exile also. But that was not the end. They embarked upon a massive campaign of recruitment and training exercises for the November 12 Invasion and the civil war.

Charles Taylor was one of the first to flee the country in the early part of 1983. Taylor, a graduate of Bentley College in Boston, MA USA; fled to escape an impending government financial audit in which he was accused of embezzling under $1 million US during his tenure as director-general of the General Services Agency (government procurement office) from 1980 to 1983. He was a son of an Americo Liberian father and an ethnic Gola woman. His marriage to Quiwonkpa's relative did the bidding for him in terms of having a personal connection. In 1984 Taylor was arrested in Somerville, MA and spent 15 months in jail pending extradition to Liberia (Liebenow, 1987). He would later break jail by using a hacksaw to cut the iron window and tied bed sheets together and escaped (Sirleaf, 2009). He went to Libya and teamed up with the likes of Prince Johnson and others for intensive training in guerilla warfare and subsequently launched an armed rebellion against the country in 1989. In 1997 he was elected President of Liberia. Six years later, in June 2003 President Taylor was indicted for war crimes by the International Criminal Court on Sierra Leone. On August 11 the same year, he resigned as president and flew into exile in Nigeria. On March 29, 2006, the former president was arrested near the border with Cameroon while leaving Nigeria. He was tried in The Hague and was found guilty and is serving a 50-year sentence in England.

November 12 Invasion

On October 15, 1985, general elections were held which were marred by major irregularities and blatant rigging. (One of Liberia's leading newspaper at the time, *Footprints*, printed pictures of several ballots papers being burnt). Doe was declared winner after a 50-member commission comprising government officials and private individuals other than the Election Commission, was constituted to count the ballots. In the early hours of Tuesday November 12, 1985 the nation was awakened by the pre-recorded voice of the former Commanding General of the Armed Forces of Liberia on national radio that said in part: "Fellow Citizens, this is Gen. Thomas Quiwonkpa. The Patriotic Forces as of now have seized power. Our forces have completely surrounded the city. Samuel Doe is in hiding. There is no escape for him…" (Kromah, 2008). The invaders had entered the country from Sierra Leone by way of the Mano River Bridge to the west.

That Tuesday morning, I was just about preparing to go to work but had to cancel every plan in order to monitor radio announcements and the volatile political situation unfolding. A few of my housemates and I converged in front of the building we resided in at the corner of Coleman Ave and 17th Street, in the eastern suburb of Sinkor to listen to radio together. There were massive jubilations in the streets everywhere. Around 9 o'clock a.m., we saw hundreds of people, many of them with palm fronds and tree branches singing and dancing, in carnival-like fashion, heading west on Coleman Avenue toward Monrovia city center. Their bodies and faces were decorated with white chalk. The song being sung was a familiar tune that I had heard a 'million times' while a student and soccer star in Tappita:

Painful Journey: a Story of Escape and Survival

Gon yah puh, hee yon (The man has fallen)
Ah dae lo keh buoe(His mother will eat peanuts)

It was a popular Gio song. It was a song raised by cheerleaders on a soccer field against the losing side or against a team scored on. But that November 12 morning was no soccer game. It was literally a real game of life and death. My friends, who were of different tribes, and I continued to listen to radio while the processions went by. At the corner of 17th Street and Gibson Avenue, one block north of where we were standing, was the residence of General Alfred Glay, Aide-de-Camp to President-elect Doe. He was also a cousin of the President-elect. I recognized Glay's relatives who were also military personnel, armed to the teeth, driving to and from the house which made me to speculate that perhaps Doe was still in the Mansion. Or maybe he was truly in hiding and his loyal soldiers were regrouping to launch a counter-offensive. I began to piece together all these plausible scenarios.

Meanwhile Commanding General Quiwonkpa's pre-recorded message continued to be played repeatedly on the radio for several hours until one Col. John Nuahn took to the airwaves. Col Nuahn was also a Gio and a very close associate of General Quiwonkpa. He was one of those implicated in the anti-Doe gatherings at the General's residence in the barracks and the temporary residence on Carey Street. The Colonel was part of the group that was pardoned by Doe and he was reinstated in the army. But he did not go into exile with the General. That morning when the Colonel heard his buddy's voice, he ran to the radio station to offer his support but turned out hurting the process.

Col. Nuahn was heard on radio calling on soldiers of the Executive Mansion and the First Infantry Battalion in Camp Schefflin to lay down their arms or else they would invade those garrisons. The First Infantry Battalion was commanded by another Doe's cousin, Col Moses Wright. Hearing Nuahn's orders and seeing the aide-de- camp's well-armed relatives going in and out of his house, made me to conclude that Doe was still in the Executive Mansion. I then gave my opinion to the gathering that Doe was still in the Mansion. At that moment, one of my housemates, Kollie (name withheld) shouted back at me in a rather threatening tone: "Doe still in the Mansion ehn? Wait y'all damn Krahn people, y'all will see what we will do to y'all tonight." I was shocked but not frightened, shocked that a person considered a friend who and I belonged to the same soccer team, lived in the same house with me, ate from the same pan some days, with whom I played the games of checkers and Scrabble, was harbouring such evil intent against me and my family simply because we belong to the tribe of Head of State Doe. My major concern was Joanna who was pregnant with our son Gerald. I went in the room to tell her to get ready in case we had to leave the house for the night. I came back to the gathering where I remained for the rest of the day.

Crowds of people were still milling about on nearby streets. But we did not have a clue about what was unfolding in the downtown area of Monrovia. By 2 p.m., President-elect Doe spoke on the radio and told the nation that Gen Quiwonkpa's attempted military takeover had failed and that he was still in control. All the streets got effectively emptied of people at once. By 6 o'clock p.m. the Doe government television broadcasts showed early morning footage of arrests and detentions of cabinet ministers and other government officials captured by Gen Quiwonkpa's supporters. Many of the arrested officials were physically assaulted, verbally abused, stripped naked, and publicly humiliated. In one of the scenes, General Quiwonkpa was seen at the TV and radio station attempting to justify the reason for the "takeover" while at the same time speaking against bloodshed. He had also captured the Barclay Training Center military barracks which was in close proximity to the Executive Mansion. Other military facilities that briefly fell to the General were the arsenal, a few blocks up the road from the barracks and the defense ministry, one block west of the arsenal. Subsequently, the government ordered a nation-wide manhunt for the General after the coup failed.

After Doe reasserted state control, the next morning November 13, we gathered at the usual spot in front of the house to monitor news broadcasts again. I had completely forgotten what transpired between Kollie and me the previous day when his roommate Gardea (not real name) signalled to talk to me. I momentarily stepped away from the group to hear what he had to say. Surprisingly, Gardea began to plead for forgiveness on behalf of Kollie. He said the young man had fled the group moments after Doe spoke on radio and had hidden under their bed. At the time Gardea was talking with me, it was around 11 o'clock a.m. November 13 and Kollie was still underneath the bed. Upon hearing that, I burst into laughter and proceeded to make fun of Kollie. I followed Gardea to their bedroom and yelled at Kollie to come out. He was still shaking and scared to death. When he finally heard me laughing out loud, he came out. Kollie had thought that as a Krahn man, I would have complained him to officials that he threatened me during the brief period General Quiwonkpa was said to have been in control. I told Kollie not to be afraid for I was bigger than that. In order to make sure the issue was resolved, Gardea brought a few bottles of beer from the fridge and we "knocked glasses." From that day on, Kollie got very close to me. He worked in the projector room at the Relda Cinema where he used to take me to watch movies. At Kollie's urging, I watched all the 1986 FIFA World Cup games free of charge at Relda when Diego Armando Maradona and Argentina won the World Cup.

Kollie was somehow justified in being scared. During the aftermath of the botched November 12 invasion, many people seen celebrating in the streets or suspected of supporting the Commanding General were believed to have been detained, killed or dismissed from their jobs. It was the same time a young and vibrant radio and TV journalist, Charles Gbeyon was killed. His death still remains a mystery today. The guilt by affiliation syndrome that Kollie had applied on me was used by both the coup makers and the government security forces during the November 12 military conflagration. During the few hours that General Quiwonkpa was seemingly in control, his supporters who were mainly Gios and the linguistically related Manos went on a rampage victimizing Krahns and looting their homes. Those excesses created the opportunity for a cycle of revenge and recrimination that followed. Emmanuel Dolo, a prominent Liberian scholar who is also a son of Nimba County, indicated that even though Quiwonkpa had called on his supporters to refrain from any acts of violence, a large number of Mano and Gio people did the opposite. They allegedly raped women, murdered Doe's loyalists, particularly Krahns and Mandingoes and also engaged in the wanton destruction of their properties. Dolo also pointed out that physical violence, such as public flogging of Doe's loyalists were pervasive in Sinkor and other parts of the country (Dolo, 1996).

When the tide turned against the General, all hell broke loose in Nimba County, home of the Commanding General. According to reports, LAMCO Plant Protection Force Director Charles Julu who was in hiding, re-emerged and began rounding up people. During the Nimba Raid, Julu's house was attacked and his son killed. Now that the coup failed, it was seen as an opportunity to exact revenge. Julu was accused of murdering several Gios and the linguistically related Manos including a prominent Nimba politician, D K Wonselea (Berkeley, 2001). Hundreds of residents of Nimba fled into exile as a result of the broader campaigns of reprisals carried out by government security personnel. Consequently the seething rage and plot to unseat Doe and mete out violence against the Krahn people thickened. This plot is best summed up by Dr. Alfred Kulah, a prominent Nimba scholar. (Introduction).

In the aftermath of the failed coup, in December 1985, the Doe government carried out a policy of massive lay-offs of hundreds of public employees, a move the government described as an austerity measure intended to boost economic recovery. But many critics accused the government of purging out of its ranks, persons suspected of celebrating during the abortive coup. Some heads of government ministries and public corporations allegedly used the policy as pretext to rid their offices of "potential enemies." In a country that absolutely has no unemployment insurance opportunity or any kind of safety net, an employee laid off is practically on his own. Not only is he on his own, so are the number of family and extended family members who depend on him/her for support. Hence the December 1985 massive lay-offs created the opportunity for more anti-government or anti-Krahn sentiments.

CHAPTER THREE

Making the Run

"There is no greater sorrow on earth than the loss of one's native land"

– Euripides 431 BC

It was Wednesday, June 27, 1990. The mid-year morning sun was still struggling to burn its way through the stratus-cumulus clouds that had gathered in the sky. The day looked gloomy and unpredictable. A week ago, the National Patriotic Front of Liberia[8] (NPFL) rebels cut off water supply to the city and all speculations pointed to electricity being cut as well. I woke up that morning with a terrible feeling as if something of catastrophic proportion was about to happen. At that point I embarked on an unyielding process of negotiating with my mind on whether to stay home for the day or reluctantly show up for work. As a matter of fact, chronic absenteeism had become the new normal for the employees at National Housing Authority, a public corporation where I worked as Administrative Assistant to the Deputy Managing Director for Administration.

I finally mustered the courage to go to work. It was two days before pay day and maybe Managing Director Paul Mulbah would do an early release of paychecks which would enable employees to stack up food and other essentials before the war entered the city. I sat at my desk completely oblivious of what was unfolding outside when a co-worker

---

[8] The National Patriotic Forces of Liberia, led by Charles Taylor initiated the war in Liberia on December 24, 1989

barged into my office to give me the terrifying news. When we looked out the window we could see people running helter-skelter because of the massive shooting that was taking place. Soldiers from the Barclay Training Center military barracks on the south side of the city started a shooting spree that soon engulfed the entire city in record time. At first it seemed like the rebels were already in the city. Panic gripped everyone in the office and we started packing up to leave and be with our respective families in case the war was actually in the city.

Down the streets in the Waterside business district which was always over-crowded, there was massive evidence of a state of confusion and pandemonium. People were running to and from all directions of the city but did not know why there was such a large scale shooting. Amid the heavy gunfire, the only thing I could hear people saying was, "*Ay na easy over there o*" which apparently added more fuel to the confusion. Of course some Liberians are fond of feeding the rumor mill like that. Those running from Waterside toward city center were mentioning that "it was not easy in Waterside." Likewise those running from city center toward Waterside were saying the same thing. No one was in a position to give an explanation of what was actually happening.

I quickly packed up and jetted out of the office toward city center and saw the same situation playing out. Moments later, the city got emptied of all commercial vehicles, so I had to walk home across the bridge north to Battery Factory but still not knowing why the shooting was going on. About 1 o'clock p.m. military police officers in vehicles were seen driving up and down all the major streets of Monrovia yelling out cease-fire orders. Another hour or so would go by before the trigger-happy soldiers stopped shooting in the air and the real story was then told by many. The story was that a soldier who had been convicted by the military tribunal for war crimes was sentenced to death by firing squad. During the march to the beach, the convicted soldier escaped into one of the housing units of the military barracks. One executioner shot in the air, then another, and then another until soldiers in other parts of the barracks and the city joined in. The shooting also coincided with an organized demonstration that was happening on Lynch Street near the military barracks in which the protestors were chanting "monkey come down", an apparent reference to President Doe to step down. One thing, the shooting was clearly a prelude of what was to happen when the real war entered the city. The shooting incident helped to hasten my resolve to get out of the country.

One of the things in life that I do not believe or will not ever subscribe to is the possibility of having a psychic or a soothsayer predict my future. Twenty-five years ago if someone had told me that I was going to leave Liberia for safety reasons and spend 20 years in exile, I would have questioned the person's sanity. I would have probably added that the person was recovering from hangover after consuming a large quantity of alcohol the previous night. As a matter of fact, the civil war started basically not only as a war intended to dethrone the government of the day but also to cleanse the country of the Krahn, the tribe that I belong to, which I alluded to earlier. Therefore safety for me and my family was the first and foremost important thing I needed to provide since the state could no longer do so. All along during high school days, like most Liberians my age, my dream was to travel to the United States after completing university studies to obtain higher educational credentials and return home. Not one moment in my wildest imagination did it ever cross my mind that I would become a refugee spending most of my productive years in a foreign country.

Why was fate so inconsiderate, cruel and ridiculously conspiring against me now? Why must the war come at a time when I was about to graduate from university after all the years of unyielding struggle and hard studies? Why did Taylor choose this era to bring war to the country? I wrestled with the many *whys* that had populated my mind. The more I asked myself why the more difficult it was for me to arrive at any clear answer. My father, even though illiterate, always pushed me to go to school when I was a kid growing up in Kakata, a city about 35 miles east of Monrovia. And when I reached the age to determine the importance of education, seeing my classmates in St Christopher's in Kakata being driven to school by their parents or driving themselves to school while I walked six miles every day to and from school, made me stronger and I pushed myself even harder also. However, my desire to get an education was always characterized by a long string of unending struggle. By sheer coincidence during my school years, I always lived three to five miles east of all the schools I attended from where I would walk to and from school five days a week. It was not by calculated design. In Monrovia 1982 while attending the University of Liberia, I lived with my sister in the Sherman Bar compound of 16th Street, Sinkor the headquarters of Liberia's 1st Division team, Mighty Barrolle. I remember sometimes walking to and from the University of Liberia which was about three to five miles just to save my bus fare for lunch. I would sometimes go the whole day on campus without a meal. After the first school year in 1982, I dropped out for three years because my sister could no longer afford to sponsor me.

After I relocated to Tappita from Kakata in the early 1970s, I lived in the east end Gibson Town suburb of the city. From that location, I used to walk six miles to and from the Tappeh Memorial High School each day. Consequently, after going through this litany of unyielding struggle mentioned above, I was looking forward to a great deal of prosperity and a promising future for my family and me. But all that changed.

It all started when Clan Chief Jerry Gonyohn reported to the government of some subversive activities intended to destabilize the country being hatched in Nimba County. Being a chief and not wanting to see his kinsmen subjected to government heavy-handedness again like the reprisals that occurred in the aftermath of the 1983 Nimba Raid and the November 12 invasion, whistleblower Gonyohn felt the right thing to do was to inform the government. In mid November 1989, President Doe immediately appointed Internal Affairs Minister Edward Kumo Sackor to launch an investigation. The Minister then delegated authority to Nimba County Superintendent, Stephen Daniels to carry out the investigation. Minister Sackor, a son of Nimba commanded tremendous respect among his people and was a trusted confidante of the president. At the end of the investigation, the Minister reported to the President that the information was baseless and unfounded. Consequently whistleblower Jerry Gonyohn was relieved of his chieftaincy and incarcerated.

During the same time in 1989, while Monrovians were planning for the Christmas and New Year's Day celebrations, rumor mills were churning with news that a lady in Nimba County had given birth to a child, which immediately spoke in English prophesying that deadly rains would fall on Christmas Day. After giving the prophecy, the child died. As usual we treated the rumors for what they were and carried on with life. Consequently, when the government reported news of an incursion, everyone pointed to the deadly rain story as a continuation of the vicious rumors which government critics believed would be used as a viable pretext by government security personnel to clamp down on the people of Nimba once again. In the wake of the attack the government arrested a group of NPFL fighters who had infiltrated the city waiting to strike at the opportune moment. The dissidents were paraded before national TV in which the main culprit, Harrison Mentoh Diakpo (not sure if related to Cummings Diakpo) confessed taking training through Burkina Faso to Libya. Almost all the arrested NPFL infiltrators spoke of one Yeagbehee Digbon as the chief recruiting officer. In spite of all the drama unfolding on TV every night, many Monrovians questioned the authenticity of the confessions. Most believed those were choreographed confessions orchestrated by the government to implicate the people of Nimba in another episode of subversive activities. Not until the *Daily Observer* newspaper printed photographs of victims of the attack on Butuo in one of its editions and BBC Radio interviewed Charles Taylor on New Year's Day who claimed responsibility for the attack, that some started paying attention. Of course the deadly rains turned out to be an invasion of the country on December 24, 1989. The NPFL had invaded Liberia through Butuo, a small town in Nimba County situated on the northern border with Cote d'Ivoire. Chief Gonyohn was vindicated and later released while Minister Sackor was relieved of his duties and replaced by my former high school principal and football/soccer coach Ansumana Kromah, another son of Nimba County.

When the NPFL launched the war, I was completing the final courses for a Bachelor's degree at the University of Liberia. In extra curriculum activities I was also serving as President of the Public Administration Students Association. On February 16, 1990 while participating in the graduation ceremonies along with several hundreds of my classmates at the University of Liberia Fendall campus, the fighting had spread in Nimba County about 180 miles north of Monrovia and was entering the central Liberian county of Bong. And it was clear that the NPFL and the government soldiers had no intention of abiding by the laws of war, nor to the laws governing the protection of civilians during war time. All the factions acted with a sense of complete impunity.

By March, the City of Monrovia was beginning to heavily feel the pinch of the war. The population of the city had swollen to astronomical proportions. Monrovia had by this time become the only safe haven for all the displaced people from the leeward counties. Families, the elderly, motherless and fatherless children could be seen arriving in droves from dawn to dusk each day. Many Krahn people who lived in counties closer to Monrovia other than Grand Gedeh, relocated to Monrovia. Ethnic Gios and the linguistically related Manos who were in similar situation also relocated to Monrovia. The Krahns for their part feared being pointed out to the rebels by members of other tribes who had been living in the same communities with them. On the other hand, some Gios and Manos who relocated to the city did so in order to escape reprisals from government troops in other parts of the country. It was a known fact that Taylor's NPFL rebels comprised mostly Gios and the linguistically related Manos.

Even with the explosion of the population, by 4 p.m. downtown Monrovia would look like a ghost town as everyone was leaving the city centre as fast as they could. By 5 p.m. one would stand for hours on end downtown Broad Street waiting for a vehicle in order to leave city center. No one wanted to be caught up in the middle of the fighting between government forces and the insurgents.

That still did not deter me from attempting to satisfy my grandiose thirst for more knowledge. I still hoped against all odds that the situation would be better. In March 1990, I enrolled in the Louis Arthur Grimes School of Law at the University of Liberia to study Law. The law school is located on the southwestern end of the university campus across the street from the Executive Mansion, the presidential seat of government from where the war was being prosecuted. Classes would be disrupted by the constant roaring of military vehicles and equipment leaving the Mansion yard. That always scared the living hell out of me. Thus I finally resigned myself to the hard fact that the war could not be contained by the government despite government officials and top military brass attempting vainly to allay the fears of the citizens by claiming to have "things under control" and "conducting mopping up" exercises. The war was escalating and the situation was rapidly spiraling out of control. In addition to the NPFL's battlefront successes, Taylor and his aides were also winning the propaganda war. By 1700 Greenwich Main Time (GMT) the entire population of the city would be glued to the radio to listen to BBC World Service news followed by 1709 GMT *Focus on Africa* news. BBC frequently updated the country about activities of the war. The government-owned radio station was no longer credible to bring verifiable independent news reports from the war zone. Therefore classes would be disrupted and all the students and professors would assemble in the courtyard to listen to the BBC news broadcasts. As usual, Taylor or the NPFL defense spokesman Tom Woweiyou would take to the airwaves fighting the war psychologically. That worked in their favor immensely.

Between March and June 1990, as rebel forces drew closer to Monrovia, the Liberian army unleashed a reign of terror on the capital after the President called on Liberians to take up arms, machetes, and knives to fight the rebels. Civilian disappearances became commonplace, and bodies began to pile up in the streets. Monrovia thus teetered on the brink of anarchy. Predictably, it was civilians of the Gios and the linguistically related Manos associated with the NPFL who were the most vulnerable. First it was the body of an Americo-Liberian businessman Robert Phillip whose throat was gruesomely slit from ear to ear in his home. Four days later the bodies of two other persons murdered in a similar gruesome fashion were discovered. In late May, another three headless bodies were found in the northern suburb of Gardnersville with their hands bound behind their backs. It was increasingly apparent that the Liberian army was losing the war at the battle front. As they lost territory to the approaching rebel forces, the government's administrative authority rapidly collapsed. The army took over, imposing military rule. Tribal elements within the army hierarchy first isolated and then began killing troops from other tribes, mostly Gio and Mano soldiers, whom they assumed to be sympathetic to Taylor's NPFL (Ellis, 1999).

Additionally, government troops engaged in the systematic process of rounding up civilians and charging them as "rebel collaborators" which carried with it, more serious punishments of lengthy detention, mysterious disappearance, or death. Even petty criminals and street hustlers would prefer other names to being labeled a rebel collaborator. One evening, while waiting for a taxi cab at the Johnson and Broad Streets intersection, I saw a group of persons pursuing a street hustler from the Crown Hill area located east of where I was standing. People in the group were yelling out, "rogue, rogue" (thief) but the hustler would not stop. Then someone yelled, "rebel, rebel." As soon as he spotted two well-armed soldiers accosting him, the suspected thief stopped running immediately to dissociate himself from the rebel label, "*I na rebel; I rogue*" (I am not a rebel but a thief), the suspect blurted out in Liberian Pidgin English. At first the soldiers laughed but took him aside for more questioning. I later found a taxi and went home. The suspect's action may have seemed funny to the soldiers and other onlookers, but the most essential thing was that the man was fighting for survival. The best way he felt justified in preserving his life was to agree to being called a thief.

Hundreds of ethnic Gio and the linguistically related Mano people who lived in Monrovia along with their kinsmen who relocated to the city from other parts of the country, did not feel safe in their homes in Monrovia. Many of them sought refuge in the St Peter's Lutheran Church compound and the Don Bosco Polytechnic campus, a Catholic Church-run institution, both located in Sinkor. Other frightened displaced sought refuge in the UN compound in Congo Town, a suburb of Monrovia. At the same time, some fled east of the city toward the territory under the control of the NPFL to enlist.

On a number of occasions, I visited some of my friends at the church and at Don Bosco.

In similar fashion, young Krahn and Mandingo men in Monrovia, who were encouraged by prominent government officials, began undergoing quick military training in Camp Schefflin, a military barracks about fifteen miles east of Monrovia and given arms to defend themselves against the rebels. They were referred to as the "volunteer soldiers."

Unfortunately, the UN compound was raided in the latter part of May by armed men who killed the guard on duty and abducted several people believed to be mostly Gio and Mano internally displaced people.

Even though I was back in school, with the constant news of rebel gains on the battlefront and their rapid advance to the capital, I could

Painful Journey: a Story of Escape and Survival

not practically comprehend what was being imparted under the atmosphere of heightened tension and rising insecurity. Was it time to leave the country? If indeed I planned to, how could I do that with no savings account from which to buy a one-way ticket to relative safety? In addition to this nagging question was the fact I could not afford a ticket for myself, let alone the possibility of providing for family household members of six persons or more. Every passing day presented new challenges and questions which answers I could not provide. The atmosphere in the city grew tense day by day as there were trucks filled with people and their belongings fleeing the city. Foreigners were also leaving the city in droves. I wanted to take my family to Grand Gedeh in the southeast and if possible cross over to the Ivory Coast. But the road to Grand Gedeh had been cut. Traveling by sea and by air were the only ways to get to the southeastern counties of Grand Gedeh, Sinoe, Grand Kru, and Maryland.

Military planes were available at the James Springs Payne Airfield. The airport was located in the Sinkor suburb east of the city. I attempted three times to negotiate for a seat on the military plane but I was not successful. To secure a seat on the military plane on a daily basis, one had to have connections with the power elites at the Executive Mansion and that connection I did not have. I had grown up in Tappita, Nimba County and not in Grand Gedeh. Therefore I was not acquainted with most top government officials in the Executive Mansion most of whom were from Grand Gedeh. My other liability was that I belong to the section of Krahn in Grand Gedeh County that is closer to the western border with Nimba County which was marginalized and persecuted by other sections of Krahn.

Because of the area's close proximity to Nimba County, Krahns from that section were (and still are) given a stereotypical name of "Terramycin Krahn."[9]

---

[9] Terramycin Krahn is a stereotype given to a section of Krahn called Gao, which is an indication of a second or third class Krahn, or not a full-blooded Krahn. Terramycin (tetracycline) which is an antibiotic used to cure infectious diseases is a capsule of yellow and red colors. Thus to equate that section of the Krahn with being Terramycin Krahn is to say practically that they are half Krahn and half Gio because of their location on the east bank of the Cestos River, the boundary between Nimba and Grand Gedeh Counties. The Gao Krahn is also on the west side of the river in Nimba and they are referred to as Nimba Krahn.

Jerry Gbardy

I vividly remember in January of 1986, two months after the abortive invasion of Liberia on November 12, 1985, President Doe had invited all citizens of Liberia hailing from Grand Gedeh County for a unity meeting in the county capital of Zwedru. As a person coming from the county, I made the trip too in one of the buses provided by the president. When we arrived in my hometown of B'hai which is about two miles east of the border with Nimba, I asked the bus driver to stop so that I could speak to my parents. The temporary stopover was also necessary to allow passengers to get out and stretch their legs after a long ride. My parents' house was situated by the main highway to Zwedru. Before we could disembark, someone asked: "Are you a Terramycin Krahn too?" The whole bus erupted with "Terramycin Krahn, Terramycin Krahn"! It felt terribly shocking and disappointing. I thought Krahn was Krahn. Perhaps due to some level of naiveté, I could not accept the perception or fact that there was a section of Krahn – the one I belong to - which was totally deemed to be lower in stature than the others. My trips, therefore, to the Springs Payne Airfield on a daily basis in search of a seat on the military plane, were indeed a fruitless venture.

Another reason for the area's disappearance off President Doe's development radar was the issue about the executions in August 1981 of two prominent sons of the so-called Terramycin Krahn area, Col Nelson B Toe and Col Harry Johnson of the military council for allegedly plotting to overthrow the military regime. From that point, Doe never made any conscious effort to visit that area in his capacity as president even though the area is within his county. The so-called 'Terramycin Krahn' area was perceived to be anti-Doe. So being a Krahn from that area, the odds were stacked up against me to get a seat on the military plane. So I finally abandoned the pursuit as it was not worth the effort.

In another light, my wife Joanna and I seriously considered the possibility of relocating to another part of the city where we thought our non-Krahn neighbors would not be able to identify us. Being Krahn and or working in the public sector provided the grounds for summary execution by the NPFL fighters. I was guilty of both. I worked in a public corporation, the National Housing Authority and I am Krahn. I could not change that. Monrovia being a relatively small city, it was pretty much impossible for me to live in another area without being recognized. I played soccer and was an avid supporter of one of Liberia's biggest clubs, Mighty Barrolle. I also attended the University of Liberia. Therefore socially, I was well-known. Nevertheless I still gave relocating to another part of the city a try. We found an apartment on the other side of the city. On the day that Joanna and I went to pay the deposit, I saw people in that area that knew me. At that point, I changed my mind.

By the final week of June, all the major roads connecting Monrovia were cut off. The NPFL and the INPFL, a splinter group of the NPFL which was headed by Prince Johnson, controlled the roads. Monrovia by the day was getting very dangerous and unlivable. Water had been cut off and residents were getting water from wells which were judged to be unsafe. The next amenity that would go as we suspected was electricity. At that point there was much urgency to propel our departure for anywhere outside the country. We got news that the road leading west toward Sierra Leone was open and passable. But I did not want to risk traveling on the road with my family without first getting concrete assurance from someone that had travelled on it before in order for me to venture out on it. Like a miracle unfolding, I got the unexpected break that I did not think would have ever come. The day was Friday June 29, 1990 and the time was 1709 GMT when the NPFL defense spokesman Tom Woweiyou granted an interview on BBC *Focus on Africa*. He revealed that the NPFL had cut off all the roads from Monrovia except the one leading to Sierra Leone. He further mentioned that they had the capacity to close the road but were deliberately leaving it open to provide safe exit for civilians. He further warned that anyone who ignored the warning and remained in Monrovia would be considered a soldier, a Krahn, or a supporter of Doe and that meant death. Prior to this, in previous interviews, Woweiyou and his boss Charles Taylor were heard mouthing on BBC that the only good Krahn man was a dead Krahn man or the only good Samuel Doe was a dead Samuel Doe.

I did not need further elaboration. There is a common Liberian adage: "When a blind man threatens to stone you, he already has a rock in his hand." The threat was absolutely real. After the Woweiyou interview, we concluded that it was time to leave the country. I reckoned that, no matter how much virulent anti-Krahn, anti-Doe, anti-government propaganda the NPFL officials spewed on international airwaves solely intended to score more battle front points, there was always some measure of credibility in it. It had been like that from Butuo at the northern border with Cote d'Ivoire where the war started up to this point. I did not trust whatever the government was saying about "having the situation under control." The frontline was going to be at our doorstep any time soon. I was therefore not willing to risk it and wait any longer.

I immediately assembled my family in the living room and solicited the view of my wife Joanna and our friends Richard Kamara and his fiancée, OJ who were also sharing the three-bedroom house with us in Gardnersville. Joanna and I met at the National Housing Authority in December of 1984. She had gone there to do vacation job when I was already working there full time. She was born in Tappita, Nimba County and grew up in Zwedru, Grand Gedeh County, while I am from Grand Gedeh but I grew up in Tappita. Her hometown is Zodru in Kpiaplay Chiefdom, Nimba County. I did not know her prior to our meeting at the National Housing Authority. She lived with her sister, Annie and husband, Mr. Chea Nayou, the eldest brother of Dr. Harry Nayou who once served as Minister of State and Co-Chairman of the Election Commission in the Doe government. Old man Chea Nayou relocated to Zwedru with his family including Joanna, (the old man passed on in 1992). Joanna, who is from a very large family just as I am, completed the Bishop Juwle High School, a Catholic institution in Zwedru in 1982 before going to Monrovia in search of better opportunity. We met and began dating in January 1985 and have been married since that time.

Her father, Johnny Zleh Krayee, was one of the most powerful and well-respected old men in Kpiaplay Chiefdom. His popularity, wealth, and power had been measured by the number of wives and children he had, which, to this day, is normal and culturally acceptable in many sub-Saharan African countries. From the polygamous relationship, he would give life to many children including Joanna and her siblings: Frances, Annie, Valarie, Janet, Emmanuel, the late Alfred, Augustine, and many others.

Joanna was seriously at the forefront of the relentless campaign for us to leave the country. Her home chiefdom of Kpiaplay was one of the first places attacked by the NPFL rebels in the early part of 1990. Hundreds of Krahn people were killed and the rest fled north to the Ivory Coast. After the NPFL rebel attack on the chiefdom, Joanna's uncle was missing in the bush and was found several weeks later. Her mother Kweh also spent almost two months in the bush before eventually crossing the Cestos River to the Ivory Coast to join her husband who had fled earlier.

Kpiaplay Chiefdom in Nimba County is predominantly inhabited by ethnic Krahn people otherwise referred to as Nimba Krahn. The chiefdom is situated on the west bank of the Cestos River at the point where the river forms the boundary between Liberia and the Ivory Coast and between Nimba and Grand Gedeh Counties.

We all agreed that it was time to leave Liberia as painstaking as it was. Sometimes leaving your country voluntarily was hard, leaving under those circumstances – forcibly leaving to preserve our lives because we belong to the "wrong tribe" – was not only harder but utterly painful. Right after the meeting, my family boarded Kwame Ireland's car for Sierra Leone. Kwame and I became friends when we did a couple of courses together at the University of Liberia in 1982. I stayed behind because of lack of room in the car to accommodate me. That Friday night, electricity was cut off from the whole city by the rebels. My worst fear had come to pass.

The next morning, Saturday June 30, 1990 I ran to the parking station of vehicles going to the Sierra Leonean border. I was later joined by my nephew Richard Parker. Together we hopped on the first commercial vehicle leaving Monrovia for Bo Waterside, Sierra Leone. My journey out of Liberia – the one and only country I had known and lived in since birth - had just begun. It was painful. It felt like I was just going for a ride down the road to return a few hours later. No, I was escaping the horrors of war. I was running away to save my life and going to the land that I had never before seen. This is the day that will forever remain etched in my mind. As we drove north from Water Street into Bushrod Island, rivers of tears began to flow from my eyes. Everything Joanna and I had worked for and owned remained in the house. Janet, Joanna's younger sister who was living with us was left behind. I also left behind my mother, step-mother, siblings and other relatives in far away

Grand Gedeh County. They fled to the Ivory Coast later that year. Was I going to come back in a couple of days, weeks, or months? A large dark cloud of uncertainty took hold of me.

In any event, I joined my family later that afternoon in Bo Waterside-Liberia where they had spent the night in a motel. The town with a population of about two-hundred was the last town before crossing the Mano River Bridge, the border between Liberia and Sierra Leone. Together we crossed into Sierra Leone and settled in Bo Waterside-Sierra Leone, just half mile from the border.

The next day Monday July 2, 1990, Kwame and I chose to go back to Monrovia for some obvious reasons. I was going back to the National Housing Authority to pick up my paycheck, cash it and procure some provisions for the family and cross back into Sierra Leone the same day. We boarded Kwame's car and headed to the bridge, a minute's drive from the house we resided in. Bo Waterside-Liberia which was still under the control of Liberian government soldiers had three checkpoints: one on the east while entering the town from Monrovia and the other two on the west end before going to Sierra Leone. It had a small military detachment, customs and immigration, and the Special Security Service (SSS) offices. The border outpost was overrun on November 12, 1985 by the invading forces under the command of former Commanding General Thomas Quiwonkpa. After that abortive invasion, the Liberian government somehow improved the communication facilities at the post. So the SSS, the presidential security unit had direct communications link with the Executive Mansion.

When Kwame and I crossed the bridge and entered Liberia, the soldiers lifted the first gate but not the second. So the vehicle was now stuck between two gates.

"Where y'all going?" asked a soldier in Liberian English.

"To Monrovia."

"What y'all going for?" the second soldier demanded to know.

"We are going to get our things to come back."

"Y'all na know we fightin' war then y'all going up and down?" the second soldier asked again.

"We know. That is why we are going to get our things to come back," I replied.

Painful Journey: a Story of Escape and Survival

"Y'all know then y'all leaving us here?" the other soldier chimed in.

"But we are not soldiers," I tried to get smart with him.

The response drew the ire of the soldiers. I had earlier suspected that behind those questions was some hidden motive that soon came to the fore.

"Where is the bill of sale for the car?" one soldier asked.

Kwame opened the glove compartment and pulled out the facsimile copies of the vehicle registration documents and handed them to the soldiers.

"That photocopy, ehn? Where is the original?" the first soldier quizzed holding the document upside down. I doubt whether he ever knew what was written in the bill of sale.

"I left it home."

"Why you *na* (not) put it in the car then you bring the photocopy?" the second soldier added.

"I am keeping it at home just in case something happens to the car," Kwame explained.

"You keepin' it home ehn? You *na* bring it the car *na* (not) going nowhere," the first soldier demanded.

All our efforts to explain to the soldiers that it only made sense to keep the original copy at home just in case the vehicle got stolen, proved futile. The intimidation and harassment began and continued in earnest because they wanted the car.

"In fact give me the keys," the soldier ordered.

We refused. During the heat of the verbal argument, I walked away momentarily from the checkpoint to see if I knew any officer at the customs and immigration offices located about hundred yards away who would probably intercede on our behalf. Even though I did not know anyone there my trip was not entirely in vain. While walking down past the SSS office which door was wide open, I stumbled upon a conversation between the radio operator and somebody in the Executive Mansion in Monrovia who probably might have been a superior officer, giving orders to be relayed to the larger military barracks in Tubmanburg, a few miles to the north. The message was that rebels had attacked Monrovia on two fronts: Caldwell Road junction (west) and the Paynesville Red Light suburb (east). The caller stressed that as he was speaking, fighting was raging between NPFL insurgents and Liberian government forces.

Upon hearing that, I hastily returned to the checkpoint and whispered the information to Kwame. We both agreed that it was not safe for us to journey on to Monrovia because the only way to Monrovia from Bo Waterside was through the very Caldwell Road junction, the scene of the fighting. We went to the soldiers and told them about our change of plan and that we wanted to go back to Sierra Leone.

"What you hear over there?" the soldier inquired about why the sudden change of mind.

"Nothing," I said.

To tell them what I heard was going to be grounds for more problems for us. They would have accused me of being in contact with the rebels and would have probably charged me with being a "rebel collaborator" which was a serious charge then. Refusal to give out information was a lesser charge than being labeled a rebel collaborator, so I chose the former. That infuriated the soldiers and they detained us for another hour, making a total of three and a half hours. When they finally realized that I could not divulge any information to them, they released us but only lifted the gate behind the vehicle. We backed up on the bridge and all the way into Sierra Leone.

CHAPTER FOUR

Beginning of Refugee Life

My refugee life began on Sunday July 1, 1990. It was the day my family and I crossed the bridge to Sierra Leone. We joined Sister Payennon who had been there since May. We had traveled with some money from Liberia but our major worry was what would happen if the money ran out. The country we had run to was itself a developing country where resources, job opportunities were gruelingly scarce. That Sunday night I could not sleep. When I closed my eyes, I could see a group of refugees, with bundles on their heads, fleeing the fighting in the south between John Garang's Sudan People's Liberation Army (SPLA) and the government of Sudan. The Sudanese refugees looked emaciated and terrible. I could also see images of particularly Sierra Leonean refugees who fled political violence from the very Bo Waterside area that we were now in. I could play in my mind how those refugees were camped out in the open on the Liberian side of the Mano River. Yes it was still fresh in my mind how Head of State Samuel Doe personally brought some relief supplies to those Sierra Leonean refugees in 1983. The biggest questions running through my mind as I was visualizing those images retrospectively were: Was this the way it would be for us too? Why did it come down to this? What did we do wrong to deserve this? Or maybe we might not be there for long? How could we carry on for months or years if the war did not end soon? How would our children go to school? When would the war end? By then we were clueless about aid agencies providing relief assistance to people like us with no home, food, clothing, or shelter.

Those many questions produced three schools of thought as I lay in bed that Sunday night. In the first school of thought in respect of my situation, I summed up the definition of the word refugee in an unconventional way as one who has persistent and insurmountable problems. The name refugee was synonymous to unabated struggle, pain and deprivation. All of what one owned before in terms of material gains and family members are lost. This school of thought further added that life as a whole was characterized by hopelessness and uncertainty.

The next school of thought that weaved through my exhaustive mind that July 1 night was that as a refugee, one was somehow glad to be far away from danger which forced you to flee for life and liberty. No sounds of gunfire heard again. No threat of rebel advancement. No more threat of one being pointed out to one's enemy for being member of the wrong tribe. No more horrific scene of summary executions and brutal murders. Life was somehow better in a way that one was dependent on the government of the asylum country to enjoy maximum security protection provided. Hence life was too precious and worth the living.

I was between sleep and wake. The thoughts flowed freely as if I was reading a piece that I had written earlier. Anyway the school of thought that finally popped up in my mind was that no matter the condition, refugees were real people who given the opportunity, would contribute to the good of their receiving society. At that point, the names of the following personalities came to mind: Philippines President Corazon Aquino, Spanish President Felipe Gonzales Marquez, and the great physicist Albert Einstein. They too were refugees. If they could come out of the refugee situation and become renowned personalities, I too could one day. I might lose my homeland at the moment, I might lose my family members and material possessions at the moment, but once I still have my life, I should look to the future with cautious optimism. I reminded myself of this wise saying: "Suffering produces perseverance, perseverance produces character, and character produces hope." I jumped out of bed and went outside. At that point, I committed the lives of my family and mine to the Almighty God.

The chiefs of Bo Waterside-Sierra Leone (Gendema) welcomed every refugee that crossed into Sierra Leone. By late June to early July, refugees began streaming across the bridge daily in high volumes with what they could carry. Later, it proved to be in the interest of the chiefs and the local population to open their door to refugees. The presence of about two-hundred thousand refugees in Gendema and surrounding towns and villages opened up the area to more economic activities. This once quiet town of about two hundred inhabitants had now become the epicenter of business activities in the entire Pujahun District and beyond. The town was situated half mile into Sierra Leone across the Mano River Bridge. By Saturday, which was market day, many people would come from surrounding towns and villages and from across the bridge in Liberia to trade. Of every ten persons, especially NPFL fighters that crossed on a given market day, seven or eight of them knew me. They were people that came from Tappita where I previously lived. Some of them would invite me to visit them across the Mano River Bridge. I would just smile and say to myself, 'these guys have no idea how I feel.' The town had a large police barracks situated up on the hill overlooking the Mano River Bridge. We practically stayed in that border town under the false illusion that the war was going to be over in the next four to five months and it would have been relatively easy to cross back into Liberia. In that light, we rented one bed-room in a motel. Sister Payennon and her six children, our aunt, and my family of four, crammed up in that one bed-room. My younger brothers Beto and Zaire; nephews, Kaffie, Darlingboy and Boone; and cousin, Votee built their own house and moved in it. My friend, Kwame and wife Valarie and their children rented a house near the marketplace. He later got a job with an NGO. At year's end, they moved to Bo, Sierra Leone's second largest city.

The highway to Sierra Leone was temporarily closed after the July 2, 1990 attack at the Caldwell Road junction. The following week the road was reopened after the Liberian government soldiers beat the invaders back. The lull in the fighting afforded many refugees the opportunity to cross the border into Sierra Leone carrying whatever their vehicles could hold. My brother Beto and nephew Kulah Parker seized the opportunity to join us in Bo Waterside-Sierra Leone. Kulah and Richard spent a couple of weeks with us and left. Kulah went to Freetown while Richard continued the journey to Cote d'Ivoire. A week later, specifically mid-July, Gen. Charles Julu, Samuel Doe's military chief at the Executive Mansion crossed into Sierra Leone. Julu's crossing that afternoon created a huge stir among many Krahn and Mandingo refugees in the area. His departure they believed – and rightly so – signified that the Doe government was losing the war. Julu, who was from the same Gborbo Clan in Grand Gedeh County as the President, was accused by the refugees of abandoning his clansman at the time Doe needed him the most. In the wake of the 1985 November 12 invasion, Julu was appointed army general and assigned in the Executive Mansion. Prior to that appointment, he was the commander of the LAMCO Plant Protection Force, the iron ore mining company in Yekepa, Nimba County. He was accused of committing atrocities in the county.

That mass influx of refugees provided the perfect opportunity for Sierra Leonean local government officials and citizens to exploit. From the chief police officer (CPO) down to the constable and local chiefs, everyone was in the habit of scrambling for "valuables" from the refugees. They would buy household items, electronic equipment and vehicles from refugees for little or nothing. I personally witnessed a business transaction between a Liberian friend of mine and a Sierra Leonean in which the Liberian was grossly duped. Due to the lack of knowledge of the value of the Sierra Leonean currency, the Sierra Leonean bought the four-door sedan valued at $10,000 US for 5000 Leones, an equivalent of about $500 Liberian dollars. At that time, a Liberian would be so exited upon hearing the words "thousand Leones" and automatically assumed that it was the equivalent of thousand United States dollars, only to find out later during spending that its purchasing power was lesser in value than even the Liberian dollar, let alone US dollar. A thousand leones was good enough to buy about two to three plates of rice in a local eatery. Other times the locals would take the vulnerable and destitute refugees' possessions under false pretense. Many border guards would unrealistically demand to see receipts of personal items that the fleeing refugees had just crossed the border with. If there were none, the border guards would seize the items for themselves.

It was July 23, 1990 at 5 o'clock p.m. We had just gathered around the radio to listen to BBC news when there were sudden bursts of heavy artillery and small machine gunfire across the bridge. The Liberian border post was under attack by the NPFL rebels. Within a few minutes, we could see Liberian soldiers, customs, and immigration officers running across the bridge into Sierra Leone while some swam across the Mano River to safety. Others were not so lucky. About thirty minutes later, the shooting subsided. But from our vantage point, we could see flames of fires and thick pall of smoke billowing in the sky over the town from burning houses, clear evidence that Bo Waterside-Liberia was now in NPFL hands.

Days later, the influx of refugees increased considerably. They came only with items they could carry on their heads and not in vehicles anymore. The International Red Cross came in. Through Mr. Thomas Parker who was head of the Liberian refugees, Red Cross empowered us to begin registering new arrivals and all of us who had crossed the border earlier. Thus I began to work as volunteer assisting the Red Cross in registering old and newly arriving refugees. Everyday there were hundreds of Liberians crossing into Sierra Leone who told horrific, gut-wrenching stories of physical and mental brutalities meted out by the rebels across the bridge. According to many refugees, there were several checkpoints along the Babangida Highway leading west into Sierra Leone. To leave one town or village to another, a person had to be issued a travel pass which was the *modus operandi* of the NPFL security apparatus. A person without a pass could be charged with being a Krahn, a Mandingo, "Doe soldier" or a spy which would be grounds for summary execution. But getting a travel pass to travel from Clay Junction to Gbah (a very notorious checkpoint manned by a ruthless killer called "Gbah Ray") to Tienne to Bo Waterside along the highway, took weeks and sometimes months. Once the refugees crossed into Sierra Leone, they were safe and would report to our booth situated by the roadside in the courtyard of a local chief for registration. All of the refugees whom we registered between late July and late November looked emaciated and severely dehydrated.

On the morning of July 30, 1990, a month after I fled Monrovia, BBC Radio news reported that a group of armed men had attacked the St Peter's Lutheran Church in Monrovia the night before (July 29, 1990) killing about 600 people mostly Gio and Mano women and children. One Col Yonbu Tailey, a hunter-turned AFL volunteer soldier admitted being the mastermind in commission of the heinous crime (Youboty,

2004). Stephen Ellis describes it as the war's worst atrocity in its first period (Ellis: 2001).

In late August, my uncle's wife Anna and her children arrived along with a group of refugees carrying bundles on their heads. She and the children were dehydrated and hungry. I was excited to receive them. After registering them, I excused myself to take them to the house. She told me that Uncle Thomas "Uncle T" Giah was still across the bridge trying to negotiate his way to Sierra Leone. The NPFL fighters were doing rigorous screening of men before giving them travel pass. Maybe Uncle T would have to be across there for an undeterminable period of time or maybe he might not come at all, I thought.

Uncle T, as he was commonly called, was my favorite among my five maternal uncles. He also contributed significantly to my high school education in the 1970s. I used to spend my summer vacations with him in Monrovia at the time he worked with the Liberia Electricity Corporation. Before the war we lived in Monrovia but he was in the borough of New Kru Town. The war had separated everyone.

An hour later, to everyone's surprise Uncle T arrived. He showed up by way of the back of the house using a footpath.

"Oh, that's Uncle T!" his nephew Votee yelled out.

I ran out to see him. I could not recognize him. His head was bigger than his entire body. He had an unkempt bushy afro hairdo reminiscent of a guy who had been living in the wild for months. His beard was about four inches long and wore a mustache that covered his mouth. He had not seen a razor and had not showered for quite some time. Uncle T appeared terribly mashed up and ruefully woebegone.

'Uncle T, thank God to see you! How did you come from the back instead of walking across the bridge?' I asked.

"Jerry James," as he always called me, "I swam across the river."

"What! You swam? How did you do that?" I asked with more curiosity beckoning.

"When I watched Anna and the children walking across the bridge, which was when I made my move." He continued, "I walked down stream pretending to be a resident of the town going to the farm."

"Wow!" Joanna exclaimed. "You were lucky the rebels did not see you."

"Yes I was. If I was caught, I was not going to live to tell the story."

"So Uncle T, tell me how you did it."

"I walked further down and when I was completely out of sight from the town, I went to the river's bank. I took off my clothes, tied them on my head, and waded into the water. A Sierra Leonean was on this side of the border waving me on. As soon as I was safely across, he showed me the footpath that led me behind the house."

"Uncle T, thank God to see you o," my sister added.

His story was incredibly fascinating. Taking such a calculated risk to evade the rebels and swim across the wide Mano River required a character of a dare-devil adventurer as Uncle T. He was fearless. His escape to safety brought relief to all of us. When he had settled in, he confirmed most of the horrific stories told by refugees who crossed into Sierra Leone earlier. As a Krahn man traveling with his family, he denied his tribe every step of the way before swimming across the Mano River. At the end of September, another relative Mlanyonnoh Mamie Sohn crossed also. As for her, my sister had given up on her. We did not know her whereabouts when the war hit Monrovia. She joined other internally displaced and fled to Tubmanburg, a few miles to the north across the Mano River. As a Krahn woman, she had survived in rebel held territory by posing as a member of another tribe.

A local business woman, Madam Mamie Sao owned about four buildings in a compound one of which we were renting. But if an NPFL fighter offered her twice as more money for a night than what we were paying per month, Mamie Sao would come with a bunch of police officers and evict the refugee the same day in order to make way for the rebel tenant. The NPFL rebels had more money and looted goods, so they used that immensely to their advantage. She harassed my sister frequently threatening to evict us based on such notion. This had nothing to do with non-payment of rent. It had all to do with the landlady proving that it was her country, she owned the property, and she could do as she pleased. As a matter of fact, my sister still had three months' rent advance payment with the landlady but that did not matter at all. As fate would have it, we contacted a local chief who leased to us a plot of land to build a thatched-roof house.

The trouble started for me in October when I used a file to sharpen a machete to cut sticks to build the house. I had not done such manual work for about fifteen years. The file did not have a wooden handle as was supposed to be. So the constant rubbing of the file on the machete blade with the sharp metal end in my left palm, created a friction which produced a huge blister in my hand. An hour or so later, pus developed in the blister and it became extremely painful. After three days, I visited the clinic and the nurse I suspected, used a non sterilized blade to cut into the blister in order to drain the fluid. The wound got infected thereafter. For three months I was in excruciating pain, unable to sleep or eat. At certain time I could not wiggle my fingers as I had lost all the nerves in my left hand. In late December 1990 with some miracle my hand healed. It took weeks of physiotherapy to enable me use my left hand again. I still carry a big scar in my left hand up to today. Sadly Uncle T and my brothers completed the house without my contribution. It was a four bed-room house with thatch roof, mud-daubed wall, and dirt floor. Due to increasing pressure from Mamie Sao, we moved in the house in November when the floors and the walls were still soaking wet. The premature occupancy made all the children ill from the moisture. Every day and night we built what appeared to be campfires in all the rooms in order to dry the floors and the walls. The very first night we moved in, heavy torrential rains came down and flooded the entire house due to its location at the foot of the hill. The next morning we had to start the camp fire exercise all over which lasted for several weeks. We made beds from bamboo and mattresses from grass to sleep on. Albeit, we began to gradually adjust to the new realities of living life as refugees. We had no choice.

One sunny afternoon later that year, when hundreds of refugees gathered in the customs and immigration building to distribute food rations, former Chief Justice of the Supreme Court of Liberia, Counselor Chea Cheapo arrived in a black Mercedes Benz with a retinue of NPFL bodyguards. Interestingly, to this day, where ever Counselor Cheapo arrives, there is no shortage of excitement and controversy. The counselor is a fearless outspoken Liberian politician and lawyer. He has a "shoot from the hip" personality.

Painful Journey: a Story of Escape and Survival

Cheapo was legal counsel of the Progressive Alliance of Liberia in 1979. He guided the political organization to its registration as a political party (Progressive People's Party), which was later banned (Chapter 2). The Tolbert government incarcerated him along with Baccus Mathews and other party executives. The counselor was freed from jail moments after the military coup of 1980 and appointed Minister of Justice succeeding Joseph Chesson, the man who had raised him. (Chesson and twelve former government ministers were executed by firing squad ten days after the coup). Later in 1981, Cheapo fell out of favor with the junta and was dismissed for allegedly stockpiling arms. He went into private legal practice for a while until he was nominated for the position of Chief Justice of the Supreme Court of Liberia in July, 1987. Even that nomination did not go down without a modicum of controversy. He was rejected in the first confirmation vote by the Senate Judicial Committee. During the next round of re-nominating Cheapo, President Doe publicly scolded two Senators from Bong and Monsterrado counties for voting against Cheapo's confirmation. Cheapo was subsequently confirmed in the second round of voting.

A few months in office, a major controversy arose that led to a constitutional crisis. Probate Court Judge Harper Soe Bailey and an insurance executive, Muna Stubblefield were thrown in jail for allegedly trying to bribe the Chief Justice. According to Cheapo during a press conference, Bailey and Stubblefield offered him $2000 bribe as an inducement for him to approve of employees of the Temple of Justice to be covered by Stubblefield's insurance company. Cheapo then asked the two to come back later in the afternoon. Moments before the appointed time, he brought in journalists from the information ministry down the road and hid them in the closet of his office. He only brought the journalists out when the alleged bribery attempt was in progress. At that point the Chief Justice ordered their arrest and detention at the South Beach Prison. Upon hearing the news President Doe drove to the prison and ordered the release of the two detainees. The President's action angered Cheapo. He accused the President of unconstitutionally interfering in the affairs of the Judicial Branch of the government for which he tendered his resignation. President Doe rejected the resignation but proceeded to bring impeachment charges against him anyway. During the impeachment proceedings, Cheapo stormed out of the Senate and accused Vice President Harry Moniba of presiding over a "kangaroo court". In early December 1987 Cheapo was impeached by the Senate.

Upon his arrival at the Sierra Leonean immigration building, Cheapo was swarmed by a group of refugees greeting and welcoming him. He requested to speak to the immigration officer in charge who then ushered him into the office. Pretty close to thirty minutes, Cheapo came out of the office and with a folksy smile, yelled out to his NPFL bodyguards to go tell Taylor that he was not going back to Liberia. The crowd roared in excitement, "Cheapo, Cheapo!" He boarded the car and headed west toward Zimmi.

The area within Bomi and Cape Mount Counties (Liberia) was under the command of one Col. Oliver Varney of the NPFL. The rebel commander was revered by Sierra Leonean local government officials so much so that when he crossed into Sierra Leone with a retinue of armed bodyguards for "bilateral talks," they gave him a tumultuous reception befitting of a foreign head of state. He came in a convoy of about fifteen vehicles that was escorted to the police barracks by more than ten Sierra Leonean police officers on motor bikes, a truckload of armed Sierra Leonean soldiers, and SSD officers. Once in the barracks, the police would not allow any refugee near the barracks including those Liberians who lived with Sierra Leonean families in the barracks until the rebel commander left.

Information obtained later after the visit spoke of ways in which the NPFL regional commander would strengthen business relations with the Sierra Leoneans. After the visit, truckloads of looted goods and produce came from Liberia quite frequently. The area became the playground for NPFL fighters who were so-called "friends" of local officials. A rebel commander who went by the pseudonym of Rambo would frequently visit the CPO wearing a skirt and a head scarf like a female. He used the visits to build a "better working relationship" with the Sierra Leoneans. But little did the Sierra Leoneans know that the NPFL fighters were trained guerillas who could not be trusted. They were using their frequent visits and shady business ties to gain the Sierra Leoneans' confidence and to also surreptitiously map out the area for a surgical military attack as we will see later in the next chapter. This speaks volume of an old adage that says: "He who rides a tiger always ends up in its belly."

Initially the trade relations between the two groups were so strong that the rebels would entrust their Sierra Leonean counterparts with looted goods which they would sell and return the cash proceeds later. That arrangement would last for a couple of months until the Sierra Leoneans breached that trust. They too proved that they could not be relied on when it came to keeping their words on money matters. The Sierra Leoneans would sell the looted commodities but would refuse to remit the proceeds to the NPFL fighters. However the NPFL rebels ultimately had the last laugh. Truckloads of goods stopped coming. The visits of Rambo and others became infrequent. Then in the early part of 1991, rumors swirled around that relations between the NPFL fighters and their Sierra Leonean counterparts had strained.

Inherently the Sierra Leonean police officers in Gendema had a huge penchant for money and looted goods which the NPFL fighters had aplenty. The police officers were underpaid by the government of Sierra Leone as such, they would engage in corrupt activities to make ends meet. Therefore when it came down to police conduct, the words morality, credibility, integrity and professionalism were taken off their list of vocabulary years before the refugees arrived. There was a common saying in Bo Waterside which encouraged, condoned, and perpetuated bribery and other forms of corruption: *Usai den taye cow na dey ee dey eat* (Where they tie the cow is where it should eat). That literally meant that an employee/worker was supposed to get other benefits, perks, largesse - illegal or otherwise – at his place of assignment aside from his compensation.

That also referred to extortion, accepting of bribe, engaging in larceny, and so on. Therefore the local police officers accepting bribe in the open was commonplace, acceptable and a normal way of life. Corruption among public employees in Bo-Waterside was a culture. Those days, the scenario always played out like this: A complainant filing a case with the police would first have to pay for the pen and the sheet (s) to be used for statement-taking and would also pay the constable to take the statement and to summon the defendant. Well when the defendant arrived, it was time for the real game to begin. At that point, decision or verdict to be rendered in the case would not be determined by what was right but conditioned on who had the fattest wallet. In other words, justice was for sale and was dispensed in favor of the highest financial bidder. I do sincerely hope all that has changed for the better after the country experienced one of the most horrific civil wars ever recorded in history.

The local police department's relationship with the NPFL fighters was so cordial that the fighters could do no wrong in Bo Waterside. Several times, NPFL female fighters coming into the Sierra Leone market would taunt ethnic Krahn and Mandingo women by making comments such as "I want to drink Krahn or Mandingo woman's blood" which would spark a serious verbal confrontation that police would be called in to break up. When the case got to the CPO or his deputies, they would scold the refugee women and order them to go back to the market.

One night around 7 o'clock p.m., while we stood around under a shelter in a market place analyzing BBC news reports as usual, we saw a group of Sierra Leonean soldiers and police officers walking toward the border seemingly antsy. About twenty minutes later, they came back. And then their numbers increased. Our attempt to find out what was going on was met with an order to "leave the road and go to your respective houses." An officer would later confide in someone from our group that a senior police officer was in captivity across the bridge. What an embarrassment for the Sierra Leoneans! The rebels allegedly lured him across the bridge and vowed to continue holding him there until all their money owed was paid. The entire barracks was restless. They were forced to raise the money that night in order to secure the release of their comrade.

By late November, many of us resigned to the full realization that the war was not going to end anytime soon as Taylor was settling for nothing less than the presidency. After the capture and execution of President Doe on September 9, 1990, there was a fresh war raging between Taylor's NPFL and the West African peacekeeping force, ECOMOG which Taylor saw as a stumbling block towards claiming the ultimate prize. Therefore life for us in the new country must go on. With the help of two Liberian Football Association's FIFA batched referees in persons of Clay Albert Gibson and Alex Nagbo, we organized regular football tournaments that brought together refugees and Sierra Leoneans alike. In effect we started the local integration process until all that changed. Clay and Alex joined us in Bo waterside not by choice. They had been in Freetown refereeing an international soccer match July when the airport in Monrovia became a battle ground. Since indeed they could not fly back to Monrovia, they came by road to Bo Waterside to attempt to go to Liberia but got stuck also. The NPFL was now in control of the border town.

During their fight with the Taylor's NPFL, the peacekeepers secured Monrovia to allow civilians to leave the city. Many refugees arriving from the barracks and the mansion in Monrovia told us the news about surviving and dead relatives and loved ones. It was reported that my uncle, J Norman Bantoe whom I lived with in Tappita was murdered by some of his co-workers. His crime was that he was Krahn and had worked for the Bureau of Immigration and Naturalization after leaving Tappita.

Why didn't he agree to flee like other government officials did? Was that blind loyalty or stubbornness or miscalculation of severity of the war? I remember on Friday June 29, 1990, the eve of my departure from Liberia, I had gone to his house on Congo Town Old Road and unsuccessfully tried to persuade him to leave like I was doing. He said, "Talk to Junior and Frederick to go with you. For me I will stay here." Norman Jr and Frederick were his sons. He had taken them to Pujahun in Sierra Leone in May to leave them with his Sierra Leonean family friends but the children refused to remain there claiming that there was "no life" in the town. Fortunately for them they survived the war but their dad did not.

CHAPTER FIVE

Seventy-Two Hour Trek to Safety

Boom, boom, ka, ka, ka, pow, pow, pow! Those were the sounds of heavy artillery and assault rifle fire coming from the Liberian side of the border that woke us up during the early morning hours of Wednesday, April 3, 1991. An invasion of Sierra Leone was effectively underway. Within a few minutes, the combined forces of the Revolutionary Forces (RUF) and the National Patriotic Forces of Liberia (NPFL) had encircled the entire town of more than 10,000 inhabitants. The town was engulfed in absolute pandemonium. Everyone - refugees and citizens - was heading inland west toward Zimmi 27 miles from the border.

The RUF, a Sierra Leonean rebel army was created by dissident Cpl Foday Sankoh in 1991. Sankoh trained in Libya along with Charles Taylor of Liberia in the 1980s. The rebel army would later become notorious for brutal practices such as mass rapes and amputations during the Sierra Leonean civil war. Rebel leader Sankoh would later be arrested in Freetown after his soldiers gunned down a number of protesters outside his home in 2000 and he would later die of complications arising from stroke in 2003 while awaiting trial for war crimes.

Heavily groggy and confused, I sprang from bed, accidentally head-butted the door and fell to the floor on my tailbone. My first reaction was, "Those bastards are here." I rubbed my eyes in order to clear my blurry vision and sat on the floor for another three to five seconds. When I finally composed myself, I grabbed two pairs of my shoes, a few clothes, and two books which I threw on the bed. I hurriedly pulled the bedding over those items and stepped in the hallway. My next move was to search the remaining rooms to make sure no kid was hiding in the corner. Once I was satisfied, I threw the bundle on my left shoulder and ran out being careful not to run in the direction of the shooting.

Situated atop a hill a few yards from my house, was a police barracks which was the open target for the invaders. The Sierra Leonean government built it in the early 1980s to house the Sierra Leone Police (SLP) and the Special Security Division (SSD). It was built in the wake of the political violence that rocked the area during that time which led to mass exodus of refugees into Liberia.

Of the two law enforcement agencies sharing the barracks, only the Special Security Division that officially bore arms. The SSD was initially known as the ISU (Internal Security Unit) when it was set up by the late President Siaka Stevens due to continuous threats to his regime in 1972 (Ero, 2000). It was a paramilitary force solely created to protect Stevens and his government and put down riots and demonstrations. The government sent many of the first recruits to Cuba for training and years later, they began training in Sierra Leone. From the looks of things, the SSD seemed poorly equipped. On many days, they would be seen in their gray weather-beaten, thread-bare camouflage uniform and wearing flip flops, heading to their guard posts with AK-47 assault rifles on their shoulders.

I hurriedly went up the hill through the barracks to get to the main road to Zimmi. When I turned the corner and reached the center of the barracks, shells began to rain heavily on the barracks. An SSD personnel who was as startled and scared to death as I was, rushed from his house with an AK-47 rifle in hand. He tried to shoot in the direction I was running from but the rifle jammed. While struggling with the rifle his pants also started falling from his waist. In the process of attempting to dejam the rifle and preventing his pants from falling, the gun went off accidentally sending several hot pellets past me by a whisker and other shots lodged in the ground near me. Being so terrified, I fell and the bundle on my shoulder went flying with its contents scattered about. As if I had not seen enough danger yet, I got up and started picking up the items one by one. Finally when the SSD officer realized that I was not hit, he yelled at me in Creole: *"You refugee, commot dey."* (You refugee, get out of there).

Painful Journey: a Story of Escape and Survival

I ran down the hill as fast as I could while shells were still heavily raining on the barracks. Flying bullets were not in the business of distinguishing between refugees, police officers or ordinary Sierra Leoneans. The Chief Police Officer (CPO), protector-in-chief of NPFL fighters, was one of the first to flee because he was extremely lucky to own a vehicle that he used to get away as fast as he could. We walked past him sitting in front of a house in a town called Gonwah, few miles west of Bo Waterside-Sierra Leone. Till this day, I still wonder what was flowing through his mind that fateful morning as he sat on a bench with his chin ducked in palm. As for his deputy the Officer Commanding (OC), he was in pajamas and fleeing barefoot like some of us. The guy who suffered the most humiliation was the number three man of the police detachment. He ran out of a refugee woman's house in his underpants. The lady's friend had to help him with a blanket which he wrapped around himself. Some service personnel, who briefly stood up to the RUF/NPFL barrages before eventually fleeing, were seen by the roadside taking off their uniform. "*I na dey come die for that bastard pekin Momo*" (I will not stay and die for that bastard, President Momo), some could be heard saying. We saw some of them disassembling their weapons and casting them away. The NPFL/RUF had just drilled the final nail in the coffin of the unholy matrimony of convenience between themselves and the police detachment.

I was surprised to see and hear some Sierra Leonean soldiers and SSD officers shamefully engaging in the cowardice and unpatriotic act of disrobing themselves and castigating their president and commander-in-chief, while at the same time disassembling their rifles by the roadside. I asked myself, 'O mighty Sierra Leonean army where is thou gallant soldier who was singlehandedly capable of dislodging NPFL battalion and capturing several rebel fighters as had been regularly trumpeted to Liberians?' Before that early morning RUF/NPFL invasion, here was a popular Creole one-liner heralded in Gendema and many parts of Sierra Leone: "*One grain Salone soja man fi catch, catch beaucoup Charles Taylor ree-bells.*" (One Sierra Leonean soldier is capable of capturing several Taylor rebels). It was a comment that Sierra Leonean service men and civilians alike constantly used to herald their soldiers' tactical capabilities at the same time, berate and scoff at Liberian soldiers-turned-refugees as being untrained and incapable of withstanding the tactics and firepower of Taylor's so-called rag-tag army. 'This is the time now for that imaginary one-man army, *a la* Hollywood character John Rambo to show up,' I thought out loud. But that John Rambo was invisible, as everyone - soldier and refugee was running from Taylor's so-called "rag-tag army" in droves.

The RUF backed by the NPFL had served sufficient warning to the Sierra Leonean government long ahead before they attacked Bo Waterside. Ten days earlier, the rebels first attacked the country in the northern border town of Kailahun on March 23, 1991. That was purely a diversionary tactic for the impending attack on Bo Waterside that the government did not see coming. I think the government should have fortified the Bo Waterside area. As for the refugees, some of us worried that once certain part of the country was attacked, it was possible that our area would be attacked also. But nothing some of us could do in terms of relocating inland to other towns and cities. In the absence of resources and not knowing where to go, relocating was virtually impossible. That was the dilemma many of us refugees faced. Therefore when the attack was launched that morning many of us refugees lost a lot of our possessions,

From the barracks, I finally joined the thousands of people fleeing west toward Zimmi. In the crowd on the main highway, I began to search for my sister and her children who were between the ages of 5 and ten. I was not too worried about my brothers Beto and Zaire and nephews Kaffie, Darlingboy and Boone. They were young boys who could take care of themselves. About five miles into the journey I accosted Mlanyonnoh (Mamie) among a group of refugees fleeing west. She was retracing her steps in search of Taryonnon.

"Big Jerry, did you see Taryonnon on the way? Aunty Payennon is sitting by the roadside crying for her daughter," Mamie said.

"Where is Sister Payennon?"

"Up the road," Mamie added.

We both went to where Sister Payennon was sitting. She was barefoot and very distraught. When she saw me from a distance, she shouted in these words:

Painful Journey: a Story of Escape and Survival

"Big Jerry, I can't see Taryonnon o." In Liberian Pidgin English, "o" is often added at the end of a sentence to express seriousness. She continued: "If I na see her I will go back so Charles Taylor rebels can catch me too o."

Sister Payennon vowed not to go further unless she found her six-year old daughter Taryonnon. Upon seeing her in the total state of despair, I immediately turned around and went towards the fighting in search of my niece. Carefully I started checking among the thousands of people coming towards me. It was a calculated risk. I could have easily been accused by fleeing Sierra Leonean authorities of going to join the invaders. About twenty minutes down the road, I saw Taryonnon with no clothes on. She had run out of the house like that. I took off my T-shirt and put it on her. I put her on my back and we continued to where I had left her mother sitting by the roadside in the other town called Malema.

By noon, all the kids were hungry and badly bruised due to the long trek on the gravel road. We got some cassava from the townspeople along the way and cooked some for all of us. After that I urged the group for us to continue the journey. I did not want us to be caught behind rebel lines. The rebels were moving at their own pace. They had no resistance. By 7 o'clock p.m. we arrived in Zimmi. Six miles north of Zimmi toward Kenema, Sierra Leone's third largest city, was another border crossing which could possibly be used by the rebels. So I advised the family for us to go by way of Potoru to the south. We spent part of the night in Bambako, a few miles south of Zimmi.

Around 3 o'clock a.m. Thursday April 4, 1991, President Joseph Momo of Sierra Leone gave a BBC interview in a rather emotionally upset tone accusing the Liberians of invading his country. He said Liberians were ungrateful. He rhetorically questioned why Liberians would bring war to his country after all that they had done for Liberians. Was that the proper way to say thank you to the nation by declaring war on its peaceful citizens? That interview effectively set the tone for reprisals and organized mob actions that would greet the Liberian people for several weeks.

Even though seriously poor by UNDP standard, Sierra Leoneans are generous people. But the invasion of the country by the combined forces of Charles Taylor's NPFL and Cpl Foday Sankor's RUF, coupled with the President's pronouncement significantly altered the people's generosity. Every Liberian was now looked at with suspicion. We were considered rebels until proven otherwise. I advised my brothers and nephews for us to move together and to be ahead of the game by staying far ahead of the invaders as possible. News of gross human right violations and summary executions in NPFL-held territories as reported by international news media and refugees fleeing Liberia, were done during "mop up" exercises. This made me to promise myself and the boys not to ever share the same town with the invaders.

During President Momo's interview, the moon shone so brightly that it seemed like dawn when it was actually around 3 o'clock a.m. So we set out southwest on foot on a one-lane gravel road that wound through the forest to the Moa River ferry crossing to a town called Potoru. Sister Payennon and some of her kids stayed behind. Her feet hurt and so they needed some rest. By 7 o'clock a.m., we arrived at the Moa River crossing. There was a large motorized raft at the crossing which was used to ferry people and goods in both directions. But also it could take one small vehicle at a time. A cable, one-and-a-half inches thick in diameter, spanned across the river. Also attached to the cable, were two smaller ones horizontally connecting to the raft to prevent it from aimlessly steering downstream. The Moa River was about half a mile wide at its crossing point. It would take about 20-25 minutes to cross it on the raft.

It was safer to be on the other side of the river. So we boarded the raft and crossed. By 10 o'clock a.m. my sister had not arrived to the crossing point yet, so I took another calculated risk by going back toward the war zone. Some Liberians advised me against going back toward Zimmi for fear of me being falsely accused of going to join the rebels since indeed it was now apparent that the invaders were mostly Liberians.

Against all odds, I boarded the raft again and headed northeast toward Zimmi. About another three miles or so I saw my sister. She was walking with a cane at a snail's pace. I also saw a bunch of soldiers coming my way. They mentioned that the rebels were in Fairo, a midway point between Zimmi and Bo Waterside from where we had fled. When we arrived at the crossing, the number of people queuing up to cross had increased considerably. There was huge commotion. Everyone was jostling for space on the raft in order to be on the other side of the river where it was relatively safer at that moment. In the melee, a pickup truck trying to get on the raft, slid over the plank ramp, plunged into the river and submerged completely out of sight. Miraculously the driver survived. The raft might have shaken violently which caused the plank ramp to shift one side thereby making the vehicle tires to miss the ramp. The people could not get the pickup truck out as there was no tow truck or heavy equipment around. When it was partly settled, Sister Payennon and I crossed the river on the raft to the Potoru side. Couple of minutes later, Red Cross volunteers delivered some food rations. Since the kids were not strong and my sister's feet still hurt severely, we planned on staying in the river town for the night to rest and let the whole family recover from the pain and stress.

While Sister Payennon was preparing that midday meal, there was a huge shout of "ECOMOG" ringing out. All the internally displaced Sierra Leoneans and refugees were glad to see a group of about fifteen to twenty soldiers approaching the ferry on the east bank of the river. Their camouflage uniforms looked newer than the ones worn by the regulars that we were used to seeing at the border, which gave them the appearance of the West African peacekeepers and that also gave us little hope. Little did we know that they were Sierra Leonean soldiers who were also fleeing the war.

The soldiers had been driven out by the invaders from Bo Waterside-Sierra Leone. As soon as they crossed the river to our side, they melted away into the crowd. A few minutes later, there was another big roar: *"ree-bell, ree-bell"* (rebels, rebels)! This time it was on our side of the river. Some of the soldiers who had just passed us were seen physically assaulting and torturing a Liberian guy whom someone had pointed out as being an NPFL fighter. According to the story, this guy was known to the Sierra Leoneans in the Zimmi area. They said he had spent a day or two in Zimmi selling looted goods from Liberia before the invasion got underway. The soldiers were kicking and gun-butting him. There was considerable amount of blood oozing from his forehead trickling its way down his face and neck. Bruised and swollen, his right eye was almost the size of his head. Swollen were his lips that when put on a scale, they would have conveniently weighed about a quarter pound. I was feeling for the man. The soldiers dragged his near lifeless body to the edge of the river: "*Una all commot na bush*," the soldiers shouted in Creole, warning everyone to get out of the bush. They stood him up near a tree and pow, pow, pow; they riddled his body with bullets.

The sight of the execution visibly shook me. I had seen people shot before only in Hollywood war and western (cowboy) movies, but not in the real situation like the one that I had just seen. Having witnessed the summary execution, the first thought that crossed my mind was that it could have been any other person among us who could have been falsely accused and could have met his untimely end as the other guy. My whole being was now immersed in fear. I advised my sister and the rest of the kids for us not to spend the night in that river town as was previously planned. So we moved on.

Two days before the rebels struck, Joanna and our son Gerald had traveled to Bo City, Sierra Leone's second largest city to be with her sister Valarie and her husband Kwame. Valarie was Joanna's younger sister. I was glad I did not have to be taking care of my family along with my sister and her bunch of children. My burden was to a certain extent, lessened a bit. Kwame worked for an international NGO, so he had a vehicle assigned to him which he used to come searching for us. He met us in that little river town where the execution had occurred. Later, he took my sister and the children ahead to Potoru. By 6 p.m., under the cover of darkness, the boys and I continued on to Potoru through another one-lane winding forest road similar to the one we had travelled on from Zimmi. We arrived in Potoru by 7 o'clock Friday morning. There were pretty close to 100,000 refugees and internally displaced people (IDPs) in the town. The Red Cross had provided trucks that were transporting refugees and the IDPs south to Pujahun, the district headquarters. Imagine the difficulty in climbing into the truck: pushing, shoving, pulling, and knockdown, you name it! It was a situation of survival of the strongest and the fittest! It was a complete mess. The boys and I could fight our way into the truck but my sister with her swollen feet, her children, and our aunt could not. So we spent the night in an abandoned school building south of the town on the road to Pujahun.

When the temperatures cooled a bit by 5 o'clock p.m. the following day, we headed west to the main highway leading to Bo City instead of going south to Pujahun. We changed our mind about going to Pujahun, a beach city. With only one highway leading south to Pujahun, if the rebels seized it, there would have been no way out. Heading west, it was approximately fifteen miles from Potoru to the highway at a place where the highway pavement and the dusty road met. There was another river at that place. During the trek that night, my sister gave up. She could not walk anymore. Her swollen feet had so much fluid in them that they resembled a crystal clear water-inflated balloon. That night I pleaded with a truck driver to take her and the children to Bo. I gave him my nice pair of shoes that I had saved from Bo Waterside, one of the items for which I almost got shot in the barracks. The shoes were extremely useful now. I did not regret giving them away. With my sister safely gone ahead to Bo City, traveling with the boys was now practically much easier. We arrived at the other river town in the morning as usual and spent most of the day at the river washing and swimming. Good thing was that every town we arrived in there was always someone in the town willing to help. This town was no exception. The saddest thing was that most of the people had no clue about what was unfolding. Therefore they were not seen making any attempt to evacuate like we were doing. Later that year the entire Pujahun region was engulfed in the terrible war.

After all our activities at the river, we set out again for Bo City. It was the third day of our escape from the war zone. We walked several miles and arrived in a town called Koribondo from where the big Red Cross chartered truck took us to Gelehun west across the Saywah River. The town is six miles east of Bo City. There was another town called Gondamah situated on the east side of the Saywah River that had more than five thousand refugees housed on the school campus. We were about two hundred refugees taken to Gelehun.

"No Man Go Bo"

In Gelehun, the refugees chose me to lead them. My role was basically to meet with local officials and the UNHCR and the Red Cross staff in meeting the needs of the refugees. We spent about three weeks in the town. Those three weeks were emotionally and mentally draining. Almost every day, well-armed Sierra Leonean security personnel would come in a large truck during the day and order all the refugees out in the open. About two men in mufti would disembark along with armed soldiers and begin to identify "suspected rebels" among us. Once pointed out, the alleged rebel suspect would be bodily picked up and thrown in the back of the truck and taken away, never to be seen again. No questions asked. No comments. We were all living scared.

Meanwhile Bo City was in a state of topsy-turvy and the citizens were running amok. It was apparent that President Momo's BBC interview on April 4 had galvanized the citizens into organized vigilantism and mob actions especially against Liberian refugee men. Several Liberian men were brutalized including Referee Alex Nagbo. He was gashed with a sharp object on the back of his head. Another victim was a man named Anthony Sesay who was bayoneted in the ear. Miraculously he survived the physical brutality. That incident did not force him to repatriate to Liberia like others did. He relocated to the Waterloo Refugee Center where through the UNHCR and the Red Cross, he got regular medical attention. Therefore men were advised not to venture out into Bo City. Red Cross field officer, a Dane named Johannes would drive up and down the highway with a bullhorn warning men not to go to Bo. He could be heard yelling in Creole *"No man go Bo"* as he drove back and forth. The constant shout of "No man go Bo" was a lifesaving mantra that was on the lips of almost every refugee for the three weeks we stayed in that area. It was also my duty to pass the message on to all the refugees coming in from the Potoru area and other parts. In fact at some point, the Red Cross began trucking men from the extremely overcrowded Bo City back to Gelehun and Gondamah. My sister and our aunt came back with the children from Bo City to Gelehun to be near me. I negotiated with a local resident to give them accommodation.

In Freetown City, there were reports of widespread brutality and arrest and detention of Liberians in the Padema Road maximum state prison. Some of those arrested and falsely accused of being "rebels" or supporters of Charles Taylor's NPFL terror machine were released a year later as we will see in the next chapter.

In the wake of the brutality and false imprisonment of refugees in Bo City, UNHCR and all its implementing partners met with the Government of Sierra Leone and threatened to fold up their operations and leave the country if the human rights violations against the refugees did not cease. The government acquiesced. On radio they began to order their citizens not to take the law into their own hands but to report cases of suspicious activities to the police. The government also appealed to the aid agencies to stay and that there would be proper security measures taken to protect the refugees. One of such measures was for all the Liberian refugees to be centrally relocated in Waterloo, twenty-two miles east of Freetown.

Given the high volume of violence being perpetrated on Liberians, many, including Sister Payennon concluded that it was preferable to go back home no matter how the security situation was in Liberia than to stay in Sierra Leone and die. With the interim government of Amos Sawyer in Monrovia and the presence of the West African peace keepers, it was believed to be relatively safer there than in Sierra Leone. Ships were provided at the quay in Freetown to evacuate Liberians. Sister Payennon, our aunt, the children, and the boys took advantage of the first available opportunity when trucks were provided to take refugees from Bo City to the port in Freetown. As usual, I stayed behind to join my family in Bo City. When the tensions seemed to have cooled a little, close to the end of May, Red Cross field officer, Johannes reported that Waterloo was established for Liberian refugees and advised us to find our way there. I boarded the Red Cross pick-up truck with a very large Red Cross flag fluttering on it and headed to Bo City to join Kwame and my family.

The next day after I arrived, Kwame's landlord advised us to find our way out of Bo City since it was no longer safe for us there. He mentioned that some of his neighbors were in a constant habit of circulating false rumors that he was harboring "rebels" in his house. The next day after the talk with the landlord, we boarded a truck for Freetown. There were several checkpoints along the way to Freetown. Speaking with Liberian accent was an invitation for more questioning or physical violence on your person if the soldiers were not satisfied with your answer. At one checkpoint on the outskirt of Bo City, we were the only ones (refugees) ordered out of the truck and taken to a makeshift office for thorough interrogation. It was a scary moment for us. The driver, a

Sierra Leonean had to intercede on our behalf by offering some bribe to the soldiers.

This situation was repeated over and over at all the checkpoints we arrived. By the mercy of God we arrived in Freetown around 6 o'clock a.m. with no incident. We did not know anywhere in Freetown to go to but the driver did. He took us to the Robert Street Baptist Church, a church in central Freetown that was run by a Liberian pastor who had been in Freetown long before the war. As for the Liberian Embassy, the chancery and ambassador's residence were jammed packed. Refugees were sleeping outside in the courtyard and on the balcony. The church itself was crowded. There were refugees all over the place, sleeping in the church using the pews as beds. We spent two days at the church and moved to Sykes Street. My older nephew Sylvester and two other Liberians resided in that house owned by a benevolent Sierra Leonean elderly lady. They made the contact for us to join them there.

When we met the owner of the house, she was so empathetic to our situation because Valarie was pregnant. The lady reasoned with us that sleeping on the bare ground was not safe for Valarie and the unborn baby. She took us in. Of course every night, all the men would spread mats outside in front of the house and pass the night. Freetown, the city with open sewage system was infested with mosquitoes larger than household flies. Due to increasing mosquito bites, Valarie got sick. My son Gerald got sick and so was Alexander, Kwame's younger nephew. It turned out that our host owned a house in Waterloo Township which is three miles from the newly established refugee center. We arranged with her to move in the house since the area was closer to the Waterloo Refugee Center.

On Sunday evening, June 2, 1991, we went to Waterloo Township with the landlady. She introduced us to the caretakers of the house as her new tenants and left for Freetown a few minutes later. It was around 10 o'clock p.m. Kwame and I began cleaning the place to make it livable especially for the pregnant woman. The caretakers felt cheated. They thought the landlady treated them unfairly by giving the place to "rebels" in the middle of the night, even though they were told beforehand. So they devised a scheme by telling the police that we were rebels. Around

11:30 p.m., three police officers arrived while we were finding food to eat. They arrested all of us and took us to the police station.

Kwame and I told the police that we were not rebels. If we were, we would not be traveling with two women (one pregnant) two young boys, one six years old and the other 12, and Aletha, a 13 year old girl living with us. The police understood but advised that it was safer for us to spend the night at the Waterloo Police Station. By 7 a.m. they released us and directed us to the refugee center.

Meanwhile at the quay in Freetown, Sister Payennon and the rest of the family along with hundreds of other Liberian refugees were camping out in the open and in shipping containers waiting for the ship to arrive to take them to Monrovia. I visited them every other day carrying them food items and other provisions. They spent about three weeks at the port before going to Liberia. One part of my problem had again been solved. Therefore my going to Freetown was only on a need to basis to visit my younger nephew Kulah (Sylvester's younger brother). Kulah later joined us in Waterloo and departed for United States a year after. He has an undergraduate degree in accounting and works for Wells Fargo Securities as Senior Securities Specialist. He is also working on acquiring a CPA designation. His brother Richard resettled in the United States also. He is Captain in the US Army and holds an MSc. in Information Technology. Both are now residing in Brooklyn Park, MN,

CHAPTER SIX

Waterloo Refugee Center Chairman

The Waterloo Refugee Center was opened in the early part of May 1991. Before the refugees came, the area was wildlife, uninhabited by humans. It was home to a number of different forms of animal life. It was located about four hundred yards north of the Freetown-Bo Highway and south side of an oil palm plantation owned and operated by the notorious Padema Road State Prison in Freetown. An old World War II air strip three quarters of a mile long, previously used by the British, was located in the middle of the Center. There were several large cashew trees as old as the air strip itself planted on the south side between the air strip and the main highway. The Center was located in the Timne heartland three miles east of Waterloo Township and 22 miles east of Freetown City. Within mere months of its opening, the Center had become "home" for the many Liberian refugees who flooded it. The numbers increased rapidly on a daily basis with the population climbing to approximately 100,000 in 1991. The Center was carved into sections from A-ZZ. Each was headed by a Sectional Head who reported to the Center Chairman. By 1994 however, the population had dropped to about 20,000 after a series of third country resettlements, voluntary repatriations, and individual relocations to Guinea, Cote d'Ivoire, and Ghana.

We arrived in the Center on the morning of June 3, 1991 after our release from the Waterloo Police Station and reported ourselves to the aid agency representatives for registration. For the next full week, our bed was the open-air weather-beaten tarmac. By day, my wife Joanna and her sister Valerie would prepare food under the big cashew trees, an area shared by several other refugees and their families. But when the rains came, which it often did, all cooking had to cease, as fires got drenched and died. The women would have to seek shelter under the trees and wait for the rains to stop in order to start a new fire and continue with the meal preparation. This continued for about a week before we were supplied with tarpaulin and sticks to build our shelter which measured fourteen feet long and nine feet wide. That was the standard measurement by humanitarian aid agencies for a family size of more than five. Those with smaller families received a plot of land measuring six feet by nine feet. Once the shelter was built and we started receiving regular material and food supplies, the process of rebuilding our lives began all over again. Our address was Section H, shelter number 5 (H-5). On June 16, 1991, I was overwhelmingly elected by thousands of refugees to serve as Chairman of the Center (To this day many former Liberian refugees from Sierra Leone still call me by this title). As Chairman, I was head of the Executive Committee. It was a job that came with enormous responsibilities because I was charged with managing the daily operations of the Center. Joseph Gayekra was elected co-chairman for operations and Kromah, co-chairman for administration. A month later, Kromah repatriated to Liberia and was succeeded by Ansu Dolleh. A year later Dolleh too repatriated to Liberia and was succeeded by George Tarn.

We worked with the UNHCR and its implementing partners in meeting the needs of the refugees. It was our job to advocate on behalf of thousands of traumatized, homeless but proud people who had lost loved ones along with all their worldly possessions and who were now dependent on international aid agencies for survival. It was a very daunting task for me but one that I accepted with humility. I vowed to do everything in my power to see to it that the needs of the people were met as much as possible and that they were properly represented.

At the height of the Liberian war in 1990 when thousands of Liberian refugees crossed into Sierra Leone *en masse*, some were accommodated in private homes, allowed to rent homes, or allowed to build their own homes like we did in Gendema (Bo Waterside). However, most of the refugees in Freetown City were housed on the campus of Approved School, which was not a typical refugee camp but was needed as an immediate short term solution until the Sierra Leonean government could figure out how best to respond to such a crisis. The Waterloo Refugee Center was then opened so that all the refugees could be housed in one location, making it more manageable for the government to provide security protection for us. This had become necessary owing to some amount of physical threats that were made and violence that was perpetrated against Liberian refugees by locals whose generosity had run thin because of the invasion of their country in March and April of 1991 by the rebels of the combined forces of the NPFL and RUF. The government was therefore forced to issue nationwide bulletins for all the refugees to go to Waterloo for their safety. The UNHCR made it mandatory that in order to receive material and food assistance, even if you were residing in Freetown City, you had to relocate to the refugee center. Despite this, some refugees in Freetown simply refused to relocate.

By early June, the outbreak of cholera and other infectious diseases had reached epidemic proportions in the Center due to the large influx of refugees who were living in substandard and deplorable conditions. Lives were lost - the primary victims being those among us who were the most vulnerable – babies, children and the elderly. The same month, as preparations for the celebration of the annual Africa Refugee Day drew near, I busied myself with documenting the major concerns of the refugee people to whom I was accountable. I was to speak on their behalf. On June 20, 1991 with thousands of refugees present, as well as representatives of the UNHCR, and other UN systems, representatives of international aid agencies, Sierra Leonean government officials, the United States Ambassador to Sierra Leone, and other members of the diplomatic corps, I delivered my speech, calling for more educational, health and recreational assistance to be given to the refugees.

Whether or not they were in agreement or in a position to assist, my appeal brought the dignitaries to their feet, applauding loudly. Neither could my fellow refugees be quieted. They applauded the loudest and the longest. For them, the speech was a slam dunk. All that they had been complaining to me for days before had been well articulated on their behalf to heads of the international bodies that were present.

Immediately after the ceremony, I was swarmed by hundreds of pleased and hopeful refugees who wanted to congratulate me profusely for allowing the grouses to be heard. For weeks, that was all you could hear people at the center talking about. They felt as though they had accomplished something. Several months later the UNHCR and its implementing partners gradually began to honor our requests. These came in stages. First, an ambulance was provided to the Center for referring patients to the main hospitals in Freetown. Later, a modern clinic with in-patient wards, which functioned on a 24-hour basis, was built. The Center seemingly started to function like a regular town, as a four-room office block that housed the UNHCR field office, its implementing partners and the refugee leadership was also constructed. Six hand pumps were installed in various locations of the Center along with a supplemental water tank that was situated in the middle of the Center. This was fed by a large reservoir in the oil palm plantation office located nearby. By 9 a.m. and 5 p.m. daily, the Center's refugee water and sanitation man, Joe Pour was on hand to turn on the machine that pumped in several thousand gallons of water to the supplemental tank. The only major amenity lacking in the Center was electricity. Howbeit, the residents did not make much of a fuss about the lack of electricity because the nation's capital, Freetown itself did not have electricity. (The lack of electricity in Freetown had earned it the dubious highest distinction of the "Largest Village in Africa"). There were however, a few solar panels and a power generator that kept the refugee clinic functional on a 24 hour basis. There were also two well-equipped elementary schools: one built and run by the UNHCR and the other, a private one built and operated by Pastor and Mrs. Solomon Juah.

A month after the Africa Refugee Day celebration euphoria dwindled, the first major test of our leadership came. During the night of Liberia's Independence Day celebration of July 26, 1991 a nasty fight broke out involving an older Liberian, a group of teenage refugees, and some Sierra Leonean Red Cross volunteers. At the end of the fight, one man was hospitalized, a soldier assaulted and his uniform torn to shreds. The case was big. It brought together the UNHCR and heads of all its implementing partners. The Center leadership, the police detachment, soldiers, and several others were fully represented.

The police and soldiers made a big deal of it for the fact that a soldier was assaulted. They wanted the refugees jailed for an inordinate long period of time and for them to pay a huge cash amount for the cost of the ripped uniform. It took a week of intensive deliberations and negotiations to settle the matter. In the end, the UNHCR agreed to pay for the uniform on behalf of the refugees. The case was then dropped by the law enforcement personnel. This incident brought to the fore, what we had been skirting around for some time now - the need for regular meetings to be held among all parties who had a stake in the refugee center. It had now become a matter of urgency, as tensions over other matters at the Center were also mounting. Finally, the UNHCR, heads of the various agencies, the police and the refugee camp leadership agreed to sit down to regularly scheduled weekly inter-agency meetings to address the various problems that were rising in the Center as well as the challenges that the residents were experiencing. These meetings were as beneficial as they were necessary. They not only helped to build trust among the different groups of people involved with the Center (refugees and other groups), but they ultimately allowed for a smoother coexistence. During what was regarded as the "emergency period" of the settlement stage for instance, was a period that was fraught with problems related to settlement, many of which required that they be handled at the inter-agency level. For example, an area that produced the most tension was at the food distribution center. Refugees were in the constant habit of accusing the volunteers of "stealing" their food rations and this sometimes led to verbal and violent confrontations. When this was brought up at the meeting, the proposal was made, and received the approval of the UNHCR, to have some of the refugees work alongside the Red Cross volunteers during food distributions. That arrangement was hugely successful. Consequently, as the tensions subsided and more issues got addressed, it was agreed that the frequency of the meetings be decreased. They went to fortnightly and then to monthly.

On record-keeping, the name of one Liberian refugee stood out. He was one of the smartest persons I have ever met. Danny Philip was a born statistician in his own right. He was a Red Cross volunteer in charge of records of residents of the Center. By the end of 1992 he had mastered the names and faces of all family households residing in the

Center. Single-handedly, he knew the demographics of almost every family in the Center. At the food distribution center his knowledge of names of individuals, their shelter numbers, and composition of their family structures helped to prevent food ration theft and confusion. Moreover anytime our committee needed records of family households, he would provide the information right off the bat without the slightest attempt at flipping through pages. Such incredible natural gift endeared him to the Red Cross and the refugees alike.

By late 1991, the Center had by this time had a few well-trained Sierra Leonean and Liberian medical practitioners operating the clinic, but it still needed a medical doctor to be in charge. The UNHCR proceeded to hire one "Doctor" John (last name withheld to protect identity) to fill that position. His work ethic and behavior however, left much to be desired. One rainy day, UNHCR field officer Cosmas Chanda brought him and introduced him to the Center leadership. As we figured that it would have been beneficial for him to be introduced to all the Sectional Heads, we arranged a proper "meet and greet" session for another day of the week. It was expected that the meeting would be conducted in an atmosphere of cordiality between a bunch of refugees and the gentleman who was charged with the responsibility of taking care of their medical problems. We wanted to ensure a good working relationship among all parties and more than anything for the doctor, in particular to be sensitized of some of the challenges being experienced by refugees at the Center. He arrived promptly at 11 a.m. for the meeting, so we were able to start on time. I spoke on behalf of the refugees and welcomed him to the Center. After a brief introduction, those of us at the meeting who didn't know him were appalled at his behavior. He was unmasking right before our very eyes. The doctor began talking down questioners, going as far as uttering verbal insults. "Don't ask me that stupid question," was one of his responses to a member at the meeting. In the middle of a comment being made by another member, Dr. John placed his index finger to his sealed lips and uttered, "*sh*", blatantly telling the person to shut up. He was rude and obnoxious. After-all, who did he think he was talking to? We weren't children! And neither were we stupid!

We certainly did not take kindly to his body language, his talk-down ranting, or to his verbal insults. We made it clear to him that though we were refugees; we had not lost our dignity. We reminded the doctor of his onerous responsibility and that if he intended to succeed in his career in the Center, he should consider treating us with respect. And at that point, the meeting got out of control. The following day I informed the UNHCR about our distasteful and unpleasant encounter with the doctor. A couple of days later, Dr. John requested to meet with us again. During that meeting, he was a more conciliatory and apologetic Dr. John. We agreed to move past the misgivings of our first meeting. Several months later, to our horror, the doctor was accused of slapping Shalty, an adult male refugee. He had apparently slapped the man so violently, his finger prints remained imprinted on Shalty's face. What had come over him, for him to have acted in such an unbecoming manner, no one knew. Poor Shalty, he must have been so horrified by the ordeal that he did not even fight back. I was happy that he did not, as that would only have made matters worse. Who knows what that one act could have spurred? When I inquired, the doctor did not deny his action but expressed regrets. At that, my only thought was that the UNHCR had hired an unprofessional person. I immediately took Mr. Shalty along with me to the UNHCR office in Freetown where I submitted a written complaint. That incident turned out to be the *coup de grace* for the doctor as his services were withdrawn from the Center.

We built a basketball and volleyball court at the entrance of the center and a soccer field on the outskirt. Soccer, volleyball, and basketball tournaments were held regularly. We also had a large cultural troupe called *Gumbu Zoes*. In another light, two young refugees who were interested in the practice of journalism opened an independent weekly newspaper called *The Spy-Glass* that reported on activities in the Center. It was good to see all the young people in the Center getting totally involved in the sporting and cultural activities. With the financial donation from the Swedish government, we built a large state of the art bulletin board for posting the newspaper and other important documents. We allocated some amount of the donation from the Swedish government to build a modern playground on the elementary school campus for the kids. A UN World Food Program (WFP) Rubb Hall made of tarpaulin was transformed into a center for organizing recreational activities such as dance, screening video/movies and hosting town hall meetings.

Prior to that, it was used to store refugee food supplies, household items, building materials, tools and other equipment before they built the concrete warehouse that would later house those items. Town-hall meetings served the purpose of discussing issues relevant to health and sanitation but in general, the discussions revolved around the general upkeep of the Center. Some refugees opened provision shops and the women operated a large open market. We were adapting. If anyone was thinking then that the war in Liberia would end soon they were sure wallowing in fantasy. It had become clearly conspicuous that Taylor in Liberia wanted nothing less than the presidency, and his partner in crime, Cpl Foday Sankor of the RUF was also pushing hard to seize power in Sierra Leone. Thus the war in Sierra Leone that had driven us from the border, was raging on unabated.

The Center was not free of petty crimes. There were numerous complaints of thefts of food rations, tarpaulins, household utensils, and there were domestic disputes too. A grievance committee headed by Mr. Soko Sheriff, a former judge in Sanniquellie, Nimba County was therefore established to settle disputes between and among refugees. Cases of a grand nature that were beyond Mr. Sheriff's jurisdiction were sent to the Waterloo Police Station for investigation. Through a request by the UNHCR, a shelter was built at the east entrance of the Center to house a few police officers assigned in the Center. The police shelter was strategically situated 100 yards north of the tarpaulin Rubb Hall as a means of warding off potential thieves and petty criminals. This was however not as effective as we had hoped, as one night thieves used a sharp object and tore through the north side of the hall, the very side on which the police residence was located and made off with fifty bags of rice, several cartoon of oils, rolls of tarpaulin and other supplies in a truck. A few of us surmised that it appeared to have been the handiwork of the local NGO employees in charge of distribution of materials and food supplies with the complicity of the police in the Center. When the UNHCR Field Officer Chanda, Red Cross Representative, and I went to assess the damage, we were in awe at the magnitude of the theft and destruction that was allowed to happen under the police's nose. Clearly, they must have heard or seen something. We simply could not fathom that all the theft and malicious destruction could have happened

Painful Journey: a Story of Escape and Survival

without anyone being caught. The UNHCR Field Officer was raging mad. "What happened here?" he asked the officer in charge. "*Mr. Chandra, ar luk ya, ar luk ya bot ar nor luk yanda,*" the man responded in Creole, all the while gesticulating that he kept watch on three sides of the hall except the north side. This only infuriated Chanda some more, for here was a classic case of "where you tie the cow is where it is supposed to eat" revisited.

In addition to the grievance and other subcommittees such as health & sanitation, education, market, and sports, we also set up a liaison committee that comprised local chiefs and elders of the Center. The primary purpose of the liaison committee was to handle complaints made by locals against refugees accused of pillaging their virgin forests by felling trees for fire wood or prematurely pruning palm trees for thatch. Cases such as forced cultural enrollment into the Sande Bush[10] were also handled by the liaison committee. However, during my tenure, the only case brought to us was by a refugee woman who complained that her twelve-year old daughter was allegedly forced by the locals into the traditional school. Due to its culturally sensitive nature, the case brought together more than ten local chiefs and several refugee elders in the Center for settlement.

There were also numerous complaints of ULIMO fighters – whose families resided in the Center – visiting the Center from the war front in their military uniforms. Such complaints were transferred to the Sierra Leonean military post located at the northeastern entrance of the Center to handle.

One day in August, I met a 12-year old boy who survived the July 29, 1990 Lutheran Church massacre in Liberia. He had a very unique male Mano surname unlike names such as Saye, Zarwolo, Nya, and Wuo that are immensely popular and easily recognizable. As camp manager, I stumbled across the name while performing my duty and I immediately took interest in it. The uniqueness of his name drew my attention to it, forcing me to inquire from a lady accompanying the kid.

---

[10]Sande society is a women's association found in Liberia, Sierra Leone and Guinea that initiates girls into adulthood, confers fertility, instill notions of morality and proper sexual comportment. The opposite of this is Poro a complementary institution for men.

She was his mother. She had lived in Yekepa when the boy was born. Therefore I did not know her. The lady told me the kid's dad's name, whom it turned out, was my friend in high school, Saye Z (name withheld to protect his identity). We used to spend vacation at his parents' home in Sanniquellie during our school days in Tappita in 1979. At that point, I took the kid like my own. The kid explained a harrowing, blood-cuddling story about the massacre that kept me spellbound. He had survived by the mercy of God by playing dead when several gunned down bodies fell on him. His story was a testament of the groundswell of barbarism in which the country sank for 14 years.

"When I say 'Mahoot!' say 'Stormy weather!'" instructed Augustus.
"Mahoot!"
"Stormy weather!" the class responded.
"Mahoot!"
"Stormy weather!"

This was a trade union rallying cry that was introduced to us in the workshop. The workshop was organized by Augustus and George (last names withheld to protect their identities) in collaboration with an International Labor Organization (ILO) representative, a Sierra Leonean who had come in from Geneva, Switzerland at the end of 1991. I did not know Augustus and George personally prior to coming to Waterloo. All I knew about Augustus was what I heard on radio back in Liberia. In the early 1980s I had heard about him and his trade union activities on national news when workers were in labor dispute with management of Bong Mines, an iron ore mining company about 46 miles northeast of Monrovia. Augustus was their union representative. As for George, I had not heard anything about him prior to our meeting in Waterloo. Both men were among some of the last groups of Liberians to relocate to the Center from Freetown late 1991.

The workshop lasted for a week. During that time, both men took the liberty to tell us stories of their past activities in labor unions. It was a bonding experience. Looking back, I think we were having way too much fun. And unbeknownst to the rest of us was that George and Augustus were having a serious disagreement with the ILO representative, which they had kept under wraps. However the disagreement surfaced menacingly during the formal closing program that was held at the Catholic Church in the Center. The Liberian Ambassador and the First Secretary were in attendance. During the ILO representative's address, an angry George walked up to the podium and attempted to push the gentleman aside. It was unbelievable. I had not seen anything like that in all my years of attending various functions. In my capacity as leader of the Center, I was put in an uncomfortable position, for having spent several weeks in George's company to the point where I considered him a friend and to now see him behave in such a manner, was embarrassing to say the least, notwithstanding the fact that it was my responsibility to intervene. I immediately began to question our newly formed friendship. I shoved back my chair, got to my feet and in a stern voice demanded that George move away from the podium to allow the gentleman to complete his remarks. This he did. However, when it came time for George to speak, he had some of the nastiest things to say to the ILO representative. The program almost ended in chaos save it not for some of the cooler heads who were present.

"My son, that ILO man is a crook," George muttered in my ear at the end of the program.

"Why do you say this?" I questioned back, because I was really curious to know the reason behind his behavior.

"He 'ate' all our money."

"What kind of money?" I pressed.

"I will give you more details later," he replied.

Now, curiosity had really gotten the better of me. I really wanted him to tell me right there and then what exactly he was talking about. But wisdom prevailed. I did not press him any further, instead decided to wait until the appropriate time when he would tell me. The night came and went, days passed, and he still hadn't told me, so I left it at that. As far as I was concerned, money about their trade union was none of my business. I was not a trade unionist, as simple as that. What that entire hullabaloo suggested to me was that the issue was much deeper than what had surfaced. Since that incident, the ILO representative visited the Center on a number of occasions before leaving for Geneva but the air between him and George was sour. Their relationship was so badly bruised, there was no way it could have been repaired before his departure to Geneva.

Several months later rumors began swirling in the Center that George had uncovered information that the UNHCR had been "hiding" from the refugees. The rumors had it that all the more than 100,000 refugees in the Center had been entitled to monthly cash allowances from the UNHCR. And that the UNHCR-Freetown office had embezzled $75, 000 of the refugees' money. That money, according to the rumors, was from the "taxes our great-grandparents had been paying to the UNHCR." It was also being said that in addition to the cash allowances, each refugee was to have been issued the UN Convention Travel Document (UNCTD). Wow!

Amid all the rumours my co-workers and I were trying to deal with, tragedy struck my family in the early months of 1992. First, Joanna and Valarie's mother passed away on March 11, 1992 in the Ivory Coast. Two months later on May 20, their father died also. Joanna and Valarie were devastated. It was a painful time for our family. We made plans to travel to the Ivory Coast but because we were unable to obtain reentry visas that would allow us to return to Sierra Leone, we did not go. It felt so tragic. The Liberian war had made everyone's life a living hell. We felt angry - angry at those who started the war in the first place and angry that we were so helpless. Joanna's parents died while they were in a refugee camp and here we were in another country, also trying to live our lives in another refugee camp and were unable to as much as attend her parents' home going. We were saddened by the two losses. Joanna and Valarie wept bitterly for days – words were of little comfort to them. In December 1992 Kwame, Valarie and their children left for the Ivory Coast. From there they resettled in Livonia, MI, USA.

In the days that followed during the period of my bereavement, I was inundated with hundreds of questions from refugees regarding all these rumors – and that was what they were – rumors of the evilest kind. The perpetrators knew how vulnerable the refugees in the Center were. They knew that if just about anyone had come in the Center and said that there were truckloads of rice on the way, without verifying the information, the refugees would run to their shelters, grab their containers, and run to the distribution center. George and Augustus recognized

Painful Journey: a Story of Escape and Survival

that vulnerability and they exploited it along with the refugees' avowed gullibility. At every corner that I turned in the Center, there would be someone saying, "Mr. Chairman, they say this," "Mr. Chairman, they say that" and that made my job so much harder. I was faced with the daunting task of calling a series of town hall meetings to demystify the many "*they says*".

One day George came in from Freetown with a folder containing a bunch of documents clutched under his arm. "Mr. Chairman", (this time it was not "my son") I want you to see something," he said, rubbing his Adam's apple and looking around nervously, not looking me in the eyes. "We just sent a letter to the UNHCR. Those people are crooks!"

George was in the habit of calling other people crooks, so I was careful not to believe any accusation that he was coming up with against others. He accused the ILO representative, who was his benefactor, of being a crook. Here he was again, accusing UNHCR international staff of being crooks when to date, he had still not yet given me the detailed information that he had claimed he had against the previous ILO representative. I felt tired of him and his lies and accusations.

He handed me copy of a document that outlined all the rumors that had been circulating. The document was signed, "*George, Chairman, Concerned Refugees.*" The information in the document was not new. No surprise there, for it was being circulated for a while now. What was new was that a clandestine organization headed by George had been formed. Previous to the document being written, we had done our own home work regarding the so-called great-grandparents' taxes, refugee passport, and allowances. UNHCR had organized a two-week workshop in mid-July 1991 in Freetown City. The Center's Co-Chairman for operations, Joseph Gayekra and Georgia Saylee attended the workshop on behalf of the refugees. It was basically held to discuss refugees' rights and responsibilities. At the end, each refugee who had participated in the workshop was given copy of the book, *Collection of International Instruments Concerning Refugees*. That book was like a Bible to us, the leaders of the Center. We read it regularly so that we were adequately informed about our rights. Besides, I had already taken it up on myself to further research on how UNHCR got its funding. I made it my duty to know all these things so that I was always in a position to make informed decisions. Armed with the knowledge, I did not believe the accusations about a refugee passport and great grandparents' taxes. On the sweeping indictment about "UNHCR people eating our money," I thought perhaps George had uncovered more information that I perhaps was not privy to. Howbeit I was cautious; I would not rush to judgment. It was one thing to accuse someone of stealing and another to prove it. We gave George the benefit of the doubt. Two days later the UNHCR Representative, Mr. Godfrey Sabiti came in the Center and requested that I call a town hall meeting where George, the Center leadership and the refugees would attend. I was assured that Sabiti himself would be there. I told George and the date was set. That was early 1992.

At the appointed time, everyone except George assembled at the UNHCR office in the entrance of the Center. By coincidence, George had just come in from Freetown and was walking past us when Mr. Sabiti arrived. The office was jammed packed. I stepped outside to let George know that the meeting was about to start. His body language suggested to me that he did not want to be there. Reluctantly he told me that he was going to his shelter and would be back in five minutes. Five minutes turned to thirty going on to forty-five. Everyone had become impatient. Mr. Sabiti wanted to leave, so I sent someone to let George know that we were waiting for him to get there for us to begin the meeting. The burden of proof was on him the accuser to prove his case.

Finally George appeared, looking like a mouse that the cat had dragged in. The UNHCR representative spoke and then gave him the opportunity to prove his case in the presence of hundreds of his compatriots. George was nervous. He shifted his weight uneasily from foot-to-foot, glancing around the room nervously, not looking at anyone in particular. Then he began. But instead of addressing the accusations he had made, he began rambling on about how he too was an administrator who had traveled to Geneva, Switzerland and to other developed countries of the world. I sat there wondering to myself about the man's state of mind. Why was he telling us of his travels, pursuits and achievements? That information had no bearing on the issue at hand. I really did not care about him and his previous travels and neither was anyone else. The people assembled in the hall were interested in one thing – and that was to hear him address the scathing attack that he had made on the UNHCR diplomats.

After about a minute or two had passed of hearing his self-glorified ramblings and some baseless generalities, Mr. Sabiti interjected and reminded George that he needed to get to some meaningful specificity, as the audience and especially he, was growing impatient. For five uninterrupted minutes, George could not speak to the allegations contained in his own document. I was beginning to wonder whether he was the sole author of that document. If indeed, he was, why couldn't he speak to at least one point among the myriad of accusations he had listed? Every attendee in the meeting watched him as he fidgeted nervously. They then started to murmur amongst themselves. Though I was not the one who had leveled the allegation, I think I was factually more embarrassed for him than he was for himself. I was however not surprised that George did not have any explanation to give. The fact was that without any shred of doubt, I was convinced that he did not have any information to back his claim. I thought that in order for him to be able to prove convincingly that UNHCR staff had embezzled $75,000 he either would have been working in the office to have had secret or unfettered access to some confidential documents. Or, he would have had to, at some point, be an international independent auditor with access to financial records of the UNHCR branch office. George did not fit any of those profiles.

I was embarrassed. My embarrassment stemmed from the fact that George had falsely accused international diplomats of theft of international public money and had failed miserably to back his claim in a public forum. As head of thousands of refugees, I was the one charged with the responsibility of sitting with those very international personalities to negotiate and advocate on behalf of my compatriots for better socioeconomic conditions. To see one of my Liberian brothers making unsubstantiated allegations against them – especially in a case of embezzlement - to me that was not only embarrassing, it was utterly disgusting. Such behavior was not unique to George. His behavior epitomized the overall national problem of the average Liberian. Too often a Liberian or group of Liberians driven by greed, jealousy, or envy will accuse their leader or someone in authority of some wrong doing that they are unable to prove. "They are eating our money" is a very popular comment heard in a number of Liberian communities at home and in the Diaspora. George was simply displaying one of our national frailties to the public. After several minutes of waiting patiently without George offering anything concrete, Mr. Sabiti got up, dismissed George's document as "rubbish" and boarded his car for Freetown.

As it relates specifically to the issue of refugee passports, Article 28 Section 1 of the July 1951 Geneva Convention relating to the status of refugees, which I will quote in part, states: "The Contracting States shall issue to refugees lawfully staying in their territory travel document for the purpose of travel outside their territory…" (UNHCR, 2007: 17). The UNCTD is not a food ration card that every refugee in a camp should have. It is a travel document which is only issued to a refugee scheduled to travel for medical, academic or vocational training, workshop, religious conference, convention or pilgrimage. Other times it is issued to a refugee going on third country resettlement program. However, in most resettlement cases for developed countries such as the one carried out by the United States Refugees Resettlement Office and sometimes the Canadians, it is not necessary for the refugee to be issued a UNCTD. These developed countries collaborate with the International Office of Migration (IOM) to facilitate the resettlement process.

As for our so-called great-grandparents' taxes, UNHCR relies on donations from individuals, philanthropic organizations and developed countries to take care of refugees. Between 1990 and 1995, all the UNHCR monthly publications containing names of individuals, organizations and countries that contributed to the world relief efforts, "Liberia" did not appear anywhere in those documents. In the case of Waterloo, information inscribed on monthly rations of bags of rice and containers of oil read: "Gift from the government and people of the United States of America."

In other situations, cash allowances are given to refugees who do not live in a camp-like setting. In the case of the Liberian refugees in Waterloo, we lived in shelters in which we did not pay rent. Additionally, were supplied food rations free of charge periodically: first it was fortnightly and then monthly; and we were provided free health care and free education.

Painful Journey: a Story of Escape and Survival

Despite the fact that George was unable to show support for his claims against the UNHCR representatives, he and few members of his "concerned refugee" group, continued to move about spreading rumors and more disinformation, constantly talking to any and everyone who would listen. In May 1992, he took it a step further and embarked on a clandestine act of soliciting signatures of Sectional Heads by getting them to sign a document that he had falsely produced. He had given the Sectional Heads the impression that they were signing for the bags of rice that were to be distributed to their respective sections. George had told them that he had solicited rice on behalf of the refugees. Others' names were forged. After getting some of the signatures, he attached a cover letter which stated that the Center's leadership had been changed and that he was now the Chairman. The letter was sent to the UNHCR. That he had done this was preposterous indeed, but it was even more laughable. George had become a desperate man. And once again he had played on the vulnerability of the refugees. He used rice. It was not a hidden fact that if you wanted a refugee in Waterloo to move a mountain, all you needed to do was to make promises of rice. Rice, Liberia's beloved staple is consumed three times a day by the average Liberian. If food supply to the Center was delayed beyond its due date for any reason, the whole population would be on the edge and the Chairman would not rest. "Mr. Chairman, what time our food will come?" I would be asked every day and every second of the day by every resident until the truck came. And when the food truck arrived, there would be massive jubilations throughout the length and breadth of the Center. All for rice! If nothing else was in the truck, there had better be rice.

Knowing what he had done, George stayed away from the Center for several days. When the information surfaced, I called a mass meeting of Sectional Heads to discuss this new development. "That George again?" one Sectional Head asked wryly in the Liberian parlance. They spoke of being deceived by the man, indicating that he had garnered their signatures under false pretense. And so, together they all disassociated themselves from the document from George. He had really outdone himself this time. Months ago he had antagonized his benefactor and pointed accusatory fingers acrimoniously at the UNHCR. Now he was on another campaign of creating confusion in the Center. He was slowly but surely making enemies – and enemies of powerful people at that. He was labeled a big time rabble-rouser who the UNHCR and its implementing partners did not want to work with. In the wake of George's sheer tomfoolery, UNHCR Field Officer Chanda was sent to attend our community meeting, at which point he reminded the refugees about upholding the principles of democracy and cautioned us against engaging in clandestine activities. From then on, George was no longer a credible source in the Center. No one took him seriously anymore. He became history!

At the height of the war in 1990, hundreds and thousands of Mandingo refugees who had fled Liberia went to Guinea and Sierra Leone. The Krahn refugees who lived in Monrovia, including those who had relocated to Monrovia from other parts of the country, also fled to the country that was closest to Monrovia, Sierra Leone. In 1990 the Mandingos and the Krahns were the two tribes most persecuted by the NPFL invaders in the Liberian civil war. By early 1991 however, exiled Liberian politicians, soldiers, and businessmen began devising plans to go back to Liberia. That meant organizing into an armed faction to fight the NPFL and RUF invaders. The Liberians had realized that they had run from Liberia and there was nowhere else to go. Therefore they would stand up and fight the NPFL/RUF aggression. Consequently, when the combined forces of the NPFL and the RUF attacked Sierra Leone on March 23, and April 3, 1991, General Albert BS Karpeh, Liberia's Ambassador to Sierra Leone who once served as minister of defense in the military junta in Liberia, offered his support to the Joseph Momo government to forestall the rapid advances of the invaders. The US-trained Special Forces officer founded the Liberia United Defense Force (LUDF) which later morphed into the United Liberation Movement for Democracy (ULIMO) in May 1991. The movement received its military support from the Sierra Leonean government and ECOMOG (Ellis, 1999) and it recruited most of its fighters from among the Krahn and Mandingo refugees in Sierra Leone and Guinea.

ULIMO made significant gains on the battlefront. They took the Bo Waterside area from the invaders and entered Liberia. Thereafter, the *Liberian Way* set in. At the close of 1991, the constant reports of ULIMO battlefront successes also came with news of leadership in-fighting, a problem that was viciously threatening to divide the armed group on ethnic lines. Gen Karpeh constantly complained to the elders in the Center that most of the fighters were not taking orders from him or his leadership team based in Freetown. The in-fighting ultimately claimed the General's life. The General had gone to Kenema situated about 182 miles east of Freetown when he was gunned down in cold blood in his home on June 1, 1992. It was unclear who pulled the trigger, according to *BBC Focus on Africa* news report.

Two years later in 1994, the in-fighting that had claimed the life of a US-trained Special Forces officer was carried over into ULIMO headquarters in Tubmanburg, Liberia and split the armed group into ULIMO-J (Roosevelt Johnson, Krahn) and ULIMO-K (Alhaji Kromah, Mandingo) and culminated in the death of hundreds of ethnic Krahns and Mandingoes. The two most persecuted tribes of the war in 1990 had turned their guns on each other. Uncle T was counted among the dead in Bomi County. I was in Cairo when the news hit me. I was devastated. Years later in 2007 when I visited Monrovia, Uncle T's nephew told me that he and some other Krahn men were locked up in a container and left for dead, according to a ULIMO fighter who survived.

Two years after the Waterloo Refugee Center was opened, the process of local integration had gradually started to take shape. Refugees seemed to look much better off in appearance at times than even some of the residents of nearby towns and villages. Just imagine an elderly Sierra Leonean man old enough to be a grand dad would look at a 25-30 year old refugee and say: *"Pa ting tranga, ar kin get wan kop ress sef?"* (Father, times are hard, can I get a cup of rice?). If an old man would call a young refugee man "father" and ask for hand-out, it spoke volumes in two ways; a) refugees seemed better off socio-economically; and b) the villagers were in dire socio-economic straits. On Sundays a visitor entering the Center for the first time would hardly believe the place was owned and inhabited by refuges. Nearly everyone would be smartly dressed going to or leaving church. Because the people looked better off, we the leaders of the Center found it increasingly difficult to convince the annual UN World Food Program Food Assessment

Mission from Geneva that we needed more food rations. In fact after every visit, our food rations would be drastically reduced reinforcing the fact that we were better off than many other refugees around the world who possibly needed the food the most.

In terms of places of worship, there were five actively functioning churches of various denominations and a large mosque established by refugees in the Center. One of the churches, the Assembly of God Church deserves much attention. It was built by a group of young men some of whom were released from the notorious Padema Road Prison in Freetown. Emmanuel Zabay, Kpor Julu, Randolph Dorleh, Paul Pyne and Alexander Garbah were released into the custody of the UNHCR several months later and brought into the Center to live. Unfortunately Doe, another member of the group did not survive the harsh prison conditions. Sierra Leonean prison authorities claimed he died of tuberculosis. They were a group of refugees picked up on June 22, 1991 by Sierra Leonean security authorities from the Approved School Campus, a temporary camp for refugees located a few miles east of Freetown and imprisoned at the Padema Road State Prison in Freetown City in the wake of the RUF and NPFL attack of Sierra Leone in March and April of 1991, which I talked about in the previous chapter. The Liberians were falsely accused by Sierra Leonean authorities of being "rebels" or RUF/NPFL supporters. The released refugees looked dehydrated and terrible in physical appearance owing to the horrible prison conditions. They spoke of life of a living hell in the prison. The Center leadership was relieved to see their compatriots released from prison.

The released refugees were absorbed in the system and immediately they began to rebuild their lives after spending several grueling months in prison. Combined with Victor Cheade, Nehemiah Gbaba and others, the young men built the Assemblies of God Church in the Center that was the largest in terms of the size of the edifice and number of congregants who worshiped there regularly. The church finally relocated to Monrovia when the RUF attacked the Waterloo area in April 1995 with Emmanuel Zabay as its current pastor. Located in the Sinkor suburb of Monrovia, the church is one of the largest in the city. As for Julu, he resettled in Boston, MA where he is pursuing a degree in medicine.

Painful Journey: a Story of Escape and Survival

It was the middle of 1992 and the peace that most refugees and for that matter, most Liberians craved for, still remained elusive to the country. The quest for peace had taken the Economic Community of West African States (ECOWAS) mediating group and the warring factions from one West African city to the other. During that time there were a total of eight peace conferences held but with no end to the war in sight. Mr. Charles Taylor was still up to his usual tricks of stalling on the implementation of those agreements by denouncing the agreements and at some point, denying his own signature also during interview with BBC's Robin White. He strongly felt that militarily he had the advantage and therefore he held the trump card to the peace process. Even though ULIMO had captured a swath of territory of his controlled area, Taylor still controlled the rest of Liberia. Therefore he strongly believed he could dictate the terms of the peace agreements. At the same time he was also in trade deals with some unscrupulous international business entities that were earning him million of dollars annually in timber, rubber, diamond, and iron ore. Between 1990 and 1994 international trade had raked in an average of $75 million per annum for Mr. Taylor (Ellis, 1999), which he used to build his empire. To complicate matters and dampen the hopes of thousands, in October 1992 Taylor's NPFL launched Operation Octopus, a multi-pronged military assault on Monrovia intended to seize power by any means necessary (Sirleaf, 2009).

In spite of the fact that Taylor attacked Monrovia and on numerous occasions had denounced peace agreements, sometimes claiming that he had signed under duress, given the fact that there were a multitude of armed factions springing up here and there, in the grandest scheme of things, some of us still looked to the future with optimism no matter what. I always did self-counseling and self-assurance by constantly reminding myself of the old adage that says, "no matter how long night may seem, day will just have to come." Even though Liberia was going through the darkest period of its existence, I was cautiously optimistic that all that would end one day. We therefore chose to constructively engage in finding solutions to the national problem by organizing a one week peace symposium in the government ministerial building in Freetown. This was held in mid-1992. On February 20, 1993 I also played host to former Zimbabwe President Dr. Canaan Banana who was then serving as OAU Eminent Person on Liberia. We had a one-day discussion on devising strategies and solutions to the peace process in Liberia.

In as much as the international community was engaged in frantic efforts towards finding a lasting solution to the civil war, the waiting period was indefinite. There was a proliferation of armed factions in Liberia that was exacerbating the already complicated civil strife. At the same time, we were entering the local integration stage of our stay in the refugee center but the torrential rains in Sierra Leone had begun to take a toll on us. All the shelters in the Center had tarpaulin roofs that had worn out due to constant battering from the rains and sun. We therefore had to first ensure that our living conditions were improved before being able to take on other political tasks. Some refugees began replacing their tarpaulins with local materials called *papo*, a roofing sheet woven out of palm fronds. But the papo roofs were temporary as they would shrink in a couple of months under the baking African sun. We set up an *ad hoc* committee headed by George Saylee to conduct a feasibility study of what and how much it would cost to change all the shelters' roofs to zinc (corrugated iron sheet). After a month of an exhaustive compilation of data, the committee submitted its report which put the cost of the roofing project to about US$30,000. We submitted the report to the UNHCR office and they in turn, forwarded it to their headquarters in Geneva. Months later, the proposal was approved and the HCR contracted the services of a local firm, Multi-Systems International, owned and operated by two brothers, Abel and Ernest, to undertake the roofing project. By May 1993, the more than 1000 shelters in the Center had their roofs changed. At that point some refugees intended on making the Center their permanent home.

One sunny afternoon circa late 1992, UNHCR Representative, Mr. Godfrey Sabiti informed the Center leadership about the impending visit of the Interim President of Liberia, Dr. Amos Sawyer. Sawyer was a guest of the Sierra Leonean government but was using the visit to see his people in the Center. Liberia by then was divided into Greater and Lesser Liberia. Dr Sawyer was elected Interim President in August 1990 at the ECOWAS sponsored peace conference on Liberia in

Banjul, Gambia. In that political gathering, it was reported that only a few members from various political parties who could afford to travel, had participated. At the time of Sawyer's election, Samuel Doe was still the President of Liberia and was holed up in the Executive Mansion (presidential palace) in Monrovia. Also in August the ECOWAS committee meeting in Banjul, voted in favor of the formation of an intervention force (ECOMOG) for the Liberian civil war. As head of the NPFL, Mr. Charles Taylor vehemently opposed the intervention of a peacekeeping force which he saw as an obstacle toward claiming military victory. As a matter of fact, Mr. Taylor was a heartbeat away from the presidential seat of power. According to the BBC correspondent in Monrovia, Elizabeth Blunt, Mr. Taylor's NPFL rebel forces had taken up positions around the city except for the Executive Mansion and the military barracks nearby. He vowed to fight the peacekeepers if they entered Liberian soil. And fight he did. From the Atlantic Ocean, the peacekeeping force, ECOMOG engaged in fierce firefight with Taylor's rebel forces before landing at the Freeport of Monrovia on August 24, 1990 where they set up a garrison.

On September 9, 1990 President Doe was captured by INPFL leader Prince Johnson at the ECOMOG headquarters and mutilated while alive. Many conspiracy theorists believed that the President was lured to ECOMOG headquarters. He was supposedly there to confer with the peacekeeping force commander, Ghanaian-General Arnold Quainoo when rival rebel leader Prince Johnson and his INPFL fighters burst onto the scene, killed majority of President Doe's security operatives who had earlier been disarmed by the peacekeepers, and took the president away. According to a Waterloo resident and survivor of the Freeport debacle in a conversation with me, former deputy Executive Mansion Guard Battalion commander, Col T Cheyee Gowah, Prince Johnson and his fighters had already secretly taken up positions at the seaport prior to Doe's arrival. At the time of publishing this book, Prince Johnson is a Liberian Senator, elected overwhelmingly by the people of Nimba County in the 2005 national elections.

After the death of Doe, the peacekeeping commander, Ghanaian General Quainoo was replaced by a Nigerian-General Joshua Dogonyaro who moved swiftly to impose his authority on Monrovia in order to install the interim government. Dogonyaro used air and ground power to drive Taylor's NPFL from positions in and around Monrovia. Taylor's NPFL forces had taken up positions on the University of Liberia campus across the street from the Executive Mansion after Doe's death. In the wake of ECOMOG's relentless bombing, Mr. Taylor conceded in a BBC interview in October 1990 that he was ousted from Monrovia but not out of the bushes. He took control of the rest of the country, calling it Greater Liberia. He then set up a parallel government with headquarters in Gbarnga, Bong County. On 22 November 1990, after driving Taylor out of Monrovia, ECOMOG was known to facilitate the installation of the Sawyer-led Interim Government in the city where it was based and protected by the peacekeepers.

The Center was in a celebratory mood as news of Dr Sawyer's impending visit reached everyone. Plans were set in motion to welcome the President in true Liberian style. Elementary and high school students were mobilized – they would line the tarmac to welcome the Interim President and most importantly, participate in the main indoor activities that we had planned for the day. The UNHCR provided us with the logistics and our refugee volunteer carpenters set about building a large platform in the middle of the Center where the Interim President and his entourage and other dignitaries would be seated for the formal indoor program. Interim President Sawyer's emissary Dr. Alfred Kulah, chairman on the refugee repatriation and reintegration committee of the Interim Government, was on hand to ensure that everything was in place and ready. Most of us who had already heard of Dr Kulah, had heard that he was a very intelligent gentleman – I guess he would have had to be in order to be in the position that he was in, but little did we know that he had such a great sense of humor. It did not take long for him to connect with everyone who worked with him. He worked alongside us as we clocked in several man hours of massive preparations to ensure that the stage was in good order for the Interim President's arrival.

When we were satisfied that it was ready, Dr. Kulah left for Freetown with the promise of returning to the Center later in the day with Dr. Sawyer. The children stood nervously in the scorching sun, awaiting the arrival of the convoy that would bring the Interim President in the

Center. Surprisingly it was only the UNHCR vehicle that arrived and the place went dead silent. The door opened and Dr. Kulah stepped out. Dr. Sawyer had not come. Faces drooped with disappointment and it seemed as though a shadow had been cast over the Center. The students, more than anyone else were profoundly disappointed. They had spent so many hours in preparation for this moment. They were shattered. The message was that the President was no longer able to make it to the Center, as he had to leave so that he could catch the last ferry going to Lungi Airport from Freetown. He had sent word with Dr. Kulah requesting that I accompany Dr Kulah to meet with him on the ferry to the airport.

After consultation with other members of the Center's leadership, I respectfully turned down the invitation, not out of disrespect for the Interim President but more out of loyalty to the thousands of refugees who had been standing in the sun all day waiting for the President to arrive. I could not in good faith betray or compromise that trust. The refugees wanted their president to see them in the conditions they were in and not for their chairman to meet with the Interim President alone.

Dr Sawyer was one of those politicians during my high school days who I had tremendous respect for. He had challenged the ruling Americo-Liberian oligarchy, when no one thought that it was possible, by running for mayor in 1979 against the ruling party candidate, Francis Chu-Chu Horton in Monrovia which the Tolbert government had unceremoniously postponed indefinitely when it became apparent that Sawyer would win (Sirleaf, 2009). Sawyer had also delivered an inspiring commencement address at my high school in 1976 when I was completing Grade 9. Three years later, at the invitation of my friend Saye Z. whose son had survived the Lutheran Church massacre that I spoke of above, I attended the Sanniquellie Central High 1979 commencement convocation, at which I had the pleasure of hearing Dr. Sawyer give the keynote address. Then in 1982, while I was a student in the Business College at the University of Liberia, Dr. Sawyer also served as Dean of the College of Social Science and Humanities. At that time, I however did not have the need to meet him. Now, he was Interim President of Liberia and even though I might have had some fundamental disagreements with the arrangement that brought him to power, I was nevertheless tremendously excited at the prospect of shaking the hand of one of the progressive Liberian politicians of the late '70s. It was deeply disappointing when he did not show.

A few months later, the Interim President sent the Speaker of the Interim Legislative Assembly, Bismarck Kuyon and the Planning and Economic Affairs Minister, Amelia Ward to the Center to convey his regrets for not visiting the Center as was planned. As a token of those regrets, during a town hall meeting, Honorable Kuyon delivered the amount of US $2000 to the refugees on behalf of President Sawyer. The refugees accepted the money and laid the matter to bed.

In August 1993, we tried to organize an election in the Center to find my successor. Deep into the campaigning process, we observed that the planned elections were gradually developing into ethnic tensions that had the potential of engendering violent confrontations among rival groups. As a precautionary measure, I wrote and sought the advice of the State House's official in charge of refugee affairs, Lt Col. Dr. K.I.S. Kamara and copied the letter to the Officer Commanding (OC, 2nd in command) of the Waterloo Police Detachment and the UNHCR. A few days later the OC invited me in the police station for a meeting in which he specifically advised me to discard any plans to organize elections for now. I dutifully complied. Thereafter we convened a town hall meeting with all the Sectional Heads and stakeholders and conveyed the Sierra Leonean government decision. The next day, with the full backing of the Sectional Heads, I temporarily transferred power to Mr. Sam Jalloh, a former assistant superintendent for development, Margibi County, Liberia. He was expected to supervise the elections while I was gone.

Strangely on Sunday August 29, 1993, one of the candidates in the Center's leadership race, a former Liberian Immigration officer, James (last name withheld to protect identity) disagreed with the decision and filed a complaint with the Waterloo Police Station claiming that I was liable to reimburse him the amount of 75,000 leones which he claimed to have spent on the election campaign. The complaint, as I suspected, was fueled by a selfish desire laden with deep-seated jealousy and envy that were intended to prevent me from travelling for studies. The sinister motive was discovered when James continuously requested that the

OC seize my passport. Knowing that it was a civil case and not one in which I was accused of committing a crime against the state; I refused to surrender my passport.

For a number of years, I had worked tirelessly in search of educational opportunities for all the refugees including the complainant. I too had succeeded in being granted a conditional scholarship but I could not immediately receive it, as I was still awaiting a letter of admission from a university. When I finally got the admissions letter and was poised to travel in pursuit of my academic dream, my detractors became dangerously envious. A few days after I had transferred power to Mr. Jalloh, I started having some terrifying dreams. In one of my first dreams, I was practically cornered by a huge snake that lay in wait for me in the tree - its jaws wide open, gaping at me. A day later an old man by the name of Tamba who had openly told a gathering that he would ensure that I did not travel, appeared in my dream with a small voodoo clay pot, set up camp fire at my front door and began boiling some potion in it. I jumped up out of sleep in the middle of the night, sweating profusely. I told Joanna, and instinctively, we got on our knees and began to pray.

Having been forewarned in my dream of what lay ahead, it came as no surprise when three complainants came to my house at around 2 p.m. with the Waterloo Police Detachment's third in command to summon me to the station, the same place where we spent the night on our way to the Waterloo Refugee Center in 1991. Joanna at first did not want me to go. She logically argued that it made absolutely no sense for my enemies who had lodged a complaint against me to come with the police officer and to offer to take me to the station in their vehicle (not the police vehicle). She indicated that the scenario reminded her of how her father, who had faced a similar situation, had suffered partial paralysis after he accompanied his complainants to the next village where they had made complaints against him. Her advice also reminded me of a scene in Shakespeare's *Julius Caesar* in which Caesar's wife Calpurnia warned him not to go to the Senate where Cassius and Brutus and other co-conspirators were waiting to assassinate him. Caesar ignored the warning and paid a heavy price with his life[11].

---

[11] Shakespeare, William. *Julius Caesar*, Act II, scene II.

I concurred with Joanna but told her that my refusal to go would be interpreted as resisting arrest which could have far-reaching consequences. As Camp Chairman, I had been in the forefront of advising refugees to be law-abiding. It did not make sense now for me to be violator of the law in view of the fact that the OC had sent his deputy, not a constable, to summon me to the station. In the end Joanna and I agreed that I should go to the station but not in their vehicle. So, a friend of ours, James Kpagai offered to drive us to the police station.

We arrived at the station and were ushered into the OC's office. One of the three complainants was a Nigerian fetish priest who lived in the Center. I recall that during refugee registrations in early June 1991, he was denied registration by the UNHCR field officer because he was a Nigerian who had fled the war in Liberia. By the refugee agency definition, the Nigerian was an economic migrant and not a refugee. I had happened to be around when he was plucked out of the registration line. I had empathized with his plight and had pleaded with a Red Cross registrar after the field officer had left, asking that they register him so that he could qualify to receive the material and food assistance that other refugees received. He was registered and allowed to live in the Center with the refugees. Two years later I became his sworn enemy because of petty camp politics. And today, he was in the forefront of destroying me. I regretted my decision that I had made two years ago.

In the OC's office, the three complainants sat next to one another, each with his hands in pockets even while they stressed their points. "Strange", I thought to myself, for I know how we like to gesture when we speak. And that looked pretty unnatural. I sat opposite to them and just watched their body language. And every time I was about to respond to the OC's question, I saw the three men, in a bizarrely synchronized manner, as if performing some kind of ritual, would tightly squeeze whatever they were holding on to in their pockets – each hand respectively. I began to feel dizzy. My thoughts were incoherent, not making sense to me, and my speech slurred. I felt as though I had been diagnosed with diplopia (double vision) - my vision was blurry as hell. I started seeing two of everyone in the room, then that quadrupled. Though I was seated, my legs began to shake – they felt weak. I was now on the verge of choking - my life was slowly ebbing away. I wanted badly to get out of the office. Finally the OC ordered us all out of his office so that he and his deputy could come up with the verdict. I had never been so relieved in a long time. How I didn't fall over myself was a mystery, even to me, for I didn't feel as though I was in any shape to stand without assistance, much more walk out of the office. As soon as I stepped outside, and felt the fresh air, I felt somewhat better. Being outside was good for me. It enabled me to regain my composure while my thoughts flowed more coherently. My physical being and spirit was being renewed. I knew that The Heavenly Father was in complete control.

Fifteen minutes later we were called back into the office. I heard that I was liable to pay. Here was the irony though: the same OC who, a couple of days earlier had advised me in his office not to conduct an election in the Center, insisting that, "this is Sierra Leone and not Liberia" was now in complete agreement with the complainants. At that, I just figured that money must have changed hands. I tried to remind him of the letter I had copied his office and the meeting to which he had invited me at his office, during which he had warned me against any attempt to hold an election. But he would not listen. Of course that was *Salone* where "justice was sometimes dispensed in favor of the highest financial bidder," I thought. I was ordered by the OC to be taken to the prisoner's bench in the adjacent building that housed the prison cell. I really didn't care, I was just glad to be leaving the sight of those three lying, evil-doing people. .

On my way to the building, I briefly talked with my relatives and friends and asked them to get me a Bible from the house, which was about two and a half miles away. Kpagai had dropped us off and had driven back to the Center. My nephew Peter would have to fetch my Bible for me. Poor Peter! He had to race back to the house on foot to get the Bible. I sat on the prisoner's bench in front of the prison cell door while being processed by the desk constable. Peter seemed not to be getting back with the Bible any time soon. "How long was it going to take him to get back with the Bible?" I wondered. I was becoming greatly impatient and agitated, for I strongly believed that it was only the Bible that could be a source of my salvation. "Was I going to be consumed by the evil spirit before the Bible arrived?" I thought as I sat on the bench pondering over the predicament I was trapped in. Suddenly there was a burst of noise coming from outside. A scuffle had ensued between two police officers and a suspect they were bringing in to be locked up. When they had succeeded in getting him in, the officers started to frisk him, and lo and behold, a pocket-size Bible dropped from his back pocket and fell between my feet. I picked it up and clutched on to it for dear life. I did not return it to the police; neither did they ask me to. I immediately started rummaging frantically through the pages searching for the Psalm that would deliver me out of the hands of my enemies. I was in such a state that I began flipping through the pages and I passed by the main page over and over again without realizing. I finally composed myself, and found the book of the Bible that I was looking for. I turned to Psalm 23 and read it over and over and over again. I suddenly realized that I was worrying myself for nothing. "Oh ye of little faith," I thought. I had said it, for I knew it. Now I felt it – my God was in control. And he would deliver me. I was overjoyed and overcome with emotions. I felt powerful. It was as though electricity was pulsating through my veins, taking over my entire body - from my head, down to my neck, chest, my belly-button, and down, down, down to the tip of my toes. I was buoyant. I was strong. I was elated. I felt like I was finally and permanently delivered from the grips of whatever evil forces that were tightening the noose on me. Twenty years later, I still have in my possession that little Bible that I believe saved my life.

Meanwhile back in the Center, my deputy Joseph Gayekra had begun mobilizing hundreds of my supporters for a march to the police station. That prompted Kpagai to drive back to the police station to apprise the police of what was unfolding in the Center. In order to verify the information for himself, the OC went with Kpagai to the Center. The OC saw for himself what Kpagai had told him. Immediately after he returned to the police station, he ordered my release. I arrived back in the Center at around 7 p.m. My deputy, Gayekra, friend Kamaty Diahn and several hundreds of supporters were on hand to welcome me. Triumphant, I spoke briefly to the hundreds who had turned out to welcome me. The next morning, I went to the UNHCR office in Freetown and informed the office of what had transpired on Sunday. UNHCR Program Officer, Tilak Abeysinghe then phoned Lt. Col. Dr

K.I.S Kamara. They advised me to stay in Freetown while they went to the Center accompanied by the Chief Police Officer of the district. At the end of it all the complaint against me ended up being an exercise in futility. On October 1, 1993, I left for Cairo, Egypt.

Jerry Gbardy

American University in Cairo Campus with Jeremiah Sulunteh, 1994

Painful Journey: a Story of Escape and Survival

Certificate Presentation, Waterloo Refugee Center, 1993

Dedication of Children's Playground, Waterloo Refugee Center, 1991

Dedication of Children's Playground, Waterloo Refugee Center, 1991

*L-R: Jerry, former Zimbabwean President Dr. Banana,
George Tarn & Robert Gbei 1993*

Painful Journey: a Story of Escape and Survival

In Giza, Cairo by the Pyramids 1994

Mano River Bridge between Liberia and Sierra Leone

Jerry Gbardy

Family Photo 1997

CHAPTER SEVEN
The Cairo Adventure

I arrived in Cairo on October 3, 1993 to pursue graduate studies at the American University in Cairo (AUC). It was a noteworthy experience. The language is Arabic with an Islamic culture, which presented lots of challenges for me from the onset. It was indeed a cultural shock. Cairo is the capital of Egypt and the largest city in the Arab world and Africa and obviously the largest city in Egypt. Undeniably, Cairo is the center of almost everything in the Arab world from education, religion to intellectualism. It attracts students and professionals from all over the world for academic, vocational, and professional studies in the areas of television and radio broadcast journalism, agriculture, health sciences, maritime, water and sanitation, Islamic studies, etc. During the time I was there, the Liberian government sent groups of employees from the ministries of agriculture, health, foreign affairs, and the broadcasting corporation for training.

The population at the time between 1993 and 1995 was about 16 million. With the population that high, the city suffers from high levels of pollution, filth, congestion, traffic, deafening and nerve-racking noise. It is a city where donkey carts, humans and vehicle traffic jockey for position on the roadway. In an effort to discourage mass rural to urban migrations, the government built modern cities outside of Cairo with subsidized housing units. I had the occasion to visit two of the modern cities – Nasser and Sadat – on an academic field trip arranged by my professor. I was astounded, and so was the rest of the class, to find out that the housing facilities were under-utilized. Most of the housing units as modern as they were, sat unoccupied while Cairo was, as Author Lamb concisely puts it, "sinking under the weight of people, people and more people..." (Lamb, 2002:27), many of whom had migrated to the city in search of work and better opportunities. Also during summer, the temperature would rise up to forty-five degree Celsius.

In 1992, as head of the Liberia refugees in the Waterloo Refugee Center, with several of my executives namely: Joseph Gayekra, Rufus Duo, Francis Sarmah, Ansu Dolleh, George Tarhn, Robert Gbei, to name but a few, I had on several occasions, visited the German Embassy to solicit scholarships for the refugees. During the multiple visits, the German Ambassador repeatedly assured us that our request was forwarded to his government in Bonn with a note of caution that if the scholarships were approved, they would be channeled through the United Nations High Commissioner for Refugee (UNHCR) for effective management.

Mid January 1993, the UNHCR field officer delivered the good news in the Waterloo Refugee Center. The Albert Einstein German Academic Refugee Initiative Fund (German: *Deutsche Akademische Fluchtlings Initiative Albert Einstein or DAFI*) was approved to grant deserving Liberian refugees scholarships at universities, colleges, vocational and technical institutions in Sierra Leone and elsewhere. The objectives of the DAFI program are to:

- Develop qualified human resources to contribute to the reconstruction of the country of origin upon repatriation;
- Achieve self-reliance of the beneficiary student and his/her family through gainful employment;
- Serve as a model for other refugees to further their education, particularly female students;
- Contribute to the refugee community – as teachers or through other work – pending a durable solution or repatriation.

True to the ambassador's promise, the UNHCR was put directly in charge of administering the scholarships. The memo added that all interested applicants were advised to go to the office on Lightfoot Boston Street the next business day to apply. Like all others, I went to the office on Monday to fill out the necessary paperwork. The UNHCR Program Officer Moshood Olatokunbo assured me of the tentative approval of my application pending submission of an admissions letter from any recognized institution of learning. At that point I began to intensify my search for admission.

Prior to that, as a Convention Refugee, in 1992 I had started applying to schools around the world for admission and scholarship. I had been going to the United States Information Service Library in Freetown and compiling a list of academic institutions to which I wrote. Some would respond requesting original copies of my academic credentials. Other would not bother to respond at all. Howbeit, the fact that I had scholarship only pending submission of admission letter gave me the impetus to intensify my search. My biggest setback was that I had left Liberia in 1990 after graduation with only a student copy of my transcript. So there lay my problem. To compound the already involuntary hopeless situation, Operation Octopus, the military campaign launched in October by Taylor's NPFL to finally take Monrovia was underway. I could not get any contact with the University of Liberia.

In all of this, I applied to the Fourah Bay College (FBC), University of Sierra Leone. Founded in February 1927, FBC is the oldest university in West Africa. In 1876 it became a degree granting institution with an affiliation to the University of Durham in England, and since then has maintained a reputable tradition of higher education in Africa, producing top lawyers, academics, and politicians and other professionals in the region (www.fbc.usl.edu.sl). The university sits atop Mount Aureol the second highest peak overlooking Freetown, the capital of Sierra Leone. But by the early 1990s, FBC was a shadow of a university only thriving on past glory. There was no electricity on the campus including the city. The library shelves were full of dusty outdated books. Instructors were underpaid and unpaid for months. There were horrible stories of academic fraud which alluded to the scheme of "satisfying the professor." This meant that no matter how smart the student was, he or she still needed to satisfy the professor through some dubious means in order to clear the course. Getting an A or a B was not a definite guarantee for clearing the course.

Therefore every trip I made up Mt. Aureol to meet with an admissions counselor or the chair of the department, reminded me of the enviable task that lay ahead if accepted. The trip alone up the mountain on foot, took about twenty to twenty-five minutes. By the time I arrived up there, I was all sweaty and banged up. Once up there I would have to walk up several flights of stairs to the ninth floor to see the chair of the department because the elevators were inoperable due to lack of electricity. I made the last trip up FBC campus in April. During that visit, an admissions counselor informed me that the chair of the department had assessed my credentials including the thesis proposal that I had submitted which was previously evaluated by a University of Liberia professor, also a Liberian refugee who was then teaching in a Teachers' College in Freetown. The admissions counselor advised me to wait till May when the results would be out.

On the other hand, far across the continent, I had written to the American University in Cairo (AUC) for admission. They responded in late 1992 that as sub-Saharan African, with a Bachelor's degree, I was eligible to apply for the Graduate African Fellowship Award (GAFA) and they suggested that I apply and must also submit the required documentation in the original form. But the problem was that I had only the student copy that I fled with. I wrote back and informed them of my predicament that I could not contact the University of Liberia because of the prevailing civil war. Under such extenuating circumstances, I pleaded with them to accept the documents as they were. Consequently the waiting game began.

The American University in Cairo (AUC) is a prestigious private institution of higher education. Situated in the downtown Tahrir (freedom) Square district of the city, the university provides American liberal arts education to students from all socio-economic backgrounds in Egypt and other nations around the world, contributing substantially towards Egypt's intellectual and cultural life. The university was founded in 1919 by American Mission in Egypt sponsored by the United Presbyterian Church of North America (www.aucegypt.edu). It was dedicated to cultural enrichment and modernization. The university offers American style learning programs at the undergraduate, graduate and professional levels, along with an extensive continuing education program. It is an American institution that promotes American education in the Middle East, professional education, and lifelong learning.

Painful Journey: a Story of Escape and Survival

On Saturday July 3, 1993 while performing my camp chairman duties, I received two letters in care of the UNHCR: one from FBC, the other from AUC. Both were admissions documents. When I opened the one from AUC, voila, the award! The award covered tuitions including summer school and medical insurance, excluding books and maintenance. I could not contain my emotions. I chose the latter. I was virtually awestruck and absolutely so thrilled to be going to the birth place of civilization which I had read about in grade school over the years. I went to the UNHCR office on Monday morning to fill out the necessary paperwork for my travel to Cairo. Since I already had a scholarship pending, it worked perfectly in my favor. The UNHCR agreed to facilitate my travel to and from Cairo and to take care of my maintenance and books. A few days later, they issued me a UN Convention Travel Document, commonly known as refugee passport and applied for an entry visa on my behalf to the Egyptian Embassy near Freetown.

The trip to Cairo almost did not materialize because the embassy delayed in issuing me the entry visa. The reason for their delay was simple. I had a refugee passport. For the many trips I made to the Egyptian Embassy, the Charges d'affairs told me quite emphatically that the passport was the problem. He said had it been a Liberian passport, and with the cover letter from the UNHCR, they would have issued the visa without delay. He added that as a Convention Refugee, I could opt to remain in Cairo and international covenants would have protected me there. The embassy did not want me to be a burden on their government. Against that backdrop, there were many back and forth between the UNCHR and the embassy. They requested the UNHCR to write a diplomatic note guaranteeing to cover my living expenses while in Cairo and that I would come back to Sierra Leone after my studies. They also wanted a re-entry visa to be issued in my travel document by the Sierra Leonean Immigration. The immigration issued me a one-year re-entry visa, which within their jurisdiction was the best they said they could do. Additionally the embassy further requested that my ticket to and from Cairo be open. All those pre-conditions were met by the UNHCR on my behalf. The embassy then forwarded my document to their security headquarters in Cairo.

I made several trips to the embassy. It was from those constant visits to the embassy that I unknowingly got introduced to the fundamentals of Egyptian bureaucracy which would later manifest itself while I was in Cairo. With the run-around that I got from the visa officer, it still did not adequately prepare me for the practicum of "Bureaucracy 405" that I came face to face with while in Cairo. By the time the embassy completed meeting the requirements of their cumbersome bureaucratic process and issued the entry visa, I was four weeks late for school. And that almost spelled doom for me. That meant once I arrived in Cairo, I had to redouble my efforts because I had so much reading to do to catch up with the rest of the class. The day I arrived, Graduate Students Coordinator Carol King Reed was quick to notify me that she had sent a letter to UNHCR-Freetown advising me to wait till the next semester. However, since I was already in Cairo, I needed to work a little harder to catch up with the rest of the class. Had the letter met me in Freetown, I would have been devastated. In retrospect, I thank God that was not the case!

For the first few days in Cairo, I was homesick. I missed my family so badly especially Jeryna our daughter who was about 8 months old when I left. Leaving my family and friends behind and settling in a country with different culture and language, it was very tough for me to make the transition smoothly. At one point I was so emotionally drained that I felt like going back to Freetown. I therefore met with the UNHCR social counselor in charge of student affairs, Madam Tahani that I wanted to return to Freetown. She did not talk much. All she did was to remind me of the hundreds of thousands of refugees around Africa who would like to have the opportunity that I had. If I wanted to throw away this chance it was entirely up to me as she was ready to book the next flight for me. The message hit home as I left the office heading back to the hotel. Once I was introduced to Jeremiah Sulunteh, a fellow Liberian in the same program and several other Liberians living in Cairo, I felt at home. We started paying frequent visits to the home of the Charge d'affairs at the Liberian Embassy, Cosmos Sherman where we reminisced about the good old days back home.

Historically, Cairo boasts of having Al-Azhar University, the oldest and most prestigious Islamic university in the Arab world (Bard, 1999).

Painful Journey: a Story of Escape and Survival

In the summer of 1994, I visited some Liberian students on the campus and was surprised to see the magnitude of the structural decay of the facility. The windows and doors were broken and the dining hall had no furniture. The hallway from the dining hall to men's living quarters was sooty due to excessive hallway cooking. The school could no longer provide food for the students on a group basis, as such; every student had portable kerosene stove that they would mount in the hallway to cook their individual food. My Liberian friends who had been there from 1984 indicated that allowances from the school were not forthcoming, as such; they were left to fend for themselves.

Riding on the public transit was a complete mess. Every time of the day, the metro as the train was called, was jammed packed. Entering the train station was like being at the entrance of a soccer stadium where fans are coming out from watching a game between Spanish rivals Real Madrid and FC Barcelona. It would take about three to four trains to pass by before getting room on one – that is if you were lucky. Of course you just had to fight your way in.

As for the buses, they were always jammed packed inside and at the front and rear doors. A rider must be trained in the art of boarding or disembarking. Except for the terminal of origin and the last one where they would be stationary to allow boarding and disembarking, the buses would only slow down at designated stops along the route. Like in a Hollywood stunt movie, a rider would have to be very strategic and tactical in knowing which foot to put forward and at what time while at the same time running alongside the bus. The driver would assume no responsibility if a passenger accidently fell while attempting to board or alight. He would simply drive on. I watched an incident in Maadi, a suburb of Cairo where a passenger got rolled over by the rear wheels but the driver kept on going. In most instances the standing passengers would help the one trying to board by holding his hand and pulling him on the doorstep while the bus was in motion. Though I was from a developing country, this method of boarding was incredibly sophisticated for me. I was not prepared to risk my life. I therefore did what a safety-conscious person would do by not riding a transit bus from any point between two terminals.

On the other hand, riding a cab was not problem-free also. On several occasions, cab drivers successfully capitalized on my lack of knowledge of the value of the currency and the geography of the area to maximize profit at my expense. The encounters with cab drivers in the first week of my arrival made me partially broke before I got the hang of it. On the night of my arrival at the airport, a UNHCR employee was on hand to pick me up and drop me off at a hotel called Pension Roma which was about five minutes' drive from AUC. The next morning he was back to take me to the campus. Before he could leave, he wrote the name and address of the school in Arabic on the other side of the hotel's business card and gave it to me along with 200 Egyptian pounds as spending money for a couple of days.

On the way back to the hotel, I flagged a cab and handed the cab driver the hotel's business card. He smiled and in halting English with a very thick Middle Eastern accent said:

"May-starr, zbeak Arabic?" (note that pronunciation of letter *p* for an Egyptian and for the most part, Arabs, is *b*)

"No," I replied.

"Welcome to *Kaiee-rro*," the cab driver beckoned.

"Thanks."

He ultimately sensed my vulnerability knowing full well that not only was I a foreigner but that I was new in the country. Therefore he deliberately turned off the old Victorian Era style meter on the dash and said "*mosh-kwayis*" (not good). He drove all around and made occasional stops at almost every turn of the way to cunningly ask shopkeepers and pedestrians for "direction" to the hotel. When we finally arrived at the hotel, he charged me "*ashra gini*" (ten Egyptian pounds), five times more than the actual price. I gave the money without any question. I almost ran out of cash at week's end. What I found out later during my stay in Cairo was that Egyptian cab drivers erroneously believed that by pretending to ask for direction it would create an inflated impression that they were performing special extra service for the passengers which should deserve compensation in addition to the fare.

At the end of the week, I met with Madam Tahani, the UNHCR social counselor who was so surprised that I was on the verge of running out of money in so short a time. She then advised me that the fare for every distance

Painful Journey: a Story of Escape and Survival

within the Cairo city limit was a maximum of *ethni gini* (two Egyptian pounds). She also gave me other valuable pieces of advice that I used on a daily basis. As time went on, I knew the map of the area and also learned how to give directions in Arabic which I applied to my advantage to beat the cab drivers to their own game. As soon as a cab driver asked: "May-starr where from? Afri-kia?" my response was quick and a complete opposite of what they wanted to hear: "*Sharia Basra, Mohandessen*" (Basra Street, Mohandessen). I would then motion to the driver to drive, and in Arabic, I would instruct him thus: *ala tool* (go straight), *she-mal* (turn left), *yameen* (turn right), and *hina* (here). If he turned the meter off and said "*mosh kwayis*," I would say "*La, la Kwayis*" (No, no it is good) with a considerable twist of humor attached.

It was understandable to see a cab driver trying to extort money from foreign passengers as this seemingly happens all over the world. But for a shopkeeper to engage in such tendencies also, underscores the mindset of many Egyptians which alludes to a widely held belief that all foreigners visiting Cairo have plenty of money which must be doled out. Several times I would go to a shop to buy a pair of shoes or pair of trousers and the shopkeeper would pretend to be so nice by offering me seat and bringing several sizes for me to try on as is obvious. In the end he would neatly wrap my preferred size and stretch his hands for *bakshih* (tip) in addition to the price of the item. When I asked why, the answer that I always got was, "Because I helped you find the right size," which was kind of hilarious indeed.

Prior to going to Cairo, I had learned about Egypt in grade school as the birth place of civilization. Therefore when I got the offer to go to the country I was overwhelmed by a heightened sense of elation especially as a dark-skinned African. No sooner had I arrived than my expectation began to dwindle and turn into one of profound disappointment and absolute indignation. Many Egyptians, including AUC students believed that they are not in Africa. An Egyptian would come up to me and ask whether I was from Africa. I would respond in the affirmative with an emphasis "just like you." Their response was always quite baffling: "No we are not in Africa." We had an African Students Association on campus that the Egyptian students refused to be members of.

Most Egyptians generally love their country to the extent that they will do whatever within their means to protect or defend its name. Sometime during the middle of 1994, two young African-American students wearing baggy jeans with backpacks almost got lynched by rowdy AUC students when a cab driver pulled up at the school's gates and yelled out to a group of Egyptians that the American youngsters verbally insulted Egypt. Within split seconds angry students and passersby descended upon the two African-Americans who had just got out of the taxi in time. They literally ran upstairs to the University President's office on the fourth floor with the surging crowd in hot pursuit. Staff of the office barricaded the Americans until diplomats from the US Embassy nearby, accompanied by some armed Egyptian police, came and took the Americans away. Even the presence of the armed police officers did not deter some angry students from throwing punches at the Americans who were immediately flown back to the States thereafter. One valuable lesson learned: never to say, *"Misr mosh kwayis."* (Egypt not good)

During the fifteen months I spent in Cairo, Egyptians never ceased to fascinate me. I observed that they had taken the words greetings and courtesy, which are deeply rooted in cultural practices, to a whole new level. The act of simple greeting which Americans and Canadians and others take for granted by casually waving the hand or by saying "hi", the Egyptians perform with gusto. Two male motorists traveling in opposite directions on a busy Cairo thoroughfare would stop their respective vehicles in the middle in order to engage in a greeting process that would last for pretty close to five minutes. They would embrace, kiss multiple times on both cheeks, and embrace again, and again. Meanwhile other motorists would honk their horns and go around them. After the exchange of greetings, the drivers would board their vehicles and go their separate ways finally allowing traffic to flow again.

In similar fashion, if there were a minor vehicle collision, both motorists would disembark and engage in a ferocious thirty-minute shouting match in the middle of traffic. At the end of the shouting match in which there would be no apparent winner, both men would embrace, shake hands and part ways. *Kalaas* (Case closed)! In another instance, on boarding a minibus, two men would stand by the door, each imploring the other to board first. One would say, *"Fedhr"* (welcome or you first). The other would respond, *"La, fedhr"* (no you first). And that would go on and on while others were patiently waiting in the queue.

Painful Journey: a Story of Escape and Survival

Egyptian public employees were never in a hurry to get work done culminating into excessive bureaucratic red tape. What should normally take a couple of hours would last for days or weeks. Therefore one of the things I loathed immensely was going to the security building, *Mogama*[12] every six months to renew my temporary residency visa as was required by Egyptian Immigration laws. As mentioned earlier at the Egyptian Embassy in Freetown, I was introduced to the fundamentals of Egyptian bureaucracy, yet I was not fully prepared to do the practicum. My experience at the Mogama Building is a case in point.

As a UNHCR-sponsored refugee student, my security clearance letter would be prepared by the office and sent to the Mogama via the Foreign Affairs Ministry. But meeting all those bureaucratic requirements was not good enough to hasten the issuance of the visa. I spent a full work week in several attempts from 9 a.m. to 4 p.m. to get my passport stamped, but was unsuccessful. On the sixth business day I went back to the UNHCR to notify them of what was going on. After a few phone calls, the social counselor, Madam Tahani gave me the name of a police general as a contact person, a move that was supposed to facilitate a smooth process, but wound up adding to my woes.

I went to the general's office as advised. After introducing myself to his orderly, he stretched his hand: "*Baz-bot*." I handed him the passport and sat in the waiting room as was instructed. After about an hour or so of going in and out of the general's office with some passports, the orderly briefly stopped by me - upon seeing me rise to talk to him - and said, "*May-starr, shwaya, shwaya*" (Mr. slowly, slowly or take it easy). I dutifully sat back in my seat again. I wanted to attend nature's call, but could not lest I would lose my seat or not be around when needed. I sat there for the rest of the time without getting to see the general. At that point, I started getting increasingly impatient and frustrated again but nothing I could do. Interestingly, the general was not the one to issue the visa. He was only supposed to okay the document and send me to another office where the book would be stamped as I found out a couple of days later. At about 3:30 p.m. it was time for me to go to class. Coincidentally it was time for the general to leave also. The orderly came and said, "*Inshallah,*

---

[12] It is a large national security building situated in Tahrir Square across from AUC. It housed the police, immigration and other paramilitary organizations of the government.

bokra."(God willing, tomorrow) I was upset. When I tried to argue with him, the orderly said, *"Malesh"* (never mind) and walked away. This scenario is what Author Lamb refers to as the IBM syndrome (Lamb, 2002), was repeated for another three days. I eventually said to myself, "Welcome to Egyptian Bureaucracy EGBU 405." This same scenario used to repeat itself whenever I went to cash my UNHCR-issued checks. Every day I was told *bokra*. That sometimes would take me well beyond rent due date. Even after the UNHCR arranged for the bank to pay me directly without having to issue me a check, it would still take me about three days to get the cash. Either way it was a no win situation for me.

I noticed among other positive attributes that not only was there plenty of food on the market in Cairo but that the food, including fresh vegetables, was relatively inexpensive that everyone could somehow afford. What I also saw was the absence of crime such as theft. I would launder my clothes and hang them up on the ground floor apartment balcony for days without a single piece being lost. In fact one day a female American schoolmate forgot a purse full of cash in a cab. The following day the cab driver delivered the cash-filled purse on campus.

Meanwhile in the southern end of Cairo was the City of the Dead, a 4-mile long cemetery that was home to a large chunk of the population forced from central Cairo due to urban renewal demolitions and urbanization pressures. Other residents emigrated from the countryside in search of work and better opportunities, a classic case of rural to urban migration. I heard about the City of the Dead, but dismissed the story as an exaggeration or mere fabrication. Beyond my wildest imagination, I did not believe that people would actually live in the cemetery until I visited the place during burial of Foumba, a Liberian embassy staff. Again I was astounded to see the many BMWs, Mercedes Benzes, and Fiats parked in front of cluster of tombs remodeled as residential units. Residents of the City of the Dead did not see anything spooky about living among the dead. They preferred living in the cemetery to living in Cairo itself. The neighborhoods were cleaner, quieter, less crowded than those in the main city. The air was much cleaner also. The streets were free of traffic jams and the lawns were properly manicured. In residents' backyards, there were beautiful flowers, plants, and vegetable gardens.

Owing to the rising population in Cairo, I can logically assume that the population of the City of the Dead has grown tenfold.

During the first semester, I put my studies in overdrive. I worked very hard as had been advised by both the graduate school coordinator and my academic advisor. I had to play catch-up with ease in all the three core-courses I was doing. The following two semesters were much better. I went with the class on four academic field trips to several places. The Director of the MPA Program, Dr. EH Valsan took us on the first three while Dr Cyrus Reed, Director of the Office of African Studies accompanied us on the last one. The first trip was to the historic Suez Canal, a 100-mile man-made waterway constructed in 1869 that connects the Red Sea to the Mediterranean Sea (Bard, 1999). Blockading of the canal in 1967 by Egypt led to the Arab-Israeli War (ibid). We rode the ferry east across the Suez Canal and did a whole day tour of the Sinai desert, a portion of Egypt on the east bank of the Suez Canal that borders Israel and Saudi Arabia. The next two trips were to the government-built modern cities of Sadat and Nasser. The final trip close to the end of my studies was to the Red Sea which reminded me of a scene in Cecil Demille's *Ten Commandments* in which Moses parted the Red Sea to allow the Israelites to cross to freedom from generations of bondage. That trip was a fulfilling moment for me.

Outside of academic works, I also had the opportunity to do some sightseeing. There are three great Pyramids, arguably the most famous, fascinating and durable structure ever built, situated in the southwestern suburb of Giza. Pyramid Cheops, the largest and tallest of the three, has a mausoleum down in the basement (about three stories deep) that preserved the bodies of the pharaoh and his family. The place looked so spooky that I was glad to quickly crawl back to the surface. At the bottom of the hill below the Pyramids, is the Great Sphinx of Giza, a mythical creature with the head of a human and the body of a lion. I also visited a museum in Tahrir Square that keeps the mummified bodies of pharaohs and other archeological finds that attract thousands of tourists annually.

Except for occasional worrying news from my family in Waterloo about the approaching frontlines of the Sierra Leonean war, I had nothing else to worry about but to devote all the time to my lessons.

The UNHCR was taking care of my maintenance, and paying for all my books and other needed academic materials. I therefore cautioned myself to fulfill my share of the bargain by studying, which I did. I also hung out with my classmate, Jeremiah Sulunteh. Up to the time of writing this book, he is Liberia's Ambassador to the United States of America. In all fairness, I must openly confess that I enjoyed my academic studies at the American University in Cairo. I completed my studies with honors and returned to Sierra Leone on January 9, 1995.

CHAPTER EIGHT
The Third and Final Run

I arrived in Freetown from Cairo on January 10, 1995. I was glad I returned for the fact that I missed my family and friends and thus, I was homesick. The other reason was that the civil war in Sierra Leone was fast approaching the capital city so I wanted to be there to take care of my family in case of any eventuality. That evening when the KLM flight finally touched down at the Lungi Airport, my family was not there as they did not expect me to be on that flight. But the UNHCR had arranged for me to be picked up. My re-entry visa had expired so it created a little problem for me with Sierra Leonean immigration and custom officials. They ordered me to step aside briefly. Just as they were beginning to hassle me, a guy showed up from the baggage claim area and presented a letter on my behalf to the customs officers. The letter was written by the UNHCR with a stamp of approval by the chief immigration officer in Freetown. The customs officers stamped my UNCTD and let me through. Problem solved! The guy who had brought the letter was the driver. Instead of proceeding directly to Waterloo, I requested him to take me to MV Swaray's house in Aberdeen Village, an affluent west-end district of Freetown City where three five-star intercontinental hotels – Cape Sierra, Mammy Yoko and Bintumani – are located. I had planned to spend the night at Mr. Swaray's house before going to Waterloo the next morning.

When Mr. Swaray opened the door, he was full of surprise and excitement upon seeing me: "Oh, Joanna, your husband is here o."

"What?" Joanna asked in total amazement.

"I say your husband is here."

I could hear her waking up the children: "Mamie (Aletha,) Gerald, and Jeryna, your father is here."

They all ran to the front door and ganged up on me.

"What a surprise and coincidence! Welcome back o," Joanna said.

They knew I was coming but not that night. At some point there was confusion in the communication between Joanna and UNHCR and she was planning to inquire from them the next day about my arrival date. Well there would be no need for that now – I was in town. All of us were extremely happy to see one another again. Jeryna was now walking and also talking. She was under 9 months old when I left and was now two days shy of her second birthday. Gerald had also grown a little taller.

Although I should have been physically and emotionally exhausted after having travelled almost 48 hours from Cairo via Amsterdam to Freetown, I was not. Being with my wife and kids and Mr. Swaray and his family after two years, buoyed my spirit. I was absolutely overwhelmed by an indescribable feeling of joy and satisfaction. For the whole night we sat up talking, I about my adventure in Cairo while Joanna told me most of what had happened while I was away. Gerald had graduated from kindergarten as valedictorian delivering a very inspiring speech to the audience which was highly praised by the school authorities and residence of the entire Center. It was the talk of the Center. As for Jeryna, she had been severely ill to the point of death for which she was hospitalized in Sierra Leone's largest referral hospital for about a month. Joanna revealed that at certain point Jeryna had stopped breathing momentarily which made her to send for some of our male cousins whom she would have sent to go dig a grave. Fortunately the boys were nowhere to be found. Miraculously Jeryna opened her eyes and whispered a few words to her. She had cheated death.

While I was in Cairo, I did not in any way get a hint of the terrible news. Joanna had reasoned that - and truly so – if she had told me, that would have rendered me totally devastated which would have certainly ruined my studies. Therefore she advised everyone writing to me not to divulge news of Jeryna`s illness. I thanked her for her courage and far-sightedness and for enduring all the pain of caring for a sick child and all the children while I was away. She also mentioned that night that she did not receive the parcel I had sent her in December through the Express Mail Service (EMS) of the post office. The parcel had contained some money for their Christmas celebration. We went to Waterloo two days later. There was a tumultuous welcome reception awaiting my arrival. While we were in Freetown news of my arrival had hit the Center like wildfire. Every day, one group of relatives and friends would host some kind of get-together for me.

A few days after my arrival, I was sitting in front of our house with some friends who had come to greet me when Jeryna came to me with the following message in Liberian English:

"Gerald pa, mama call you." (Gerald's dad, mama wants to see you).

I laughed and so did everyone else. On second thought, I realized that it was not a laughing matter but one that should claim my attention. My daughter was considering me a dad of her brother, but not herself. Obviously she did not know me and understandably so, she was under nine months old when I left. Therefore I needed to work some overtime in constantly honing into her mind that I was her dad. At that point, I said, "Mainyo (the nickname I had given her before my departure), I am also your dad just like I am Gerald's dad. He is your older brother." It would take several days, weeks of telling her I was her dad before she started calling me "papa."

I gradually began to settle in, readjusting my way of life. All of the "luxuries" such as tap water, shower, flush toilet, and electricity that I had enjoyed in the apartment in Cairo were no longer available. I was back in the Waterloo Refugee Center and was compelled to adjust to my new-old realities. Also I had left Cairo during winter and arrived in Freetown where it was summer. So differences of weather conditions featured prominently into the adjustment equation. Regardless of the challenges of readjusting to the new-old realities – which were temporary I suppose – I was glad to be back in my comfort zone by being in the company of my family, relatives and the hundreds of friends in the Center. The Center had a new leadership under the chairmanship of Winston Jordan and Secretary Victor Gray. Sam Jalloh who succeeded me had repatriated to Liberia. Operations co-Chairman Hector Higgins; a holdover from my administration that succeeded Jalloh, had also resigned. And so Jordan was effectively steering the affairs of the

Center. By that time we were continuing with the local integration phase of our refugee life. Consequently UNHCR and its implementing partners decided to provide us with some incentives that would enable us to engage in life-sustaining activities. As was expected, monthly food supplies would phase out in the foreseeable future and we were definitely being prepared to be independent if the war in Liberia did not end and we still chose to continue to live in Sierra Leone. CAUSE-Canada, an international non-governmental organization (INGO) succeeded the Red Cross for the daily management of the Center. They opened a large trade shop in Section Z where they trained refugees in vocations such as soap-making, carpentry & woodwork, tie-dying, sewing, gardening, and basic home economics. The INGO also successfully ran an adult literacy school that was filled to capacity. They provided small loans to refugees who submitted applications with business proposals approved by the INGO's loan managers. Refugee market women took advantage of the opportunity also and took loans. Thus socio-economic activities began to flourish in the Center. Meantime we kept our eyes and ears to the war that was creeping toward Freetown from the east and north.

Four months after I arrived, specifically during the morning hours of April 8, 1995, there were heavy volumes of firepower from artillery and small machine guns coming our way from the east. Pow, pow, boom, boom, kraaa, kraaa, ka, ka, ka could be heard. The sounds were rapid and deafening, so powerful that it seemed like we were in the middle of the warzone. Some shells were falling on the outskirt of the Center. The war had now come close to home again. "Sankor rebels are here o," could be heard all over the Center. At that point, all hell broke loose. Refugees began running helter-skelter picking up their children and their "worldly possessions". Usually those worldly possessions were chosen in order of priority and carried on their heads: food, cooking utensils, and if possible sponge mattresses (if available) or mats, and blankets which were the trademark of fleeing refugees. We were on the run again!

"O God, is this how our lives will be…all the time running from rebels?" Joanna could be heard shouting aloud. The cry from Joanna clearly put into proper perspectives, the life we had been living for the past five years – woefully intolerable and hopeless. We ran from the NPFL rebels in Liberia in 1990, from NPFL/RUF rebels in Bo-Waterside in 1991, and here we were again on the run for the third, certainly the final time in five years. It was too much for the young lady (Joanna) and all of us to bear but we had no choice. Joanna gathered the children and began packing what we could carry on our respective heads. For all of us - except Mainyo – it was our third time running for our lives. I grabbed the remaining half bag of rice, tied the bag and handed it to Aletha to carry. We would have to eat at where ever we settled. Joanna took a few personal effects, bundled them up and stepped outside with Gerald. I carried Jeryna on my back and two suitcases on my head: one full of books brought from Cairo and the other full of clothes. Gerald at 9, was relatively old enough to carry himself. We walked three miles to Waterloo town center. As for Jeryna, she was reveling in every moment of the journey. Occasionally I would take her from my back, allow her to walk a few yards, and then pick her up again. She was having fun perhaps thinking that we must have been going to the park or something. By the time we arrived, everyone was in pain. Aletha and Gerald had sore feet from the long walk while Joanna was complaining of severe back pain. I was in excruciating pain also, in my neck, chest, and back.

Once again we had become displaced refugees. From Waterloo, everyone headed for Freetown to be far away from the warzone. We boarded a taxi for Freetown. But the soldiers at Rockell, a checkpoint between Waterloo and Freetown, would not allow us to proceed beyond that point to the capital city lest we startle the nervous city population of rebel attack twenty-two miles from Freetown. Some way somehow, I was fortunate to be let through with my family by a Sierra Leonean soldier who recognized me as "Chairman" of the refugees. The taxi took us back to Mr. Swaray's house in Aberdeen Village which was always the point of refuge for my family and me. The man was so good to us, always giving us accommodation during times of need. Hundreds of refugees who were refused passage camped out on the main highway for about two weeks in the rain and sun. A few days later, the fighting passed Waterloo and came close to the checkpoint. Thanks to ECOMOG fighter planes that consistently bombed the RUF rebels back.

In order to help the situation, from Freetown, Julius Cee, Tommy Soe, and I started working frantically behind the scenes to get the UNHCR and the Sierra Leonean government to take our compatriots from the highway, which was the rebels' pathway to Freetown. We met with the UNHCR on a daily basis. At one point during our meeting with the UNHCR, a diplomat confided to us that a government minister angrily told him that there were thousands of displaced Sierra Leoneans over-populating Freetown with nowhere to stay. Therefore it made sense for him to take care of his citizens first. As refugees, we were second priority to the government at that moment. Julius, Tommy, and I made several trips to the State House to meet with Lt Col Dr. K.I.S Kamara, the State House's official responsible for refugee affairs. After several days of relentless visits coupled with added pressure from the UNHCR, the government finally gave us an old abandoned shipyard in the back of the Jui military/police barracks about 10 miles east of Freetown. The barracks housed ECOMOG soldiers awaiting deployment to Liberia and parts or Sierra Leone.

Hundreds of our compatriots were relocated to the abandoned shipyard. Between March and August 1995, many refugees were repatriated to Liberia. When all hope seemed to be fading, my family and I thought about repatriating also but discarded the idea later, simply because around the same time specifically on August 19, the Abuja Peace Accord on Liberia was signed by the warring factions, according to a BBC news report. The agreement was based on power-sharing and expansion of the Council of State among the warring factions and civil society representatives. Each warring faction was allotted a seat in the collective presidency arrangement which meant that Charles Taylor of NPFL, George Boley of Liberian Peace Council (LPC), and Alhaji Kromah of ULIMO-K would be heading to Monrovia to begin the implementation of the Accord. I logically calculated that bringing all the three warring faction leaders in one place, each with larger-than-life ego was a recipe for disaster. And so I concluded that it was not time for me to repatriate to Liberia.

Here was my situation: since July 1, 1990 I had been a Convention Refugee when I crossed the border into Sierra Leone and got registered by the aid agency on the ground providing assistance. Records abound that millions of refugees in the world have found asylum in least developed countries or in states which cannot be expected to shoulder the refugees unassisted. Sierra Leone was no exception. At the height of the war, thousands of Liberians streamed across the border into Sierra Leone, a nation that did not have the resources and the economic capacity to take care of the refugees. Against this backdrop, UNHCR, in consultation with the government of Sierra Leone, got involved with the provision of material assistance, including food, shelter, medical aid, and in many cases, education and other social services. To further discuss the other assistance the refugee agency helps facilitate, it is first important to know who is a refugee. The statute of the UNHCR says that the organization is competent to assist any person who,

> owing to well-founded fear of being persecuted for reason of race, religion, nationality or political opinion, is outside the country of nationality and is unable or owing to such fear for reason other than personal convenience is unwilling to avail himself of the protection of that country (Goodwin-Gill, 1983: 247,270).

With that in mind here are the three durable solutions in a refugee's problem that I had to consider: voluntary repatriation, local settlement and third country resettlement (Loescher and Monahan, 1990).

There was a burning desire in me to go back home. At certain point while in Cairo, I thoughtfully reviewed the pros and cons of voluntarily repatriating to Liberia after my studies but the cons outweighed the pros. Voluntary repatriation, accordingly, has long been regarded as the most permanent solution. It is a process whereby the UNHCR facilitates the return of refugees to their country of origin. Repatriation depends on a number of factors, most importantly conditions in the country of origin. Unless it is convinced that refugees can return in reasonable safety, the agency does not actively promote return. However it may facilitate existing spontaneous movement. Judging from the uncertainty regarding the peace process on Liberia in which about 11 accords were signed as of September 1994 but nothing significant had been achieved; and also considering the fact that the number of armed factions had ballooned from two to more than six with each faction controlling its own military enclave, I took repatriation off the table.

I also carefully weighed the local settlement option which is considered the second permanent solution. Because I had concluded that voluntary repatriation was unlikely to occur in the foreseeable future, the next viable alternative was for me to settle in Sierra Leone, my country of asylum after completion of my studies. But with the war also raging in Sierra Leone which had displaced thousands of Sierra Leonean citizens and Liberian refugees in combination with the fact that job opportunity seemed to be woefully non-existent, I was faced with the choice of recalibrating my options. Additionally considering the large number of refugees residing in Sierra Leone, local integration opportunities tended to be restricted.

From the UNHCR point of view, third country resettlement falls in the third category of permanent and durable solutions to the refugee problem. For refugees who can neither return to their country of origin nor safely remain in their country of refuge, the only solution is to resettle in a third country. The third country is usually a developed country where the refugee will reunite with his or her family or start life on their own.

Consequently in August of 1994 while in Cairo, I applied for refugee third country resettlement opportunity to the Canadian Embassy near Cairo. By November my file was complete. While waiting for information from the Canadian Immigration in Ottawa to let the embassy know what province I would be living in, I completed my studies and was scheduled to return to Freetown. At that point, the visa officer advised the UNHCR to request the Egyptian Immigration for extension of my temporary residency visa to at least three months. The extension was necessary to allow me stay in Cairo while awaiting the reply from Ottawa. For three days, I shuttled between the UNHCR Office and the Canadian Embassy to make the arrangement as was requested by the embassy. The UNHCR indicated that since I had completed my studies, I would be going back to Freetown. They did not deem it practical to request the head office in Geneva for me to stay for another three months. The Protection Officer, Ann-Marie Kuiper explained that the issue of processing my case for resettlement to a third country fell within the jurisdiction of the office in my country of asylum – UNHCR-Freetown and not UNHCR-Cairo, which was only facilitating my

Painful Journey: a Story of Escape and Survival

academic pursuit. That was how the situation was before I returned to Sierra Leone. Now in Freetown and the war had displaced us again, I needed some divine intervention to get us out of Sierra Leone as fast as possible.

At the same time, like Monrovia in May and June 1990, Freetown was beginning to feel the weight of the war. Many school campuses, public and private unoccupied buildings, government wharfs, hospital compounds, and other facilities were now used to accommodate thousands of internally displaced people (IDPs) coming from the provinces in the north and the east. Many Liberians in the ship yard in Jui and in Freetown began unwillingly repatriating to Liberia.

Meanwhile, at Aberdeen Village, Joanna and I continued to ruminate about several suitable options regarding our plight. Fighting had been temporarily confined to the Waterloo area mainly due to ECOMOG's airpower and there was no guarantee the situation would stay that way forever. Maybe the war would enter Freetown. On numerous occasions I checked in with the Ghanaian Embassy near Freetown requesting entry visas and during those visits, the charges d'affairs declined my request. Finally, I wrote a letter to UNHCR-Freetown apprising them of the resettlement opportunity to Canada that was awaiting me at the Canadian Embassy in Cairo. The office followed the normal protocol of contacting their regional office in Cairo which forwarded the letter to the Canadian Embassy. In a reply to the UNHCR, the embassy confirmed the resettlement opportunity that was pending. They then advised the UNHCR to either send me back to Cairo or to Accra, Ghana. In the end HCR-Freetown and HCR-Cairo agreed that my family and I be transported to Cairo to receive the visas since Canada did not have a consulate in Freetown. It was like a dream to me. Joanna and I were still not sure until the day we boarded the ferry from Freetown to Lungi Airport. Even on the ferry, there was still some level of cautious optimism. Anything could happen: the ferry could break down, the flight could cancel or the RUF rebels, who were in the Port Loko area where the airport is located – although far from the airport - could bring the war to Lungi and that would have spelled doom.

Finally, and I must emphasize, finally we boarded a KLM flight from Lungi Airport to Cairo via Amsterdam, Holland on Sunday September

3, 1995. There was a big sigh of relief among us. The threat of war meeting us in Freetown had now been put behind us. We arrived in Amsterdam during the early morning hours of September 4. At the Schipol Airport we waited in transit for about twelve hours. We arrived in Cairo the night of September 4, with one-way tickets. Due to that, the Egyptian Immigration authorities detained us for a day. They seized our passports and placed us in a holding room with only one door. That one day detention at the airport seemed like a week to me because I did not expect to be treated in such an inhumane way especially when I had lived in Cairo for 15 months and lawfully met all their immigration requirements. We were only going there to receive our visas to go to Canada in view of the fact that Canada did not have a consulate in Freetown.

In October 1993, when I went to Egypt the first time, I was treated like a royalty. There was a driver at the airport holding a placard with my name written on it. It was easy and smooth. Why this time it was the other way around, worst of all when I had my family with me? I could not fathom it. The airport officers were just being very terribly unreasonable. I was using the same passport that I used when I resided there previously going to school. The passport still contained the previous entry and residency visas that they stamped in it while in Cairo. On this latest trip we also had valid entry visas. The UNHCR had made sure everything (document, visa) was in proper order before we left Sierra Leone. As such, there was absolutely no need for holding us at the airport. What made it very stressful and disturbing for me was that the children got ill from lying on the bare floor at the airport with no food to eat.

Immigration authorities began treating me like a common criminal. They would not let me leave the holding room to go anywhere in the airport without an officer being my shadow. If I went to make phone call there was always someone accompanying me. Several attempts to get to the UNHCR proved futile as the lines were always busy. I got through to the Canadian Embassy, but the Visa Officer indicated that, they would not want to get involved into immigration matters. He however assured me that once I crossed that point I should report to the embassy. The visas were ready for my family and me. The embassy's

Painful Journey: a Story of Escape and Survival

response was not what I wanted to hear. I wanted to get my family out of the airport. But I understood the diplomatic protocol involved. In my case it was only the UNHCR that was clothed with the authority and responsibility of handling immigration problems involving refugees.

Finally I got through to the UNHCR. Madam Tahani who was my contact person at the office was no longer there. Her successor was another Egyptian lady who did not know my case and had unreasonably assumed that I was just "another asylum seeker" detained at the airport who was seeking UNHCR's intervention and protection. While in the middle of the conversation the phone got disconnected.

"Hello, hello", I shouted repeatedly with no response. "The damn phone has cut off", I added.

I restored the phone to the hook. When I pulled it back up and attempted to insert some more piasters, the officer yanked the phone from me and restored it to the hook.

"*Telefon, la, la.*" (No more phone call).

"*La, la* (No, no). I want to complete the phone call, please," I pleaded with the officer.

"*May-starr, tahl, tahl,*" (Mr. come, come) the officer ordered.

All attempts by me to explain that the phone got disconnected in the middle of the conversation proved futile. The officer would not understand. If only he knew how I was feeling! I badly needed some kind of divine intervention. Did he and his bosses want a bribe? I did not have the money. If indeed I had the money, I would rather spend it for food for my family. Our documents were legitimate with legitimate visas issued by their embassy in Freetown. But they just held us against our will for no apparent reason.

Albeit, with much deal of anger and frustration, I stopped any attempt at putting some more money in the phone as the officer had ordered. Reluctantly I stepped in front of him and began walking back to the holding room. The walk back to the holding room seemed like a mile when it was only fifty yards from the pay phone. Each time I came back to the holding room and saw the children in pale condition and their mother speechless, I felt more dejected and wanted an immediate decision for our release. After another ten minutes, I asked for permission to go back and make a phone call to the UNHCR again. It was

153

approaching 5 p.m. and I must speak to someone at the UNHCR. If I did not get the UNHCR to do something before their office closed, we would have to stay another horrible night at the airport. Again another officer followed me to the pay phone. This latest attempt, the line did not break and I requested to talk to protection officer Ann-Marie Kuiper. When she got on the line and listened to my rants borne out of frustration, she assured me that the office was handling the situation and that I should be patient. But she did not give me details. What patience when Jeryna and Gerald were ill and hungry? Again I returned to the holding room to my family. I relayed the information to Joanna who also agreed that we should just wait as there was nothing we could do at that moment. Five o'clock painstakingly came and went on to 6 p.m. No sign of UNHCR. I gave up knowing that the office was closed. My only hope was for day to break so that I could start another round of phone calls. Or maybe there might probably not be another opportunity for me to make a call. Maybe the airport officers would send us back to Sierra Leone. They were capable of doing that in a heartbeat. Meanwhile, every time I returned to the room to my family, an officer would come to summon me to their office.

"*May-starr*, come," came another order.

I would get up and follow. In the office another officer would interrogate me. "Are they going to return our passports and let us go in the city? Or is something else up?" I thought to myself.

"*Kaiee-rro*, why come?"

"I am on resettlement to Canada but I come to get visa." They could not or maybe they pretended not to understand English.

"Canada, why come *Kaiee-rro?*"

"I am going on resettlement with my family. No Canadian Embassy in Sierra Leone. That is why I came back here."

At that point the officer ordered me back to the holding room.

"*May-starr, ruh, ruh.*" (Mr. go, go)

I returned to my family with more questions in my mind than answers. They did this to me repeatedly. When I thought the ordeal would be over, that was when it was just beginning. They were trying to wear me down mentally but I held out firmly.

Painful Journey: a Story of Escape and Survival

Two horrible hours went by. It was now 8 p.m. I went back to the main baggage claim area to buy food for the children, of course with an officer in tow. I got some fast food and returned. When I got back Jeryna was asleep but battling a heavy cough. Her mother woke her up and fed her some of the food. Gerald had his. Looking at the children eat while sitting on the bare floor only compounded my anger and frustration. They did not deserve to be treated that way. I almost came close to breaking down at one point seeing my children in the state of despondency.

Few minutes close to 9 p.m. Ann Marie Kuiper showed up. She came with some food for the children. Most important of all, she came with a copy of a letter written to the Foreign Minister of Egypt. She gave the immigration commander a copy and gave me one also. The letter was written in Arabic so I did not understand a thing in it. She chatted with me briefly, jotted down some information regarding the treatment we were receiving. She saw the state the children were in and did not need much probing. She promised to return the next day. I felt relieved that UNHCR had taken up my case with the Egyptian Foreign Ministry. About a minute or two after the protection officer left, an officer came to the room.

"Maystarr"…, he began his sentence. I anticipated another round of summoning. My heart pounded with infinite ferocity again.

"What is this officer up to again?" I thought out loud.

"… *Baz-bot*. Go inside *Kaiee-rro*," he ended his sentence and handed me the two passports.

I received the two passports, turned in the corner and shed a few tears of relief and joy. It was as if a hundred-pound load had been taken off my shoulders. I did not thank the officer. I was not obliged to for they did not deserve any from me. For almost two days I had lost weight. Thanks to the Egyptian immigration authorities. For almost two days, my encounter with them was mentally torturous to say the least. With the help of Joanna, I packed our luggage and we stepped out of the temporary confinement room. We took a taxi to Garden City, an area within the vicinity of the Canadian Embassy. It was one hundred Egyptian pounds a night – very expensive indeed by Egyptian standard.

155

The next morning I went to the campus of the American University in Cairo to see my friend Edmore Moisema but did not see him. In the fall of 1994, when I was doing my final courses, Edmore enrolled at AUC from Zimbabwe. He was a highly intelligent and ambitious young man who was sent by the University of Zimbabwe to do another Master's degree. Like all sub-Saharan Africans who from the onset would love to go to Cairo but get disappointed upon arrival owing to social and cultural differences, Edmore was no different. Like me in the first two weeks of his arrival, he felt homesick and wanted to return to Zimbabwe. He did not like the cultural and social environment. He was not in the same academic department as I was, but we had something in common. He was a sub-Saharan African in a totally different cultural environment. For a few weeks, he was in a hotel just like I was. He did not understand the language and did not have anybody to talk to after school. I was always there to fill in that void. I became a source of comfort for him by playing a "big brother" role. I would take him to the apartment where Jeremiah, James and I lived. We would cook, eat and have fun until it was time for him to go to his hotel. The next day, it was the same thing. I also helped him find an apartment. We found a three bed-room apartment in Maadi, a suburb of Cairo. I had suggested that renting a three bed-room apartment was perhaps a waste of money since he was alone. He said his wife and daughter would be joining him later on so he needed the extra space. Money according to him was not the issue. Now I was back in Cairo and needed accommodation. When I called his home he was there.

"Hello. Can I talk to Edmore?"

"This is Edmore. And who is this?"

"Jerry."

"Oh, Jerry I am happy to hear you! How is Sierra Leone?"

"No I am not in Sierra Leone."

"Where are you calling from? Canada?"

"No, I am here in Cairo."

"What are you doing back in this place?"

"I came with my family and we are on our way to Canada. Young man I need a place to stay with my family while we are waiting for our visas and departure time."

"Jerry you know the African way. We do not make phone calls to ask for accommodation. We just show up at the door and the door is opened. As for you this apartment is yours."

"Thanks. But Edmore"--

He interrupted me with this question, "Where are you now so I can come get you?"

I gave him the address and within minutes, Edmore was at the hotel to take us to his apartment. We boarded a taxi for his home, the very three bed-room apartment that I had helped him find before I departed for Sierra Leone in January. At the apartment, we were introduced to his wife Auxcillia and their two-year old daughter. Edmore told his wife not to receive any money from me or Joanna for food. He was practising the African culture which points to the fact that a guest or stranger in a village never has to bring food with him to his hosts. He firmly believed in the African culture and tradition. My family was welcomed in the home with open arms.

The next day after we moved in with the Moisema family, I proceeded to the Canadian Embassy. The visa officer was glad to see me finally after all that we went through from the war in Sierra Leone after I returned in January to the ordeal at the airport. He told me to wait for a few minutes. Away he went into the back office and returned with four packages. Each package contained a Landed Immigrant document for each member of the family. The visa officer advised me to protect the packages as if my life depended on them. Surely indeed my life and those of my family depended on them, no exaggeration at that moment. He explained that the envelopes were to only be opened by immigration authorities at the Vancouver Airport. I was also given four airline tickets for KLM. With the visas and airline tickets in my possession, it was just a matter of time before we put all the challenges of refugee life and the ordeal at the airport behind us.

At certain point Joanna started feeling embarrassed by all this royalty treatment we were receiving without our contribution. Some days, she would buy some food and sneak it into the kitchen and would beg Auxcillia not to let Edmore know. Jeryna's cough turned to wheezing and chronic cold. It was what she contracted from the airport. Edmore urged us to take her to his family doctor.

Several weeks later, on October 18, 1995 at the Cairo International Airport, we boarded KLM Flight #554 for Vancouver, in Beautiful British Columbia, Canada to begin a new life. Thus that flight from Cairo capped a painful journey from Liberia. Due to the different international time zones, we arrived in Vancouver October 18, 1995: Cairo to Amsterdam to Vancouver. At the customs and immigration counter, a female immigration called out in the lines for all Landed Immigrants to jump the queue and follow her in one room. We did. She took all the documents from me and processed them individually. After that she took us to another room to try on winter clothing and select the ones that we wanted. When we were done with immigration, the female officer accompanied us to the taxi stand and advised the driver to take us to Welcome House on Drake Street, Vancouver. The Welcome House is run by the Immigrant Services Society of British Columbia. As federal government sponsored Landed Immigrants, we were allowed to stay in there for two weeks while finding an apartment to move in.

That Wednesday evening was the beginning of our new life in Canada. We immediately communicated with Edmore and Auxcillia. At Welcome House the manager gave us accommodation in the same apartment with the Igualu family from Uganda: Martin, Maryann and their two daughters. They had come to Canada the previous Wednesday. As Africans we struck a bond immediately. That evening, Martin accompanied me to a supermarket west on Davie Street where I bought some provisions with the allowance given me by the manager. The following Wednesday, Abdulai Dukuly, another Liberian arrived also. At the end of their second week, the Igualu family found an apartment on Queens Avenue in New Westminster. I helped Martin set up their government-issued furniture in the apartment. I used that time with Martin to find the way to get mine done too.

Days later, I found a suite in Burnaby at the eastern suburb of Vancouver. We finally moved in and started the adjustment process. The next task was to find a job as the federal government adjustment assistance was going to run out at certain point. I prepared a resume at the Immigrant Services Society-sponsored job finding club which copies I dropped off at many places.

Three times I was interviewed and on those three occasions, the potential employers denied me employment under the frivolous notion that I did not have "Canadian experience." At my fourth interview, the interviewer literally told me that another company in the area was offering the same position. He suggested that I checked them out. I began wondering what was going on. I was assured of better opportunities for my family and me once I arrived in Canada. Disappointingly I was now being told that I needed to have Canadian experience in order to get a job. My education and my past experience did not matter at all?

Days later, came another phone call scheduling an interview. The caller described what I was going to be doing and asked whether it was something like that that I wanted to do. I responded in the affirmative. I prepared myself to take the Canadian experience monster question head on. As soon as the interviewer asked whether I had Canadian experience, I got into a militant mode. I instead turned into the interviewer.

"Look at my resume, what does it say about the last position held?"

"It says Camp Manager, Waterloo Refugee Center; Freetown, Sierra Leone," he said.

"Then how do you expect me to get Canadian experience when this is the very first time in my life to come to Canada? If you hire me I believe that's the only way I will get Canadian experience. If you can't, hire me, then give me back my resume." The interviewer was surprised at my reaction. He gave my resume and I walked.

Deep in the back of my mind I knew when it came time for me to get a job - it did not matter what kind of job - I would. That moment came when I got hired by a firm. They hired me the same day I entered the office and filled out the employment application form. They only asked whether I had done that kind of job before. There was no question about Canadian experience. The fun came when the interviewer told me I was to "work graveyard." I mistook it for working in the graveyard.

"What, grave yard?" I asked.

I told the manager that the graveyard was not one of those places that I would want to work. "I am afraid of the dead and do not visit graveyard let alone talk about working there. If that is the case I do not need the job." The manager laughed and clarified that it was a shift from 11 p.m. to 7 a.m. That was the beginning of my Canadian job experience.

In retrospect, I definitely made the right judgment call not to repatriate to Liberia in 1995. On April 6, 1996, war broke out in Monrovia (Ellis, 1999). The city again descended in an orgy of violence. My nephew, Darlingboy who survived the 1991 Gendema (Bo Waterside-Sierra Leone) invasion was killed.

After the April 6, 1996 war, general elections were held in 1997 during which Mr. Taylor was elected president of Liberia. A year later, another war broke out again in Monrovia. From September 18-20, 1998, Taylor government security forces conducted a military assault on Roosevelt Johnson's ULIMO-J faction on Camp Johnson Road, Monrovia in an operation that lasted for 17 hours. They employed automatic weapons, rocket-propelled grenades, and mortars. Much of the shooting occurred at night time and was indiscriminate. Credible reports indicated that as many as 300 persons, most of them Krahns, many of them women and children, were killed and in subsequent house-to-house searches and summary executions by government, according to the 1998 US State Department Country Report on Human Rights Practices in Liberia, (www.state.gov). My younger brother Beto, who had also survived the 1991 Bo Waterside attack, and my older sister, Cecelia were two of the hundreds of Krahn people murdered. Beto had been living with me in Monrovia since 1985 before we fled to Sierra Leone. He left behind two kids and a pregnant wife. For Cecelia, she had remained in Monrovia with her husband throughout the 1990 war. For weeks I was distraught. Their deaths were a major blow to me.

CHAPTER NINE

Emotional Return Home

The day had finally come. For years, I had dreamed of my return home. What would Liberia look like now? What should I expect? Would I recognize members of my family who I had left home? How would they receive me? What about my old acquaintances from the University of Liberia and the soccer fields? How would my mother look now after nineteen years of not seeing her? What about my office and co-workers at the National Housing Authority? These and a hundred more questions swirled around senselessly in my head. A kind of numbness invaded my body as I awaited my departure from the SeaTac Airport, Seattle Washington, the first leg of what was to be a 19-hour journey to Liberia.

We arrived in Washington DC on a United Airlines flight from Seattle later in the afternoon of February 4, 2007. It was a one hour stopover in order to change to a flight bound for Brussels. At the check in line, I heard a guy at the front of the line speaking with a perfect Liberian accent. I was excited to meet him as I believed he would be on the same flight with Joanna and me. I walked up to him and introduced myself. He responded also by introducing himself as Mohamed, a deputy minister in the Liberian government. Mohamed had traveled on an official trip with the President of Liberia and was now returning home. After the introductions, I said, "Mo, I am so excited going back home in seventeen years. But my major worry at this point is our luggage. There are rumors of alleged tampering and theft of passenger's luggage by airport workers at the Roberts International Airport."

"You should have no cause to worry Jerry," he assured me. "Things have changed for the better at the airport since Madam Ellen Johnson-Sirleaf became President."

We moved on to chat on other issues until we heard a boarding call on the PA system. During our conversation, Joanna made a comment that led Mohamed to give her the nickname "Big Sister." Throughout our flights from Dulles Airport to Brussels to Monrovia, the name stuck on Joanna. Our encounter with the deputy minister felt like we had known one another for several years. Of course, generally most Liberians are like that: personable, outgoing and jovial.

We arrived in Brussels early the next morning. After some delay at the airport, we finally boarded the SN Brussels flight for Monrovia. Mohamed was on the other side of the cabin. I did not get to see him again until we arrived in Dakar, Senegal. Joanna was sitting across the aisle from me while I sat next to a Liberian lady on the flight. She had such a severe headache that she could not chat with me. I called out to the flight attendants to give her some medical attention. We arrived in Dakar around 5 o'clock p.m. for an hour's stopover. The flight attendants requested us to stay on board the flight on the tarmac. At that point, Mohamed came to my seat with a young Liberian. He was smartly dressed.

"Jerry, this is Colonel Voker. He is the immigration commandant at Roberts International Airport. The colonel will be the one to tell you more about the airport." After the introduction Mo returned to his section of the cabin.

"Hello Colonel, my name is Jerry and this is my wife Joanna. I am pleased to meet you. We are returning to Liberia for the first time in seventeen years."

"I heard from Mohamed that you have a serious concern about your luggage?" the Colonel asked.

"Sure," I said. "We are travelling with other people's items they sent by us for their relatives in Monrovia. And I heard this vicious rumor that we might lose some pieces of our luggage through theft or tampering."

At that point the Colonel's facial expression changed. "Since I took over at the airport, I have been carrying out a zero tolerance policy. Anyone guilty of any unwholesome practices is dealt with in keeping

Painful Journey: a Story of Escape and Survival

with the law. So do not worry," the young colonel added. The comments were particularly reassuring and encouraging.

After the brief chat, he returned to his seat. I picked up my video camera and began walking about in the plane to meet and greet other people. A section of the plane behind me was filled with a group of government officials. They, like my friend Mohamed, were going back home after the official visit along with the President of Liberia. Seated directly behind me was an old acquaintance at the University of Liberia who I did not make out. He was now legal counsel to the President of Liberia.

"Are you Jerry?" he asked.

"Yes I am. And you?"

"I am Richard Kla," he went on.

While I was trying to remember the name, he followed up with another comment to assist me connect the dots.

"I used to be with Robert Lormia."

The Lormia that he spoke about was my boyhood friend from Tappita. At that point, I jumped on him in a bear hug. While we were reminiscing about our University of Liberia days, he introduced the lady next to me as passport director Kollie. After the brief chat, I moved down the aisle with my camera. I recognized one Lincoln Brownell. He was student council president of Ricks Institute, a boarding school a few miles north of Monrovia where we used to come from Tappita in the late 1970s to play in an annual soccer tournament organized by the school. Brownell was now a doctor of philosophy and President of the Baptist Theological Seminary in Monrovia. We chatted briefly and I moved on.

I went to the other side of the cabin to meet with a group of Liberians. They were Senators and Representatives chatting among themselves. One of them introduced herself as Senator Sumo. When I sought their permission to videotape my conversation with them, almost all of them spoke in unison: "We hope you will use it for good purpose." I promised them that it was for home viewing only. I further added that I was excited to be in the company of my compatriots who were high level Liberian government officials and that I was going to use the recordings for reference only. I was no paparazzo. Their suspicion was well-founded. During the time of my visit to Liberia, there was the "Knucklesgate," a sex scandal involving a former government official. Monrovians made a big deal of it by posting it on the internet and in print media, pictures of him and some girls in an illicit sexual act. He would later resign under pressure.

Moments later, I returned to my seat when it was time for takeoff. After what seemed like a decade later, the SN Brussels flight eventually hovered over the Harbel area. My breath stopped. I was overwhelmed with elation. But as we got closer, my excitement gradually began to turn into trepidation and disappointment. Watching the Smell No Taste and the Roberts International Airport area from the window, all I saw was pitch black, a night time blackness that swallowed the entire landscape taking the residents with it. Eventually, little specks of light, which I later realized had come mostly from lantern and candle light, could be seen to bring light to the thick blackness, enveloping it with a bad polka dot pattern. The plane touched down at about 7 o'clock p.m. Greenwich Main Time (GM). There was thunderous applause from the passengers, delighted to finally be on firm soil.

"Welcome to the Roberts International Airport," came the voice of the chief flight attendant. "Thank you for flying with SN Brussels. We hope you enjoyed flying with us." Her voice had now become a blur to me, as all I could think about, was that I was home, finally back to the land of my birth. Oh what a sweet day! A few minutes later the doors were swung open. The thick, warm Atlantic Ocean breeze that I had almost forgotten hit me. It was welcoming me home. Thank God Almighty, I had arrived home to the place that I fled 17 years ago!

For all the years I lived outside of Liberia, my heart always longed to go home. But my homeland was full of violence and depravity. In that respect, I had made a covenant with myself that as long as security conditions on the ground were not conducive for me, I wouldn't return. I am a victim of the war, a despicable war that should never have happened. I despised it and I despised all the warring factions that brought death and destruction to the nation. In February 2002, in the wake of the fresh war that was raging between an armed group, LURD and the Taylor government, I wrote a letter to President George W. Bush asking the American government to lend its voice to solving the crisis in Liberia. The letter which was published in *The Perspectives*, a Liberian online newsmagazine on March 4, 2002, reads in part:

Painful Journey: a Story of Escape and Survival

The Liberian civil strife has reared its ugly head once again. Scores of innocent people are being butchered and others turning into refugees in their own homeland, a situation reminiscent of the 1990s. Elections are slated for 2003, but with the imposition of the state of emergency in Liberia by Mr. Taylor, the idea of holding election is a goal believed to be a million of miles from reality. Taylor only imposed the state of emergency in order to clampdown on the press and opposition perpetually. Therefore Mr. President, please do not turn your back on Liberia as previous administrations before you have done. Majority of the Liberian people want Mr. Taylor out in order to restore total peace and tranquillity in the country as well as restore her place among the comity of nations. We want you to please add your voice to the numerous voices of Liberians in the Diaspora and those at home who cannot speak out for fear of retribution, to call on Mr. Taylor to step aside. You may probably be occupied with the Taliban/al Qaeda and the "Axis of Evil" issues that Liberia may not be a priority. But make no mistake, according to the November 2, 2001 edition of the Washington Post, the regime in Liberia has an al Qaeda connection, (Gbardy, 2002:4).

Accordingly, on April 23, 2002 the Bush government responded through Assistant Secretary of State for African Affairs, Walter Kansteiner in this way:

> Jerry Gbardy
>
> United States Department of State
>
> Assistant Secretary of State
> for African Affairs
>
> Washington, D.C. 20520-3430
>
> APR 2 3 2002
>
> Dear Mr. Gbardy:
>
> I am responding to your February 26 letter to the President regarding U.S. policy towards Liberia.
>
> The primary U.S. national interests in Liberia are twofold: to prevent the Government of President Charles Taylor from supporting regional armed insurgencies and to support conditions that would permit credible democratic government in Liberia. The United States remains committed to improving governance and opening political space in Liberia. We believe that this best can be achieved by supporting independent media and building the capabilities of civil society and Liberian opposition parties. In a March 1 press release, we also have made crystal clear to President Taylor what he needs to do to restore peace, prosperity and the rule of law in Liberia (enclosed).
>
> While the United States and the international community certainly will do what they can to help, Liberia's fate rests not in the hands of one or a few individuals, countries, or organizations, but rather in the hands of Liberians themselves. Their talents and resources are critical to Liberia's ability to re-create a civil and prosperous society. It is important that Liberians cooperate with each other in addressing the challenges at home.
>
> Sincerely,
>
> Walter Kansteiner
>
> Attachment: As Stated.

It thus came as a relief when in July 2003, George Bush stood in the Rose Garden of the White House and called on Mr. Taylor to leave office. Taylor complied. On August 11, 2003, he resigned from office and subsequently left Liberia for Nigeria. These and other events paved the way for national elections to be held in 2005. I felt then that it was time for me to visit my home and if possible make plans to re-establish myself there.

Before we disembarked, the young colonel requested Joanna and me to accompany him. At the foot of the stairs on the tarmac, was an army of immigration officers saluting and welcoming their boss back from abroad. We were in good hands. As the subordinate officers were saluting their boss, so too was I, returning the courtesy like the young colonel.

Painful Journey: a Story of Escape and Survival

The main terminal lay in ruins. What once stood as a symbol of pride for Liberians was now in total disrepair, showing signs of the heavy pounding it took during the turbulent 14 years of war. It was apparent that no repairs had been done. We followed Col Voker to another building adjacent to the main terminal that was by far too small to accommodate the booked-to-capacity flight that had just landed. When we arrived, he ordered his deputy to take care of us making sure that every piece of our luggage was accounted for. This building was once the terminal for the elites used in the prewar days to host the VIPs entering and departing Liberia. We were like sardines in a can. Passengers, airport security personnel, baggage handlers, you name it, all relevant personnel, packed together in one tiny space, all with the same wish – to step outside and once again breathe comfortably. It was hot and miserable inside. Noisily rumbling and squeaking, the carousel spun around like an old manual sugarcane mill. The ceiling was water-stained, displaying large, brown patches across it. In places, parts of it were hanging, manifestly displaying the evidence of a leaky roof that was terribly in need of repair. Positioned on the counter at the head of each line were large black hand-written cardboard signs, emblazoned with words, such as "Aliens/foreigners" and "ECOWAS citizens". When all was done we returned to the Colonel to thank him. Words were inadequate for us to express how immensely appreciative we were. I took his business card and promised to call him once Joanna and I got settled. Disappointingly a week or so later when I phoned him, he told me he had been reassigned.

There were about twenty-five family members and friends waiting for Joanna and me outside. They were singing and beating drums while some were crying tears of joy. I could not hold back my emotions. When I was leaving 17 years ago, I shed tears of pain, despair and despondency. This time I was shedding tears of joy for being firmly on home soil. My friend Lewis Brown who was in Columbia, MD had arranged with a guy named Olu to pick us up at the airport. Brown lived in Liberia throughout the war and had connections.

Olu dropped us off at Joanna's sister's house in Thinker's Village. My mother did not travel to the airport. She was there waiting for us. When I entered the room where she was sitting, she could not contain her emotions. The last time she saw me was in 1988, 19 years ago when she visited us in Monrovia. She fled to the Ivory Coast in 1990 where she survived the war. Even though I was in Sierra Leone, I did not get to see her. The moment with her seemed like I had resurrected from the dead.

"Sit on my lap, my son," she said in Krahn amid streams of tears.

"No" I responded, fearing that her frail legs would crumble under my 200 pound-frame. When she could not get me to voluntarily sit, she yanked me on her lap. She held me and cried for the longest. That night everyone that came to see us, including my sisters, nieces and nephews, aunts, uncles all sat in the living room till daybreak. It was at that moment that my mother told me a story which kept me spellbound. She told the story of how they would sneak across the border from the Ivory Coast into Grand Gedeh County, Liberia to gather firewood, hunt for snails, and dig some cassavas from their abandoned farms. At that time the NPFL had already taken over the entire Grand Gedeh County. It was most certainly a calculated risk that they always took. One day she sneaked into Liberia with few other women, this time to gather firewood. Upon completion, they carried the first load back to the Ivorian village where they resided with the intension of going back for the last load later. My mother said when they arrived, she felt so exhausted that she advised the other women for them to put the trip off to another day but the women refused. They went back into Liberia with a young woman, their number four altogether. Months later, only the young woman came back to the Ivory Coast but pregnant. According to the woman, the older women were killed by their kidnappers. My mother could have been one of those three women. It was only by the mercy of God that she had lived.

A few days after we had had some much deserved rest, we started visiting some parts of the city. The first visit took us to the Red Light business hub located in Paynesville, the eastern suburb of Monrovia. The area had now changed. It was only a commuters' station before the war. The Camp 72nd military barracks which was the scene of fierce fighting in 1990 was a few blocks down the road. Red Light has now become a sprawling business center with a cluster of shops and stores that attracted more than 200,000 shoppers, petty traders and travelers on a daily basis. Due to the sweltering heat, I wore short pants and

T-shirt almost every day except on days that I was going to the Foreign Ministry. So did Joanna. I carried a backpack containing a camcorder and I purchased about a dozen facial towels for constantly dabbing the beads of sweat popping up on my forehead and face. At a certain point in the street, I would buy a bottle of cold water and drench myself with it just to cool off. Every time I did that it always drew a crowd of curious onlookers watching me in disbelief.

The large crowds of people in that teeming market place seemed abnormal to me. Usually crowds large as they were could only be seen at the Samuel Kanyon Doe Sports Complex during a major soccer match but not in the Red Light area. I therefore pulled out my camcorder to take pictures for our daughter Jeryna to see when we got back home to Vancouver. As soon as I hit the record button and began to pan the scenes, I heard not only one but two, three and four voices:

"Stop taking our picture. That the thing y'all can do. Y'all take people picture and put it in the newspaper and TV in America to make money."

One of them threatened to take my camcorder if I did not stop. I stopped to talk to the one making the threat. All of a sudden, we were surrounded by several people. Joanna yelled out to me to put the camcorder away. Meanwhile one of the marketers seeing what was about to happen, summoned a police officer walking nearby. I was glad the officer showed up. After I explained to the officer what had or was about to happen, he asked me to put the camera away for my own safety. A potentially explosive situation was averted. We bought what we wanted and left the area while perspiring profusely. After the war most Monrovians had become all too apprehensive and paranoid about their picture being taken. That encounter in the market place was the first but certainly not the last as we shall find out later in this chapter.

My first week back felt like hell on earth. 'So this was what 30 degrees Celsius felt like?' I thought aloud. It seemed my western Canadian lifestyle must have turned me into a softie, for I was not coping well with the merciless heat that bore down on the city of Monrovia. It was unbearable. My exposed skin was smarting beneath the sun's rays, perspiration was dripping from my forehead and I could feel a whole river of it channeling its way down the crevice of my back. It was hot! 'It could not have been as hot as this when I was living here,' I thought to myself. "How can anyone survive in this heat, much more be expected to be productive?" While I was figuratively baking in the sweltering heat in shorts, T-shirt and sandals, I could see people in three-piece suits and ties standing by the roadside fighting for taxi. Of course, that is called becoming accustomed. But four days into my visit, I had not reached that level of adjustment yet. My plan was to visit other parts of the city within my first four days, thus despite the heat, I was determined to carry on. Heat or no heat, I was home and that was all that mattered.

I was stunned, but not entirely surprised to see the level of physical destruction of the infrastructure of the city that had been caused by the war. The Waterside Bridge connecting the Waterside business district and Bushrod Island had disintegrated. The Johnson Street Bridge was the only one in use. The streets in the Waterside area and the downtown core were lying in almost two decades of disrepair. Evidence of a broken drainage system – or lack thereof – was strewn across all the major streets in the city. Foul stench from feces in plastic bags, urine, and garbage filled the air. It was apparent that Benson, Gurley, Center and Lynch Streets had suffered the major brunt of the drainage collapse. The city was heavily overcrowded. The alleys had become urban shanty towns, housing the homeless and the internally displaced persons (IDPs) in scrap metal and tin shacks. The unfinished and damaged buildings in Monrovia and its outlying areas also served to provide additional shelters. The war had brought on a process of forced urbanization – many young people were forced to leave their villages and even with the civil war at an end, many were reluctant to return, despite high unemployment in the city. In all the areas I visited, the only public infrastructure constructed that I saw was the pedestrian overpass connecting the University of Liberia campus and the Capitol Building. The overpass was built during the administration of Mr. Charles Taylor. But it sat there like a statue with pedestrians jaywalking underneath it. For the brief moment I was on the University of Liberia campus, I did not see a single pedestrian going up the overpass and coming down on the other side of the street. What a misplacement of development priority! The Ellen Johnson-Sirleaf administration was in the 13th month of its sitting. Therefore, it would be unfair to attribute any lack of infrastructural development at that time to her administration. Taylor, the main architect of the war, was elected president in 1997 and was eventually forced to leave office six years later. Of those years that he was in office, I believe he was well-placed to carry out major facelift of the city but he did not.

Government ministry buildings such as Defense, Health & Social Welfare, Lands & Mines, and Budget that were under construction but not completed before the war, now lay in ruins, providing shelters to the hundreds of IDPs and the homeless people in the city. Social amenities such as water and electricity had not been restored. Electricity supply to the city was cut off on the night of Friday, June 29, 1990 and water was also cut a week previous to that. Most private residential buildings, depending on those who could afford, and businesses got their power from the many privately owned portable electricity generators. Water, a very basic necessity of life which once flowed through pipes into homes, had now become an expensive commodity sold in plastic bottles and bags. Armed robbery and other violent crimes were rampant! And it showed. Ten-foot high fences framed residential neighborhoods keeping their residents captive, concealing buildings that would eagerly boast their elegance and style to all who passed by, if only they weren't hidden. Windows encased by thick prison-like steel rods and doors covered by heavy metal shutters, protected those houses not lucky enough to be fenced in.

After a week, I called Robert Lormia at the Foreign Ministry and we set the date for us to visit him. The scheduled visit was hyped up. It would be an opportunity for us to reminisce on the good old days. He was assistant minister of foreign affairs. I think the time set was around 1 o'clock p.m. to give him enough time to do his office work before we arrived. On the appointed day Joanna's cousin Loretta Barshall drove us to the ministry as my vehicle had not yet arrived from Accra, Ghana. Accompanying us were Loretta's younger brother, Daniel and her associate, former presidential aspirant Cecelia Siaway. Cecelia was from Tappita, the city where I attended grade school. We arrived at the Foreign Ministry on time. The President of Liberia also had her offices in the ministry which made it a temporary Executive Mansion. The main Israeli-built Executive Mansion, official residence of the President is situated west adjacent to the Foreign Ministry edifice. An electrical power surge in 2006 had ignited a fire that caused a substantial damage to the fourth-floor office of the President in the building. The incident occurred while President Johnson Sirleaf was hosting other foreign heads of state during the commemoration of Liberia's 159th independence anniversary. The President and all the foreign dignitaries got out safely. Since the fire incident, the President has been using the Foreign Ministry as a temporary office. The main entrance of the Foreign Ministry building at the north side toward Tubman Boulevard and the University of Liberia, which was expertly manned by a contingent of female Pakistani soldiers of the United Nations peace keeping mission in Liberia, was reserved for the President only. Access to the building by the general public was from the east side. There was a security checkpoint guarded by a team of Special Security Services (SSS) officers.

When we arrived, the SSS officer granted us access to the main parking lot of the building after a thorough screening. Once parked, I reached in my backpack for the camcorder and returned to the checkpoint to seek permission for some picture taking. The last time I was in the Foreign Ministry building was May 1990 when my friend Kawa Myers helped Joanna and me to get our passports. The building, I was informed, went through some tough times during the war. It now looked beautiful from the outside. Korean expatriates were giving it an extreme make-over during our visit. So I wanted to capture it on video tape.

"Hello Officer, I am back again. I want to take picture of the building and the area. May I?" Knowing how apprehensive Monrovians were about picture taking, I wanted to make sure I got the permission especially at the place where the President works. There was no sign of any bylaw prohibiting picture-taking. No billboard with any anti-picture taking instruction, except for the sign written on the wall of a small shed in the courtyard of the foreign ministry building prohibiting anybody from urinating around there. The instruction, visible from about 150 yards away read, "Do not pepe here." Therefore I was encouraged to pull out my camcorder but wanting to make sure that I did not ruffle any feathers again. Really?

"You are welcome sir," the officer approved.

"Can I take your picture?"

"Yes sir. Go ahead."

Painful Journey: a Story of Escape and Survival

He left his kiosk and posed by the gate to allow me roll the camera. My back was turned to the building while doing the video shoot. As soon as I turned around to train the camera on the building, a plain-clothed officer yelled at me to "turn the damn camera off". Once he yelled that command, four other plain-clothed personnel joined him and they came charging at me.

"Why are you taking picture here?" one of them asked authoritatively.

Before I could answer, another added, "Don't you know that this is the Executive Mansion?" Then another, "Who authorized you?"

"Take his camera from him and let's take him to the chief," the first officer ordered.

"Damn, I am in trouble again?" I thought aloud. "How many people will question me at the same time?" I protested.

"Take the camera and bring him to the chief," another guy standing by the building commanded.

I surrendered the camcorder. They also took my portable camera and cell phone. They surrounded me and ordered me to go with them to the Executive Mansion wing of the building. Joanna, Loretta, Cecelia and Daniel followed. The officers created a scene that looked like I had been caught with contraband.

When we arrived on the main floor, a Colonel who introduced himself as the boss accosted me and began pestering with a series of questions. At the same time everyone in the group embarked upon the same round of questioning again. I told the Colonel I would only answer if the questions came in one at a time.

"Where do you come from?" the Colonel asked.

"Thinker's Village," I said.

That was not what he wanted to hear, I presumed. Speaking with a perfect Liberian accent, he had no shred of doubt that I was Liberian. He knew that I came from out of the country – from somewhere in North America or Europe. Common sense told him that it was just uncommon for a resident of Monrovia to pull out a camcorder and begin video-shooting government buildings. It was something that residents did not normally do. He wanted to know the "somewhere" that I came from.

"No. I say where you come from?" he repeated.

"Thinker's Village. This is a digital camera with touch-screen playback capability. If you want me to, I can delete the picture," I explained.

"Even at your White House they do not take picture without permission. Who authorized you to take picture?" the Colonel asked again.

In my response, I deliberately left out the part on the "White House." I reckoned that it was a clever ruse for me to tell him where I came from. But I brushed off the bait.

"Your officer at the gate gave me the permission. Just look at the video. He posed for the camera. If he did not permit me," I continued, "I could not have taken any picture."

Without looking at the picture, he said, "Stop lying to me. My officers here know the rule not to allow anyone to take picture."

"I am not lying," I said with confidence.

The Colonel ordered the gate officer be brought for questioning.

Meanwhile Joanna ran upstairs to get Lormia unbeknownst to me. Lormia and Joanna arrived when I was strongly defending myself. As soon as he saw me in the midst of the SSS officers, Lormia started to laugh. Even though I was in trouble, I laughed also while we embraced.

"What a reunion after almost two decades!" Lormia exclaimed.

"Yes, that's the way things are sometimes."

"Chief, I authorized the man to take picture," the officer at the gate confessed.

"Why, when you know that we have a policy against picture taking on these grounds?"

"Chief, he asked me," the officer told his boss in the midst of his co-workers and us. Of course he would not deny that he approved of my video shoot. The evidence was there, clear in color. As a matter of fact his uniform - navy blue pants and sky blue shirt - looked so crisp and immaculate in the video that it was wholesomely representative of his profession as a presidential bodyguard.

I guess the Colonel was embarrassed at that moment. The testimony by his subordinate might have unintentionally sapped the steam out of him. He thought he had me where he wanted. As a face-saving stratagem, the Colonel said to his subordinate, "Then I will take you and this man further." I agreed to go to wherever he wanted. At that point he ordered me to sit in an airconditioner-less glass-walled office. I told him that I was claustrophobic. Also, given the fact that I was sweating profusely, I did not want to fall prey to dehydration and heat stroke. I asked if I could rather stand in the lobby by the security desk. He agreed.

Lormia went back upstairs and came down with the overall security boss. They both talked for a while and boarded the elevator. A few minutes later, the Colonel requested that I should join him in the glass-walled office. I complied. When we were both seated, he first introduced himself and offered his apologies for "the inconvenience this episode might have caused you." He returned my camcorder, portable camera, and cell phone. For obvious reasons, I will just call him AVS.

"Thanks, young man. But this situation would have been avoided had you just agreed to let me delete the picture. But instead you guys just made a mountain out of molehill. Apologies accepted. No hard feelings."

Finally, he asked me to delete the picture. Before his eyes, I played back the video and voila, there was the uniformed officer posing like a Hollywood model wannabe! Colonel AVS and I laughed at the posing before I deleted it. I took possession of my items, shook his hand and parted ways with him. Joanna and I hopped in the elevator to Lormia's office on the fourth floor and we were joined later by Loretta and the rest. The episode lasted for more than an hour.

I left the foreign ministry wondering why the big fuss about taking picture of a big public building such as the foreign ministry. I could have been across the street on the campus of the University of Liberia without them knowing. How could they control and stop tourists in moving vehicles from taking pictures? How could they also control the pictures that were on the internet? As beautiful as the Executive Mansion, Foreign Ministry, the Capitol Building and the Ducor Palace Hotel are, they can make good post cards for tourist attractions. They present good images of the country as well. We must be proud to see pictures of those public buildings in international papers and books. Whatever the reason for preventing me from taking the picture, which I was not in the position to judge, it was profoundly disappointing. I was attempting to have something of picturesque value to show to some co-workers and others back in Vancouver who I encounter almost daily asking me whether there were tall buildings, paved roads and bridges in my country of origin.

Over-population and shortage of public transportation made finding taxi a more than tedious chore, and it didn't matter what time of the day it was. Peak hour was horrendous! Commuters would literally sit in the trunk of a taxi – the "VIP seat"- in order to hitch a ride to get to certain point. Unlike the prewar days when passengers would request to be dropped off at a destination of their choosing, they now had no choice but to be dropped off where the taxi drivers wanted. Taxis operated like transit buses – they had specific routes. Motor cycle, another mode of transportation, which is dubbed *pehn-pehn*, had been established in Monrovia and its environs. The bikes are however not insured and their riders do not wear helmets. Pehn-pehn has been the major source of injury and death among riders in the city.

As I waded my way through Monrovia and through the municipality of Paynesville, I was quite astonished to see the plethora of foreign currency changers situated almost everywhere. Each money changer sat with several stacks of money in various denominations next to him. Never before in my life had I seen such large number of money changers per capita concentrated in a city in a developing country. These were some of the entrepreneurs who were breathing a healthy life into a functioning parallel economy.

Visit to the National Housing Authority

The building of the National Housing Authority looked dilapidated. The walls were dull and in need of paint, and in the interior, the paint was peeling from the walls at various sections. The corporation which once boasted of sustaining itself from the revenue it generated from tenants was now in a sorry state. Most of the offices lacked furniture. The National Housing Authority is a public corporation that builds and manages low and medium cost housing estates in Monrovia. It is located on Water Street, in the downtown business district. This was the place I worked prior to fleeing the country. My last position held was that of administrative assistant to the deputy managing director for administration. There were about three hundred employees at the time I worked there. Before the war, it was one of the best public corporations to work for.

Painful Journey: a Story of Escape and Survival

I was hired on March 1, 1984 as a cadet, a position reserved for students attending college or university. As a cadet I was required to work a maximum of five hours per day but on my own volition, I used to work full eight hours. The year I was hired, I was in the second year of my voluntary dropout from the university due to unavailability of funding. I therefore had too much free time on my hands. The full time work also helped me get better on-the-job experience. My boss Dwede Kobbah appreciated it. Few months later, news of my hard work, better work ethics and professionalism spread like wildfire. The Managing Director, Mr. Sam Tody took personal interest in assessing and admiring my work ethics. In November of that year I was promoted to a full-time position. Subsequently in the years that followed, I rose through the ranks, serving as warehouse superintendent, chief procurement officer, and assistant chief of public relations before becoming administrative assistant. As administrative assistant, I was chief of staff of the administration department. That gave me the opportunity to know and work with every employee of the corporation. But after seventeen years of a brutal war, things had changed. I could not recognize some co-workers who looked much older than what they actually were. Others I recognized by faces but not by names. Nevertheless they all welcomed Joanna and me. It was where Joanna and I met when she did a summer job at the corporation in December 1984 and January and February, 1985. It was reminiscent of a home-coming event.

Emmanuel Wesseh, my former office assistant still worked there. He was extremely excited to see me.

"Welcome back chief. Thank God to see you o," Emmanuel beckoned.

"Thanks."

After a few jokes, he opened the door to my former office. Previously when I was using it prewar days, it had all the furniture and office equipment but it was now bare. From there we walked next door to the office manager's office which was once occupied by Mr Veto Mason. It now had only a chair and a desk. A new manager, who I did not know was in it. After a few pleasantries, we stepped out into the general waiting area of the administration department.

"Where is Mr. Mason?" I asked Emmanuel.

"He died in his home during the war." I was sad about his passing. Before the visit, I had read in Youboty that former managing director Sam Tody was killed at the Freeport of Monrovia in 1990 (Youboty, 2004) and Comptroller Oliver Farley lost his life in the war also. Former deputy managing director for administration, Thomas Ziah who was my immediate boss was in the United States. Mr. Paul Mulbah, who was the last managing director before the war, still lived in Monrovia. He had served the Taylor government in various capacities; the last position was police director.

"What about Roosevelt Blay? Marea Grigsby? Abraham Garneo?"

"Oh chief, Blay is on vacation and Marea is on the other side in the technical department. She is now gender affairs director. Come with me to her office". Marea was the assistant office manager to Mr. Mason prewar days.

"As for Abraham, he now works for the Monrovia City Corporation," Emmanuel added while we were walking down the hallway to Marea's office.

Emmanuel ushered us into Marea's office. Lord, she jumped on me and almost knocked me off my feet! "Why is the entire office space looking like an open soccer field minus a goalpost?" I asked.

"Jerry, Jerry," Marea called out, "you haven't forgotten about your sense of humor? Welcome back."

"Thanks!"

She continued, "Blame it on the war. All the furniture and equipment were looted and vandalized. We had to start from scratch. Gradually we are getting there." She also told us about her being a refugee in Freetown for some time but had to return home during the Sawyer interim government time.

"I have come to sign for my June 1990 paycheck."

"Man, Jerry stop that joke! You have come all the way from America to ask for a check from 17 years ago?" Marea jovially asked.

"Okay then, I will donate it to the office to buy some paint," which drew a good chunk of chuckle from the group of employees who had come to greet me.

From there, we walked to the finance department where I met with Agnes, Wilmot Smith, Nagbe, and several others. They allowed me

Painful Journey: a Story of Escape and Survival

to videotape them. We talked for a while and I bade them goodbye. Emmanuel walked us downstairs and I promised to go back before flying back to Canada.

The news of our visit spread like wildfire. Every day a steady stream of visitors began filing in to speak to us. The visits continued up to the day we left Liberia. Cousin Cecelia heard of my being in town and came to speak to me also. When she saw me, she began to cry, tears of joy that we had seen again after more than seventeen years, and tears of joy that she survived. When she was done crying, she revealed to me that BB, a young man who had lived with me on 16th Street in Monrovia, put her at gunpoint and threatened to kill her if she did not tell him my whereabouts.

According to Cecelia, she had sought refuge like several thousands of other displaced Liberians, on the University of Liberia Fendall Campus, about 15 miles east of Monrovia. The campus was in NPFL held territory. To get there, she had to join a group of people, specifically non-Krahn, and had to deny her tribe every step of the way. One day in October 1990, she recognized BB. He was now an NPFL fighter, armed with an AK-47 rifle. When she saw him, her heart raced. She was terrified. Being Krahn and hiding in NPFL territory, meant death if she was caught. She began to wonder what to do, either to appear to him or hide. While her mind was going through all the "should I or should I not," BB saw her and walked straight up to her.

"Big Jerry, I was so scared when BB came to me. The first thing he said was, "Ehn your name is Cecelia?" Before I could say anything, he said, "I know you from 16th Street." I said no, my name is not Cecelia. Right there he said, "Where is your brother Jerry? Where is Body Works?"

Then Cecelia added: "Big Jerry, I froze. The next thing he said was, if I did not tell him where you and Body Works were, he was going to kill me. Besides, he said I lied to him also, so he was still going to kill me. All that time he was talking to me, he had the gun pointed at me. I began to cry and I called some women who I had been sharing a spot with near a big school building, to help me beg BB. Three women came to beg him to leave me but he refused to let me go."

While that was going on, by divine intervention, ECOMOG began to bomb NPFL positions, at which time their commander ordered all

NPFL fighters to assemble and go to the war front. He hurriedly left with the promise of coming back. As soon as BB left, Cecelia left the scene and went to a nearby village where she remained and continued to evade NPFL fighters before eventually being liberated by ECOMOG when the NPFL fighters retreated east to Kakata.

BB knew Cecelia very well, no doubt about that. Cecelia and her siblings lived with their brother James "Body Works" Karrow, a former national soccer team player, in the same house where Sam Okai, Patrick, and I lived. BB had accompanied Okai from Tappita in December of 1981. In Monrovia, I was instrumental in a very big way, in making BB gain admission to the AME Zion Academy. He was in grade 10. In that house, Cecelia, her sister Sarah, and my younger sister Lacy, all lived with us and used to run errands, cook, and do some chores for us. Because he was a friend of ours, all our sisters including the eldest, Sister Payennon, took him like their brother. BB spent part of 1982 with us before returning to Tappita. But in spite of all that, he was hell bent on getting rid of Cecelia. He was a son of a former judge in Tappita.

After Cecelia gave me the news, I asked some of our Tappita friends in Monrovia for BB's whereabouts but I was not successful in finding him as no one seemed to know where he was. I was interested in hearing his side of the story now that the war was over. To this date, I am still hoping that he survived the war. I want to meet him. I just want to look him in the eye and ask him a simple question: "Why?" The episode speaks volume of the senseless nature of the fratricidal Liberian war; friends killing or threatening to kill on the basis of tribal and political difference.

When I toured the city and saw all the evidence of physical destruction, coupled with the large number of family members, relatives, and friends who were lining up at our door every day to ask for handouts, I could not help but wondered: was the war necessary? After 14 years of self destruction, the country is starting all over. And on a personal note, at the prime of my life, I was forced into exile where I spent 17 years against my will. And on the national level, I know this much: The war created the opportunity for settling scores. It also produced many warlords who were responsible for the deaths of 250,000 (Sirleaf, 2009) people and the destruction of social amenities and national infrastructure. It also led to the pillaging of the country's natural resources and decimation of the national economy. For several years, Liberia became a failed state where warlords carved the country into personal fiefdoms while at the same time, distributing the national ministries and public corporations among themselves. According to the Liberian Truth and Reconciliation Report of 2009, an estimated 70% of all the fighting forces were children who were perpetually high on drugs and killing without compunction. Yet, the war had provided the opportunity for the nation to add another "first" to its list of "accolades": the first nation in Africa to have a sitting president indicted and convicted by the International Criminal Court for war crimes committed in a foreign country. The war also expressly created a constitutional impasse that a few politicians would exploit. They hurriedly assembled in a foreign country to form an interim government while the incumbent president was still in office but holed up in the Executive Mansion. In the end, the destruction of the country made a few people get most of the country's resources while the rest got suffering and misery. The people who made the fateful decision that led up to the war had no inkling of what the consequences were going to be. Given the number of deaths and the level of destruction brought upon the people and the nation, the architects of the war must bury their heads in their palms and must offer genuine repentance.

CHAPTER TEN

Coming Full Circle

I returned to Liberia in February 2013 for the second time after my first visit in 2007. My ultimate intention on this trip was primarily to travel down the same road I had used when my family and I had to flee our home and all that was familiar. I wanted to see the place that had hosted me when I fled, to visit the house that I lived in, and above all, to see the spot where I almost lost my life. This was the one most important thing that I had to do on this trip – I thought that seeing the place where my refugee life was forced to begin, would be the first step towards bringing closure to the ordeal and trauma that I experienced 23 years ago.

I looked forward to the trip. This time, I was going alone, so Joanna and Jeryna drove me to the airport with ample time for me to catch a 9 a.m. flight to Montreal. My journey would be taking me from Vancouver, making a pit stop in Montreal before heading across the Atlantic to Europe. I looked around the waiting area and saw that mostly everyone was fiddling with some kind of gadget or the other and had earphones stuck deep into their ears. Some had even larger ones covering the entire sides of their heads. It seemed no one really cared about what was happening around them. Reality hit. I am old school, I thought. I wanted to see the sights unfolding before me. I wanted to hear the conversations happening around me (some of which I of course could not understand). I wanted to revel in the dynamics of human nature, not block it out. And sure enough, I could not help but be bemused by the pre-boarding call from the airline:

"*Priority boarding call for Elite and Super Elite passengers*", came the voice over the intercom. "*If you are an Elite or Super Elite passenger, you can step forward to board now.*" I burst into laughter and so did another passenger who it seemed, was just as old school as I was. 'Elite and super-elite? What is this world coming to? I thought. Why these crazy categories? What could possibly distinguish an "elite" passenger from a "super-elite" passenger on the same aircraft? Maybe one received a warmer face towel than the other…my mind went crazy thinking these up, and the more I thought, the harder I laughed. I love life! On the serious side though, the announcement reminded me of the courses on development administration and development economics that I pursued as part of my degree in Public Administration and also in International Studies. Topics on income disparity, power and wealth in society made up a significant portion of these courses. Through such courses, I came to theorize that "elite" was a word ascribed to blood-sucking, privileged, and rent-seeking politicians, including also, those who inherited wealth, living on the backs of the working class. At the airport I came face to face with a different kind of elite. I followed the urging of my inquisitive mind and proceeded to ask one of the Air Canada staff to clarify for me who exactly were the persons who fell into the categories of "elite" and "super elite." It turned out that such passengers were frequent flyers who received special privileges such as priority boarding and other perks as deemed fit by the airline. After the elites and the super elites had boarded, it was my turn – the economy class passengers. I guess I need to start flying more "frequently", I amusingly thought.

We arrived in Montreal on time. The flight from Montreal to Brussels was scheduled for 6:25 p.m. As I went up to the waiting area for departure at Gate 51, I immediately noticed that there were about six persons, all blacks.

"Hello, is this the waiting area for the flight to Brussels?" I inquired of them.

"Yes," came the reply from one of the men.

"Is it only black people that travel from Montreal to Brussels?" I jokingly asked.

"Oh yeah, I did not realize that," one of them said.

Painful Journey: a Story of Escape and Survival

We all laughed. The thought that the seven of us sitting there were all black males, in a predominantly white environment, waiting for the same airline, evoked more laughs. It was apparent that prior to my arrival, the men were just sitting there – each minding his own business – none talking to the other. Now everyone began to introduce himself. As it happened, one of the men was going all the way with me on the next flight to Abidjan. The rest of them were travelling to various destinations across Europe and Africa. Again we boarded as elite, super elites, and economy class. On the flight I had four seats to myself. It was time to get some rest. I was weary from being up late the night before my trip and even from the days preceding that. I raised all the armrests between the seats, laid my head down and closed my eyes. When next I opened them, we were in Brussels. It was the morning of February 11, 2013. We were welcomed by a heavy downpour of rain and freezing cold.

At 12:10 p.m. we boarded SN Brussels Flight 247 for Monrovia via Abidjan. One of the six Africans who I had met at the airport in Montreal and who is originally from the Congo, bade me farewell and disembarked. After an hour we left for Monrovia. The flight between Abidjan and Monrovia took almost an hour. Once we got over the Roberts International Airport, the scenes below us on the ground looked different from when I was last there in 2007. They looked beautiful from the sky. There was electricity all over the place: at the airport, in Smell No Taste, and in Harbel, the Firestone Rubber Plantation headquarters. The SN Brussels touched down for its final stop at 8:32 p.m. to a thunderous applause from its delighted passengers, who were only too thankful to be on firm ground. I was alone – no family or other traveling companion. Neither did I have the luxury of traveling with the airport Immigration Commander from whom I had received VIP treatment on my previous trip. I was on my own.

The airport was still reeling from the shock of a plane crash hours before our arrival that killed the Guinean Army Chief of Staff and his delegation. They were going to attend the February 11 Armed Forces Day celebration of Liberia. I checked in, picked up my luggage, and stepped out from the baggage claim area. I had not publicized my visit this time around. My experience from the last visit had taught me a valuable lesson in simple economics. The physical condition of almost everyone who had come to visit Joanna and me had compelled us to give gifts – monetary or otherwise. That had definitely poked more holes in our pockets – holes that had taken a real long time to mend. This time around, the fact that I was traveling home on my own was an indication that I was not in a financial position to be as generous. Therefore I did not make the same mistake as before. No one was at the airport to greet me except my cousin who had come to pick me up. Despite the developments that had taken place since I was last there, the main terminal still lay in ruins.

I was impressed with what I was seeing along the highway to Monrovia. The city had dropped the embarrassing designation of being one of the darkest capitals in West Africa. The city was awake. Bright lights were everywhere, and the city was buzzing. Every entertainment spot along the highway and in Paynesville was bursting at the seams with Monrovia`s socialites. We made a stop along the way to see Sister Payennon near the police academy. As she had no idea of exactly when I would have been coming, she was astounded to see me, not to mention over-joyed. After a brief stay, we left and drove past all the entertainment centers along the Monrovia thoroughfare to my cousin's residence in the Stephen A Tolbert Estate, named after Liberia's finance minister of the 1970s.

I was terribly jet-lagged from having travelled for two days across three continents; North America, Europe, and Africa. So I stayed home for the same number of days that it took me to get there, with the hope that I would fully recover. On the third day, I began by retracing my steps of 2007. I visited the Foreign Ministry as I was curious to see Lormia and to renew and get the new ECOWAS Passport. From there I walked across the street to the University of Liberia campus. The Business College had relocated to the north end in the building that was once the men's dormitory. All of my former professors except Mr. Philip Jayjay had left the University. A student from the Department of Public Administration accompanied me to the Graduate Department to see him. I then did a brief tour of the entire campus, which was kept clean but like a number of universities in other parts of the developing world, the class rooms were overcrowded. I headed to the main entrance, wanting to observe the pedestrian traffic now using the pedestrian overpass that connected the campus and the Capitol Building. I had written in preceding chapter that the construction of the overpass was waste of tax-payers' money because it was not being used. I was therefore curious to know as to whether that had changed. I was surprised. I definitely was not expecting what I saw. In the place of where the overpass once stood was a vast area of nothingness. The overpass had been torn down. On inquiring, I was told that it was ordered to be torn down by the Acting City Mayor Mary Broh. Good decision, I thought to myself. Its erection in the first place, had made no sense because it was never used.

Days later, I visited the down town core. I chose to do so on foot, rather than be confined to a motor vehicle. I toured from Lynch Street and headed five blocks west on Broad Street to Mechlin Street. From there I walked another six blocks south on Mechlin Street to Sekou Toure Avenue, where I was treated to a sea of blue and white buildings. All the buildings, except the National Security Agency building and the US Embassy nearby, were painted in blue and white and were occupied by various UN systems. Counselor James Verdier's office was in the UNDP Office. I made my way directly there. By the time I got there, spools of water were dripping from my forehead and I could feel sweat coursing its way down the middle of my back. After the security screening, I was ushered into Verdier's office. It was cozy and refreshingly cool.

"Jerry, good to see you; you look good man!"

"Man Verdier, you just appear like a 16-year old lad. I guess you still play hoops; that's what keeping you in shape?"

"Yes I do that once in a while," he laughingly said.

We talked about everything from University of Liberia days, to family, to national politics. Verdier was one of the friends I hung up with during my days at the University. He had served as Vice President of the University of Liberia Students' Union and was member of my graduating class. By the time I was ready to leave, I felt cool enough to withstand the scorching heat that lay waiting for me outside. Having been away for such a long time, I felt that it was my duty to connect with my old friends. So my next tour about the city continued east along the Sekou Toure Ave and walked several blocks to the Antoinette Tubman Football Stadium at the corner of Lynch Street and United Nations

Drive, just across the street from the military barracks, which was the scene of fierce fighting in the 1990s. Inside the stadium, there were massive preparations going on for the wake-keeping of fallen former national football team player, Frank Seator. The stadium was beautiful. It had undergone a major make-over some years back. During the 1980s, the center of the playing pitch had become grassless due to the everyday wear and tear of exuberant ball players as well as by the lack of maintenance it received. Pretty soon it became known by soccer fans as the "bald head field". The playing pitch now boasted of an artificial turf that needed practically no upkeep. I could not have chosen a better day to do my tour of the stadium, for as luck would have had it, a number of former national team players, and former referees were there, and I was afforded the opportunity of meeting them, as well as Liberia's most celebrated player, James Salinsa Debah. After a brief photo-op session, I left and continued further east to the Ministry of Information. I was seeing Monrovia in its present state.

After reporting myself to the receptionist who took my ID card to the minister's office, I was invited upstairs. As usual Lewis Brown, now Minister of Information was in an upbeat, lively and jovial mood. He had not changed. Since the war of 1990 when I fled, that was my second time seeing him. I stayed with him in the ministry for several hours until it was time to go home. At which point, he had his driver drop me off at the Stephen Tolbert Estate, north of the city.

The next two days were pretty much the same - touring the city to revisit old sites and to see what was new. This time however, I did so with the assistance of a car for a bit of the way. I made a stop at the National Housing Authority (NHA). Nothing there had changed for the better since I last visited in 2007. The office still looked poor and dilapidated. I had a lengthy chat with the deputy for technical services. He was new as far as I was concerned. Of all the employees from the 1990s, only three had remained. Most had retired and others had found job elsewhere. We drove up to the downtown core again and I alighted to tour on foot. From the corner of Johnson and Broad Streets, I walked one block south to the corner of Carey and Johnson Streets to see Marea my former co-worker at NHA who was now working with the Central Bank of Liberia. We chatted for a brief while, mostly reminiscing about the old days and about how the stupid war had thrown our lives into disarray. I then left Marea and made my way on to Camp Johnson Road, where I walked several blocks to the Temple of Justice to see another former co-worker, Vera Norman, who was now working as Protocol Director of the Office of the Chief Justice of the Supreme Court of Liberia. We spoke on the phone before she came down to the parking lot to get me. She could not believe that I was in town. While waiting for Vera, I encountered former Minister of Labour Cllr. Tiawon Gonglo. Gonglo had taught me Economics 201 at the University. We were joined a few minutes later by Richard Kla, former legal counsel to the President's office. He was now Associate Judge of the Commercial Court. This had certainly turned out to be a reunion of the sorts.

Vera came and I went with her up to her office. After the visit she went with me back to the parking lot. On our trip down, the elevator doors opened to allow us in. Vera first entered. Then, as I was about to step in, one side of the door began coming from inside to shut. Instinctively, I shoved my arm in, expecting the door to retreat but it didn't. Not only did the elevator door from hell jam me, it also sent 240 volts of electric current into my right arm rendering it temporarily paralyzed from my shoulder down to the tips of my fingers. 'Aaaaarrrggh!' my painful scream echoed through the long hallway. The door would not even retract. I had to force push it back, so I could step as far back away as possible. It was a good thing that I was only about to make an attempt at putting my foot in the door when that happened. I was therefore in a better position to step back. The door closed and then reopened. Just as soon as it did, I heard Vera's voice from inside the elevator,

"Jerry, what happened?" she inquired.

"I just got jolted by an electric power from the elevator," I responded.

"Are you alright?"

"No", I said. By then I could feel some numbness creeping through my arm. At that moment a guy sitting in a chair a few feet away from the elevator, who had heard and seen what happened quipped in plain Liberian English:

"Oh yea. The elevator can jes be jeking people here o. It jek one man few minutes ago".

"*It can be jeking people; it can be jeking people. Why you na tell me?*" I asked.

"*But I na know it was goin to jek you*", he replied rather sarcastically.

I was angry not only at the guy who knew about the danger the lift posed to riders but did not warn me, but I was also mad at the Temple of Justice building management for having those antiquated elevators in the building.

"Vera, I will not come in the elevator. I will go by the stairs," I told her.

"Ok we will meet downstairs."

By the time I walked down several flights of stairs, the numbness had partly disappeared. I kept on wiggling my arm as a form of physiotherapy to allow blood to flow and to get proper range of motion. Vera was very apologetic and expressed her empathy. I went straight home after that incident. The city did not see me again for the rest of that day. In fact I had vowed not to ever take the elevator in the Temple of Justice again. I would rather walk up the hundreds of flight of stairs.

The next day I was dropped off again around Benson, Center, Gurley and Carey Streets. In 2007 when I had visited, the place had reeked of foul stench due in particular to the huge amount of human waste that was everywhere. This time, as I went to these areas, I kept sniffing the air, expecting to be met by unpleasant scents but all that came back was a good old familiar smell - one that I had missed.

Monrovia was clean. Streets and sidewalks were properly paved with proper drainage and waste disposal systems. Randall Street, north to Water Street in the commercial district of Waterside was clean. There were garbage disposal facilities around the city. The Waterside Bridge that had disintegrated back in 2007 was rebuilt. But traffic congestion still existed despite the opening of the second bridge. The streets were well laid out with proper signage everywhere. Palmgrove Cemetery on both sides of Center Street had 10-foot high metal fence around it. The dead were allowed to literally rest in peace. City parking regulations were in force, thanks to Acting City Mayor Mary Broh. Motorists were prohibited from parking their vehicles downtown without paying the appropriate fees to do so, lest their vehicles be towed or the wheels locked.

Painful Journey: a Story of Escape and Survival

In the municipality of Paynesville, about 8 miles east of Monrovia, the situation was nondescript. Paynesville did not seem like it was a municipality in the 21st Century. Most sections of the city were akin to the Kibera Slum in Nairobi or West Point in the west of Monrovia. There were huge piles of garbage in the Red Light commercial district of the city. And apparently, the powers that be, allowed the garbage to be burned in the street on a daily basis.

Transportation was still a problem. It would take hours to get a taxi from downtown Monrovia to the suburb of Gardnersville or Sinkor. The number of *Pehn Pehn* (motorbike used as mode of transportation) had increased. In the absence of readily available statistics, I will safely put the number between 5 to 6 thousands motorbikes. There is no insurance coverage for the bikes and riders do not wear helmets. The bikes were constantly being overloaded with four persons. Little children were allowed to sit on the gas tank of the bike with three other persons sitting behind the child. I screamed every time I encountered them in the traffic. Once, when I asked a traffic police officer why it was that the police did nothing to enforce the laws pertaining to overloading the motorbikes, particularly the ones that carried children sitting on the gas tank, he gave me a rather outlandish response:

"We cannot pull over these bike riders for fear of them falling. If they do fall, it is our fault".

"But you would rather allow them to risk children's lives?" I questioned.

"My brother, this is Liberia."

"What is that supposed to mean?" I asked the police officer.

"My brother, just leave me ya," was the only thing he said afterwards.

I shook my head in disbelief and got in the car. I hope the government will pass a law that will make it difficult for motor bikes to be used as commercial mode of transportation.

On Thursday February 21, we drove to the Monrovia City Hall in order to make an appointment to meet with Madam Broh. I had wanted to congratulate her on the great job she was doing keeping the city clean. My appointment was set for Monday. A few hours after I left the City Hall, the regular radio programming was interrupted by a special break in news, "An arrest order has been issued for Acting City Mayor Mary

Broh," the voice blared over radio. I sat up straighter in my seat. What I drew from the rest of the news report was that the Acting City Mayor had gone to the South Beach Prison compound and allegedly prevented the Superintendent of Monsterrado County from being incarcerated by taking her away. Superintendent Grace Kpahn had been ordered incarcerated for 72 hours by Plenary of the House of Representatives for contempt. The actions of Madam Broh had now forced the House to declare both the Superintendent and the Acting City Mayor as fugitives, therefore ordering their arrest and incarceration for 30 days. The House also voted to ban them for life from holding public office. The next day, President Johnson Sirleaf suspended both officials from duties. By Tuesday of the following week, the Justice Ministry charged the Acting Mayor with obstruction of justice.

Since my appointment with the former City Mayor was no longer necessary, I decided to use that time to visit Bo Waterside-Liberia and Bo Waterside-Sierra Leone. I would be able to see Sister Sarah (the one Payennon is next to) and her daughter , Vester who live in Sinje, Cape Mount County couple of miles east of the border. I had not seen my sister for 25 years. It was also an opportunity for me to see Gbah the town that gained notoriety during the war. Tommy and I set out for the border on February 25 at 12 p.m. As we crossed the St Paul River on the outskirts of Monrovia, my heart began to pound harder and much faster than normal. The last time I had traveled that route and had gone beyond that bridge was in 1990 - I was fleeing for my life - too scared on June 30, 1990 of falling in an ambush set by the NPFL operatives, who had taken over the entire country. They were present in Clay Ashland, a town about five miles up the St Paul River from the main highway to Bo Waterside. It was ludicrous to think that at that time, I would have taken note of landmarks. Even if I had, chances are there would have been no way that after 23 years; this brain of mine would have remembered any of them. Besides, after 23 years, the geographic landscape had to have changed. Thinking back to those days, I still feel that the rebels were near the highway, but had not been given the order to strike due to Tom Woweiyou's statement heard on BBC Radio on June 29, 1990.

We arrived first at Po River Bridge, a bridge notorious for several battles. It had changed hands several times between several warring

Painful Journey: a Story of Escape and Survival

factions during the 1990s and the second war in the 2000s. I got out of the car, looked up and down the river but did not see any evidence that that place had been the site of such fierce and gruesome battles. The trees had grown very tall there. The scenery was beautiful. I boarded the car and we proceeded northwest to Klay and from there turned left (westward) toward Sierra Leone onto the Babangida Highway. The Highway, named after former Nigerian Head of State, Ibrahim Babangida was built in the mid 1980s by Daewoo, a South Korean company. Running from Klay Junction to the border, this approximately 45-mile highway stood as solid as the day it was built, despite two and a half decades of constant use. Like Po River Bridge, Klay Junction had also gained much notoriety and likewise had changed hands several times among warring factions.

Our next stop was in the town of Gbah. Of All the towns along the Babangida Highway leading to Sierra Leone, Gbah was the place in which several of the worst atrocities were committed. The town was commanded by an NPFL fighter who went by the pseudonym of "Gbah Ray"[13]. The name Gbah Ray meant fear, destruction and death. Many of the refugees who I met in 1990 in Sierra Leone, many of whom had barely managed to escape this man's terror, shivered at the mention of his name. They called him a ruthless killer who would stop at nothing to ensure that his last torture and kill was worse than the one before. It was reported that Ray would decapitate a person without compunction, sometimes using the severed head as soccer ball, while chanting, "*Major Taylor up, up. Sergeant Doe, down, down*". Other reports pointed to his so-called magical power of detecting in the lines of fleeing refugees, members of the Krahn and Mandingo tribes. Once caught, innocent unarmed refugees would be plucked from the line. That would be the end of them.

By the time we arrived in Gbah, my entire body had broken out in cold sweat, my heart racing and my hands were shaking from reliving such unpleasant memories. I got out of the car, walked around a bit and took some pictures. I hoped that I would have found someone who had survived the 1990 war in the town. But this was not to be - I

---

[13] Named Ray (Red) for his fair complexioned skin and because he controlled Gbah Town, fleeing refugees gave him the nickname, Gbah Ray. He was wicked, ruthless.

found no one. I had wanted to verify some of the stories I had heard in 1990 about Ray and Gbah as were told by fleeing refugees. I had also wanted confirmation about how he was killed. Unconfirmed reports told that Gbah Ray was mobbed and killed some time in the 1990s in Duala, a suburb of Monrovia by a group of market women. The new Gbah was bustling with commercial activities. It was heavily populated with teeming market and shops in the center of town on both sides of the highway. Disappointed by my fruitless search, we left for Sinje and crossed another checkpoint in Tienne. There, we took some photographs with the immigration and custom officers. The building had withstood the tests of time - the structure was still surprisingly solid. My mind went back to the mango tree that had provided me with shade and some amount of comfort for a few minutes while I sat and waited for some of the other passengers who were clearing immigration on that dark and fateful day that I fled Liberia. I had to fight back the tears that welled up in my eyes.

With permission of the officers on duty, I was allowed to tour the facilities for a little while. They knew my niece, Vester, who lived in Sinje. She was a captain in the immigration services and was assigned in Gbah. I had taken the liberty of throwing her name around hoping for any privilege that doing so might accrue. It worked. For without having introduced myself as the uncle of the captain, I would have never been allowed to take any pictures, let alone tour the area. The long fought hard years of war had made everyone suspicious of anyone with camera. Such matters were sensitive and had to be dealt with carefully, lest they accuse you of using the pictures to "bring on another war."

Five minutes later we were in Sinje. My niece was renting a house near the Sierra Leonean Refugee Camp in Sinje. My eldest sister, Sarah came out to greet me with heavy cry. She is the mother of my nephew Kula described earlier. We spent the afternoon together eating and talking family matters. We talked about her oldest son Sylvester (Vester and Kulah's oldest brother) who was living with me in Waterloo, but passed away in 1995 a few months after he repatriated to Liberia. So this was the time for us to grieve a little. After shedding some tears, we ate some food that Vester had prepared. Vester and one of her colleagues joined us on the journey to the border. It was a five-mile stretch of road but before we knew it, we were there.

It was like a home coming for me. Bo Waterside-Liberia looked different. But again times have changed markedly. The main customs building of the 1990s was destroyed. In its place was a new structure that housed all the law enforcement agencies. We met the commander, who was a friendly and receptive gentleman. After a brief chat, he allowed me to take a few shots of the new building. I was rather surprised to see that the check point up the hill where Kwame and I were harassed for several hours on July 2, 1990 was still there. . But this time there was only one gate instead of two. It was now some minutes past 5p.m and the border would be closing by 6:00 p.m., so the commander advised me that it would be best that we leave, thus allowing me enough time while the sun was still up, to tour Bo Waterside-Sierra Leone.

We got on the Mano River Bridge, the boundary between Liberia and Sierra Leone and stopped the vehicle. I now had the opportunity to get a better glimpse of the river that some Liberian soldiers had had to swim across to get to safety when the NPFL forces attacked them at 5 p.m. on July 23, 1990. Others had not been so lucky. I can still recall the wailings by many family members of service members who did not make it across the Mano River that fateful day. Captain Alfred Churh who had survived that attack by swimming, died some years back in the early 2000s in Monrovia. Another soldier who had run across the bridge with his M-16 rifle, later joined the anti-Taylor rebel organization, United Liberation Movement for Democracy (ULIMO) in 1991.

Finally we reached the Sierra Leonean side of the bridge. Oh yes, I was firmly back on the soil that had given me hope, the soil that had protected me from the Liberians on the other side of the border. Yes I was firmly back on the soil of the country that said, no matter what, "We will not reject you. We will not send you back to be killed. You deserve a second chance at life. Some of your compatriots want you dead, but we want you alive. We will keep you to save you from the inferno." I stood in awe, in utter bewilderment. It was a poignant moment for me. I looked at the checkpoint where on July 2, 1990 Kwame had backed up the vehicle when the Liberian soldiers would not let us go into our own country to get our belongings. What if I had not run across the border, would I have survived the war? What if the Sierra Leoneans had closed their border to me on that day in June? What would have happened? After a brief moment of mentally going through the many *what ifs*, I stepped into the little shed that hosted the checkpoint.

"Hello, my name is Jerry. I was a refugee in this town 23 years ago. I have come back to see the place".

"*Yu welcome, sir,*" an officer told me. (You are welcome, sir).

"In 1991 when the war entered here, I fled this place and ended up in Waterloo where I lived for four additional years before going to Canada." "*Oh yu bin dey na Watalo Refugee Camp?*" a female officer beaming with smile, inquired in Sierra Leonean Creole. (Oh, you were in Waterloo?) "*Me sef, Watalo na me hom*", she added. (Waterloo is my home town)

Momentarily I turned to speaking the little Creole that I know.

"Yes o. *Na dey ar bon me girl pekin.*" (Yes it was where my daughter was born)

"*Yu na Salone Borbor. Welcome sir.*" (Then you are Sierra Leonean. Welcome sir)

"Yes o. *Me na Salone Borbor. I comot na Watalo*". I replied with humor. (Yes, I am Sierra Leonean. I come from Waterloo)

"*Welcome, Sir*", added another officer.

"*Tenki. Tell Papa God tenki for dis contri*". (Thanks. Thank God for this country).

I explained that I was emotionally attached to Sierra Leone. It was my second home. It was the country that gave me sanctuary when some of my compatriots wanted my head because I belong to the "wrong tribe." The officers listened intently and expressed their empathies. Despite the fact that they must have heard similar stories or must have experienced similar situations, they made me feel at home. Seeing a Liberian who had lived in the country and had come back to show his appreciation, was indeed noteworthy to them. After the brief exchanges and some photo-ops, and with the help of my niece, the border guards gave us entry into the country without asking us for our travel documents.

We drove into the main town. Everywhere looked different. But I still recognized the mango tree near the road where I used to sit and register refugees streaming across the border form Liberia. Mamie Sao's motel complex no longer stood where it once was. Other makeshift shacks were now constructed there. Though new, the market stalls were still to the same place, but with different houses built around them. The house that we had built and in which my family and I had resided was long gone - it was a mud-walled, thatched-roof house. I believe it was one of the first to fall in 1991 after we abandoned it. There were many unfamiliar sights, but that was to have been expected. The main Customs and Immigration building where we used to share our food rations was gone too. A new customs and immigration building was now situated near the bridge from where we had just come. The moment of truth had arrived. From the very beginning of my trip, one of my greatest anxieties was to visit the military barracks where I was almost mistakenly shot by a panicking SSD officer. I walked up to the barracks, heart racing, and pounding heavily in my chest. Then it sank painfully. The 1990 buildings stood there as bombed-out frames amidst a sea of trees and tall grass. New buildings had shifted the barracks several yards to the west. I had not gotten the chance to take a picture of a place at which I could have been shot and worse yet, could have died. I was overcome with disappointment. I hopped back in the car and we headed back toward the border. All through the journey back, I kept thinking that all I had left of this place was memory – a memory that would in time fade and wither away. At the border we bade the Sierra Leonean officers farewell and crossed back into Liberia. My painful journey out of Liberia to save my life has come full circle.

CHAPTER ELEVEN

Rebuilding the 'House of Cards'

Even though I missed Liberia during all those days I was in exile and did not have the opportunity to go back until after seventeen years, I was relieved that I made the run on June 30, 1990. I was not in any way prepared to militarily participate or worse yet, be one of the victims in a senseless war that I did not help create. I was born in Harper, Maryland County. I grew up in Tappita, Nimba County, predominantly, home of the Gios and the linguistically related Manos. Tappita is the only place in Liberia that I know best. I am emotionally, socially, and in many ways, culturally attached to Tappita and Nimba County as a whole. Majority of my friends, are Gios and Manos, especially my two closest boyhood friends, Patrick and Lormia who I spoke of earlier who are indeed, my lifetime friends. Given all of the above, let me once again emphasize why my leaving on that fateful day was the best thing – best that I left to save my life, my family's and others'. Let me put it hypothetically this way: What if I had stayed in Liberia during the height of the war and was not killed, I could have probably done some quasi-military training in Camp Schefflin for a couple of days, like others, given an M-16 or AK-47 rifle, and eventually sent to the war front to kill my "enemies". At the front lines, I could have seen or encountered a multitude of my former schoolmates and classmates, or the many friends from Tappita with whom I had played soccer, some of whom came to the market in Sierra Leone in 1990 during the war urging me to visit them across the border; or the thousands of people who cheered me on when I played soccer in Nimba. Or worst yet, at the front lines, I could have seen or encountered my friend Patrick's younger brothers, Gaye, David, and Bouu-mehn and sisters Christiana and Catherine, the children (now adults) who called me and still call me brother. Then not too far from there, I could have seen or encountered Lormia's younger brother, Koko who ended up taking care of Uncle Bantoe's house in Tappita. Was I supposed to shoot them? Only in my dream!

Ethnically I was born unto Krahn parents but grew up in Tappita, Nimba County. I am first and foremost a Liberian more than anything else. I do not play or subscribe to tribal politics and all its trappings. That is why when I hear a person whom I am meeting for the first time speak with a perfect Liberian accent, my question always is and will continue to be: "Are you Liberian?" I think every Liberian needs to adopt such attitude. That is one of the better ways we can rebuilt our crumbled house of card, devoid of prejudices, persecution, tribalism, and all the other social ills that tend to divide the nation. The country needs to set a new agenda for reconciliation. For me I see the reconciliation drive as a natural ongoing process. All Liberians must engage this process with vigor. I am looking forward to the time I will see BB, and as I previously said, hear his side. In any event, I have already forgiven him, sincerely; just like I have forgiven Kollie who threatened to kill me during the Quiwonkpa 1985 November 12 attempted coup. In the same vein, I have already forgiven those who murdered my brother, sister, nephew and uncles. It is impossible to turn back the hand of the clock. Equally so, we cannot undo what has already been done but we can surely prevent it from happening again. The nation just has to move ahead.

In other light, bringing the nation together in a more conciliatory way requires the collective efforts of all. I reckon that that inextricably means the victims and the perpetrators must be willing to let the healing process take a natural course. To explain this measure further, let us critically consider two types of approaches to reconciliation: the government-sponsored approach and the natural approach. I strongly believe our better understanding of the two approaches will lend credence to putting our proverbial 'house of cards' back in order.

Government-sponsored approach

It is a top-down approach that encompasses a well rehearsed and well-choreographed process spearheaded by the Ministry of Internal Affairs. To facilitate this process and give it a semblance of authenticity, the ministry identifies the parties and invites them to a designated place where the president of the nation is in attendance. The government pays for the food and accommodations for all or some of the participants. At this pseudo-event often masquerading as a reconciliation convention, the government's hand-picked speakers will embark upon an endless campaign of political grandstanding and photo-ops by delivering empty speeches that do not address the main problem but hypocritically and deceitfully pledge their loyalty to the president of the nation. This approach offers a cosmetic solution that lasts only for the duration of the convention. Once the curtains are drawn and the actors return to their various locales, the entire process turns out to be a pure exercise in futility with the tax payers' money well wasted.

I say this because in November 1987, while the Doe government-sponsored reconciliation conference between the Krahns and the Gios and Manos was underway in Sanniquellie, Nimba County, the NPFL rebels were in Libya undergoing intensive training in guerilla warfare. Two years later, the NPFL launched the armed rebellion and the house of cards came crashing down. That conference did not address the fundamental problems for which it was called. In fact how would it have addressed the fundamental issues when the main actors in this saga were out of the country? This government-sponsored approach is associated with the era of President Tubman (1944-1971) and has lapsed into moribundity.

The Natural Approach

For reconciliation to be sustainable it must be tied in with economic development which will significantly contribute to the healing process. To achieve genuine reconciliation it is important to employ the concept of natural approach, a process by which natural forces are encouraged or facilitated to occur. This approach is better described in the G-Model of Post-Conflict Reconciliation Theory, G+I+Si/T=GR[14]. It is the bottom-up process that requires the Liberian government intervention but not in the way of the one explained above in the government-sponsored approach. G in this formula stands for government; *I* refers to intervention plus *Si*, social interaction; *T* for time; which results in R, reconciliation.

The government must have the moral imperative to invest in the private and public sectors for decent paying jobs for the citizens. In order for investment in the private and public sector to occur, the government must first ensure that there is an environment of political stability, free speech, and free press. It must also invest in education and training in science and technology, provide more funding and scholarships for qualified students and educational opportunities for former combatants. To invest in these sectors, the government must allocate a considerable percentage of the national fiscal budget toward achieving those goals. It must also invest in agriculture and the mining industries. Private sector investment requires partial or full exemption on withholding taxes. It also requires the provision of incentives to help businesses establish and expand operations and the granting of duty-free privilege to businesses bringing in large scale operational equipment. The government must also provide expansion funding to firms for the constructions of roads and bridges. Additionally the nation's manufacturing industry needs to be expanded. Iron-ore, wood, foods and other natural resources that are exported in the primary forms must have processing plants in the country. Instead of exporting only raw materials, the nation must also export finished products. That is the way modern economies function.

Social interaction takes into consideration the peaceful co-existence, security and equal opportunities for different families and or tribal members and their children who have a commonality of purpose and interest. The definition of social interaction in this context brings into focus social activities that subsist among people in the same locale which will induce peaceful co-existing. They may attend the same school, be members of the same social, fraternal or cultural associations or simply they all work for the same company. And with great effort,

---

[14] A simple concept that I developed while thinking through this chapter.

through *Time*, represented by *T* in the equation, a process of healing will be allowed to take place, for it is believed that time heals wounds. In practical terms, natural reconciliation which is a function of social interaction done over a long period of time is the pathway to peace, an essential ingredient for political and economic stability. Ideally when majority of the people in a community are gainfully employed and they can afford to provide the basic necessities of life for themselves and their families, send their kids to school and save some of their disposable incomes for the future with the process stretched over a long period of time, the nation will be on the way to achieving economic prosperity and reconciliation at the same time.

To further illustrate the G-Model, let's take Mount Wologisi in Lofa County or Putu Mountain in Grand Gedeh for instance. Let's suppose mining operations begin on either of those mountains, it will attract a great many Liberians – irrespective of tribal origin or social status - in those counties in search of employment opportunity. The employment of many citizens will ultimately translate into microeconomic activities flourishing in the area. Like LAMCO and Firestone where there are housing, educational, and medical facilities provided for employees, those working Liberians will settle down with their respective families and begin life anew in that part of the country where perhaps, some of them have never been before. In that light, their children will go to the same school, belong to the same sports and social organization thereby washing away all the mistrust and apprehension these people may have been harboring against one another in the past. Inter-collegiate sporting and cultural activities will help to unite the younger generation.

While it is important for the government to invest in the private sector in order to boost economic growth, it is also important to note that there must be proper regulations that will ensure that foreign concessionaires do not extract the natural resources to the detriment of the people of the areas of operations. Most of the concessionaires present the image of rent-seeking multinational corporations that may only be interested in extracting the natural resources without giving back to the community in which they operate. They hire a few locals and that is it. In the end, there are limited long-term benefits to be accrued by the locals after operations cease. Against this backdrop, I propose a tripartite memorandum of understanding between the government, local chiefs, and residents and representatives of the foreign concessionaire. Let the local chiefs and residents be active participants in the decision making process before granting operational license to the concessionaire, whether foreign or local. The locals must be allowed to submit a realistic development package to the concessionaire. The development package must include, but not be limited to, the construction of better roads, school, and health clinic, in the area. The concessionaire must be required to constructively engage the community by becoming a partner in progress. Another requirement is that they must institute proper measures for protecting the environment.

Initiatives such as provision of scholarships, bursaries, and awards for high achieving students are to be part of the package. Too often we have seen in the past such measures ignored. In the past, concessionaires were allowed to operate, exploit the areas, and leave them bare when they ceased to operate several years later. They pillaged the forest. They built roads that were only good for caterpillars to use to haul logs from the forest for export. They also built log bridges that lasted for only a year. And when the torrential rains came, the log bridges were washed away thereby rendering the roads impassable. There must be a reversal of this kind of policy. There must be measures put in place for long-term socio-economic benefit for the villages, towns, and the country. In other words, the national economy must be transformed from one of exportation of raw materials to manufacturing and industry.

I am sincerely optimistic, without doubt, that the people of Liberia can rebuild the nation themselves. At the same time I suggest that a major reform of the judicial system and investment in agriculture need to be considered. A) Judicial reform, because corruption in the system and arbitrariness by those in authority created a breakdown in the system that also led to the war. B) Investment in agriculture, because the nation needs to have the capacity to feed itself. Food, particularly rice, is seen as a stabilizing political and economic force in the country.

Judicial Reform

Arbitrariness or total disregard for the rule of law by past government officials, is one of the fundamental causes of the civil war. Those who sought democratic change during the Tolbert and Doe eras had little or no faith in the judicial system to protect their interest. Judges, lawyers, clerks were inadequately compensated. This created the avenue for bribery and other forms of institutionalized corruption. It is reported that the Liberian judiciary has been rated as the most corrupt sector of government, according to the National Integrity Forum (Karmo, 2013).

Judicial interference and abuse of power by government officials of the three branches of government rendered the judicial system weak and subjected it to manipulation and control. It does not need much over-emphasizing that adhering to the rule of law is the bedrock of any civilized society. This especially is true as an essential requirement for a country emerging from 14 years of lawlessness and anarchy. The rule of laws is better understood if it is considered in the shortened form as "the rule of law not of men". Citizens and residents must not be subjected to the discretion of those in power or the wealthy who have the capacity to do so with impunity. The rule of laws guarantees that the ruler and the ruled live in keeping with the law. The laws must not only apply to the people who are permanently situated on the lowest rung of the socioeconomic ladder of society. Government employees must equally conform to the law as are those who are ruled. American human rights activist, Malcolm X articulates this concept quite beautifully by stating that the "…law applies to the law enforcer as well as those who are under the enforcement of the enforcer" (Clarke, 1990:195). However this may probably not be the case in many respects in Liberia. The expression, "Do you know who I am?" epitomizes one of the classic examples through which some officials and law enforcement agents oftentimes use their power to evade or breach the laws.

At all times and levels, the government must have the power and authority in maintaining law and order without which there may be anarchy as was the case during the war. The enforcement of laws ensures security of person and property. Similarly it prevents people from attacking each other. Under the principle of the rule of law it is guaranteed that the government cannot punish individuals or groups of individuals arbitrarily based on the premise of dislike. There must be a case of proven violation of the law through due process. The rule of law also guarantees discretionary power by the government. That is, if the government wants to construct roads, it must have the discretion to plan the route and acquire the land and offer the construction contract through a bidding process. Owners of land must be adequately compensated at their market value and if they are dissatisfied, they can seek redress through the courts. Government's discretionary power must always be done within the framework of the rules that discourage arbitrariness (Dickerson and Flanagan, 1990).

Extension of the process of the rule of law is the system of courts – institutions that settle disputes between individuals and the state, between private individuals and public authority, and between different levels of government under the laws of the country (ibid). If one feels aggrieved the court is the best place to seek redress. Therefore the courts must be truly independent and charged with the responsibility of administering justice impartially to all citizens. Judicial reform usually aims to improve such things as law courts, procuracies, advocacy (bar), inquest, executory processes, and record keeping (ibid).

Professor Emerson Koroma of the Department of Public Administration at the University of Liberia once humorously lamented that there are three ways of doing things in Liberia: the right/legal way, the wrong way and the *Liberian Way*. The *Liberian Way*, according to the professor, takes precedence above all. It compromises the legal and right way by arriving at a quick-fix or short cut solution by any means necessary. A criminal case which is supposed to be prosecuted in court is disposed of with the accused and the accuser sitting outside of the legal arrangement to settle the case. It most often involves law enforcement officer and or the judge in the back door deal. This effectually negates the legal path towards resolution. The *Liberian way* is also the rampant abuse of power by those in authority. It is a process that has a wanton disregard for the rule of law. It encourages arbitrariness and perpetuates corruption. Setting up a 50-member commission to count the ballots outside of the constitutionally sanctioned National Election Commission as in the case of the 1985 general elections is the *Liberian Way*.

There are hundreds of examples of the Liberian way that can be found in every sector of the Liberian society, many of which defy logic and common sense. An incumbent in a community organization refuses to turn over the organization's documents and financial records simply because he lost in his reelection bid. Thus, he bequeaths to himself all the organization's money and property in his possession claiming that it was during his tenure that the association raised the money. A presidential nominee appearing before a Senate Select Committee for confirmation produces a doctored, fraudulent and falsified educational credential. The Committee discovers the fraud and rejects the nominee. Days or weeks later the president of the nation reappoints the previously rejected nominee. Within an hour of grilling the Senate confirms the nominee. That is a classic example of the *Liberian Way*. A government official is accused of obstruction of justice and resigns his/her position. In the wake of the accusation, Plenary of the House of Representatives, without due process, passes a resolution to ban the individual for life from holding public office. A few months later, the president appoints the same person to another position and the person is confirmed by the Senate. That again, is another example of the *Liberian Way*. In summary, the Liberian Way is an embodiment of all that is fundamentally dysfunctional about the system. Every citizen, irrespective of status in government has to change this mindset by abiding by the laws and doing the right thing.

One of the basic components required for judicial reform is judicial independence which encompasses freedom from political interference. It involves a number of factors: (a) Judges cannot be discharged except for violation of the law or gross impropriety. Judicial independence perhaps the single greatest institutional support of the rule of law is a valuable tool that can never be taken for granted. And such independence requires proper funding of the courts and their activities. (b) The second point is to ensure the court's efficiency. Cases before the court must be handled in an efficient and expeditious manner. It becomes a judicial tragedy if individuals are held in custody indefinitely awaiting a criminal trial or payment of compensation in a civil suit is indefinitely postponed by legal maneuvers (Dickerson and Flanagan, 1990). Judges and all the legal professionals who work in the court system must receive decent wages and benefits. Citizens need to have unreserved confidence in the ability of the court system to be the arbiter of the law. Therefore the Liberian judicial system needs to undergo major transformation.

Predictably there have been numerous reports of cases of land seizures in some parts of the country during the war. After the war, some returnees came back home only to find their land had been allegedly taken without compensation. Cases of such nature threaten the stability of the area and the country. The court is the best avenue for seeking redress. American author Edgar Allan Poe reminds us that, "A wrong is unredressed when retribution overtakes its redresser. It is equally unredressed when the avenger fails to make himself felt as such to him who has done the wrong," (Poe, 1983:1). There must never be a situation anymore where individuals will attempt to seek redress outside the legal system. That is why reforming the legal system in post-war Liberia is absolutely necessary.

The armed insurrection is a colossal example of what seeking redress outside of the court system can do to a people, to a nation. Did launching the war ever give adequate redress to those who might have felt the brunt of the injustices allegedly meted out by the Doe government? No it did not. It only succeeded in opening a huge avenue for a cycle of violence and destruction. The increase in the number of warring factions and the death of thousands of innocent Liberians in the process are a testament to the senseless nature of the war. There were courts available but they were politically controlled by the power elite. Had the courts been institutionally strong and independent, perhaps there would not have been political problems that led to the war. The results of the 1985 presidential elections would have probably been annulled through the courts given the overwhelming evidence of vote-rigging, ballot-stuffing, ballot-burning, and other forms of electoral mal-practices that were discovered in several polling stations in Monrovia alone. Additionally, when the Doe government banned the two most popular political parties, the United People's Party (UPP) and the Liberian People's Party (LPP) months before the October 15, 1985 general elections, the government's decision would have been challenged in court.

Investment in Agriculture

Liberia is a nation blessed with an abundance of natural resources. The economy is based on production and export of natural resources such as iron-ore, rubber cocoa, coffee, rubber, palm oil and palm kernel oil. Like many developing countries, Liberia is seeking development in the following sectors in order to meet its development objectives such as a) availability and expanding the distribution of life-sustaining goods namely, food, shelter, health and protection; and b) raising the standard of living of its people including provision of more jobs, higher wages, better education, and healthcare delivery system. One better way to secure these development objectives is to boost agricultural production. But producing agricultural commodities and exporting them in the primary form is a disincentive to local farmers. The government must encourage investors who will build manufacturing plants to process primary commodities in the country, which will most definitely, create better job opportunities for the citizens and boost the economy at the same time.

Liberia has everything nature has provided that will make it self-sufficient in food production. It has adequate rainfall, large tropical rain forest which includes arable and agricultural land, and an underutilized labor force. The soil is fertile and there are large bodies of waterways. The nation will be able to feed itself when there is a national policy on agriculture and adequate incentives given to farmers. Theodore Shultz, a notable proponent of this argument suggests: "Incentives to guide and reward farmers are critical component. Once there are investment opportunities, farmers will turn sand into gold," (Bate, 2005:2). Rice is a national staple but it is imported. Parenthetically, in 1979 it was due to the proposed increase in the price of this precious commodity that the rice riots occurred ultimately leading to the downfall of the government in 1980. One of such incentives is to give out loans to farmers. Another way is to increase the tax levied on rice importation which will discourage importation of large quantity of rice. But let it be emphasized that the increase should not be a shock-therapy rather it must be done on an incremental basis, between five to ten years by which time local farmers' production capacities may have reached national distribution levels. At this point in time of our national existence, the nation needs to take concrete steps to be able to feed itself. Farmers need to be given the incentives to grow more rice.

Another method of providing incentives to farmers is for the state to dismantle the bureaucracy in charge of purchasing agricultural commodities from farmers. The government has created a monopsony in which it is the sole buyer of the farmers' products. In this case the Liberian Produce Marketing Corporation (LPMC), which is the only buyer, can strongly influence the price in the economic transaction. Basically the farmers are indirectly told to sell their produce or keep it. This method disincentivizes the farmers' capacity to get more returns on their commodities at competitive pricing level. Individual farmers or agricultural cooperatives must be given the latitude to sell their products to whomever they please.

Finally, there must be due care given to students pursuing a career in agriculture. A government policy regarding provisions of scholarships, bursaries, grants, student loans or other forms of financial assistance will serve as an inducement to attract many people into the field of agriculture. After graduation in the field of agriculture, there must be financial opportunities (start up capitals) available to these professionals to make farms or engage in other forms of agricultural activities within their profession.

EPILOGUE

Looking back at what I have been through, settling in Canada with my family after making the run, was one of the best things that ever happened to me.

Our children have grown up. Gerald, who was 9 when we came, is now an adult attending Douglas University College in New Westminster studying to be a social worker. He also has a daughter of his own. His sister, Jeryna who was 2 when we arrived, is now an adult attending the Simon Fraser University with the ambition of becoming a lawyer some day. They both attended the same Catholic schools run by the Our Lady of Mercy Parish: Our Lady of Mercy (elementary) and St. Thomas More Collegiate (secondary). The future looks very bright and promising for them. My wife Joanna is a health care worker. I too work for a British Columbia transit company, the Coast Mountain Bus Company. Despite the many challenges we encountered, which of course were obvious, in adjusting in a new country during the first few years of our settlement, life has been generally good for us. Thus, we are extremely grateful for having been granted the privilege to immigrate to Canada. Since our arrival, my wife and I have had the privilege of sponsoring two nephews and a niece to join us in Canada. The men now have their own families and they are all doing pretty good socio-economically. We are certainly most grateful to Patrice Nectoux, the Canadian Embassy diplomat in Cairo who made all this possible for us. We are always looking ahead for a better tomorrow. At the same time, I look forward to the time when I will have the opportunity to return to Liberia one day and contribute to its socioeconomic development efforts.

REFERENCES

- American University in Cairo, History of. URL.http//www.aucegypt.edu. Retrieved February 2011

- Bard, Mitchell. *Middle East Conflict*. Alpha Books: Indianapolis, 1999.

- Bates, Robert H. *Market and States in Tropical Africa: the Political Basis of Agriculture*. U of California Press: Berkeley and Los Angeles, 1981, 2005.

- Berkeley, Bill. *The Graves are not yet Full: Race, Tribe and Power in the Heart of Africa*. Basic Books: New York, 2001.

- Carey, Robert C. Brief History of the Liberian Army, The. http://newliberian.com. January 2008. Retrieved March 4, 2014

- Citizenship and Immigration Canada. "Canada welcomes highest number of legal immigrants in 50 years while taking action to maintain the integrity of Canada's immigration system." http://www.cic.gc.ca/english/development/media/released. **2011-2013/asp. Retrieved July 1, 2013** .

- Clarke, John Henrik. *Malcolm X: The Man and His Times*. Africa World Press Inc. Trenton, NJ, 1990.

- Dickerson, Mark O and Thomas Flanagan. *An Introduction to Government and Politics: A Conceptual Approach*. Nelson Canada: Scarborough, 1990.

- Dolo, Emmanuel. *Democracy versus Dictatorship: the Quest for Freedom and Justice in Africa's Oldest Republic*. Rowman and Littlefield Publishers: Avenel, NJ, USA. 1996.

- Easterly, William. *The Elusive Quest for Growth: Economists' Adventure and Misadventures in the Tropics*. MIT Press: Cambridge, 2001.

- Ellis, Stephen. *The Mask of Anarchy: The Destruction of Liberia and the Religious Dimension of an African Civil War*. New York U Press: New York, 1999.

- Ero, Comfort. "Sierra Leone's Security Complex: Working Papers". The Conflict Security & Development Group. Kings College. London, 2000.

- Fourah Bay College. Brief History of. URL. http://www.fbc.usl.edu.sl/history.html Retrieved January 5, 2012.

- Francis, Douglas R and Donald B. Smith. *Readings in Canadian History Post-Confederation 3rd ed.* Holt, Rinehart and Winston: Toronto, 1990.

- Gbardy, Jerry. "Open Letter to President Bush". The Perspective. 2002. www.theperspective.org. Retrieved on February 10, 2013.

- Goodwin-Gill, Guy S. *The Refugee in International Law.* Oxford: Claredon, 1983.

- Karmo, Henry. "Most Corrupt-National Integrity Barometer rates Liberia's Judiciary." www.frontpageafricaonline.com. December 20, 2013. Retrieved on December 23, 2013.

- Kromah, Alhaji. Statement Presented at the Truth and Reconciliation Commission. Monrovia. August 11, 2008.(www.alhajikromahpage.org). Retrieved on September 5, 2012.

- Lamb, David. *The Africans.* Vintage Books: New York, 1987.

- _____. *The Arabs: Journeys beyond the Mirage.* Vintage Books: New York, 1987, 2002.

- Liebenow, Gus J. *Liberia: The Quest for Democracy.* Indiana U. Press: Bloomington, Indiana, 1987.

- Nimba County Development Agenda. Population by Districts. http://www.emansion.gov.lr/doc/ Nimbacda.pdf. Retrieved on March 8, 2014

- Nyanue, William. *Witness: The hand of God in the Liberian Civil War.* Professional Press: Chapel Hill, 2005.

- Office of the Embassy of the Peoples Republic of China in the Republic of Liberia. "Unemployment Rate in Liberia Hits 80% .http://lr2mofcom.gov.cn/article/chinanews/20072007. Retrieved on October 1, 2013

- Poe, Edgar Allen (1983). "The Cask of Amontillado". Philadelphia, PA. Running Press. eBook. Retrieved on October 20, 2013.

- Ray, Debraj. *Development Economics.* Princeton U Press: Princeton, 1998.

- Schwab, Peter. *Africa: A Continent Self-Destructs.* Palgrave Press: New York, 2001.

- Sirleaf, Ellen Johnson. *This Child Will Be Great: Memoir of a Remarkable Life.* Harper Collins Publishers: New York, 2009.

- Todaro, Michael P & Stephen C. Smith. *Economic Development 9th Ed.* Addison-Wesley: Boston, San Francisco, New York, 2006.

- UNHCR. *Collection of International Instruments Concerning*

Painful Journey: a Story of Escape and Survival

Refugees and Others of Concern to UNHCR. Vol. 1, June 2007.

- US State Department Country Report on Human Rights Practices in Liberia 1998. http://www.state.gov. Retrieved on June 5, 2012.

- Youboty, James. *A Nation in Terror: A True Story of the Liberian Civil War.* Parkside Impressions Enterprise: Philadelphia, 1993, 2004.

- Os aspis molorumquas sum, nem reperist, qui que siti corem quianda nduciusam sit qui dolorerum ut accaborerat et, sitae nitatec aboribusci quias sita int aut et ommolup taturi occus dipsam, sustorem qui culpa voloresto inctam eiusci commolor rempost lant inci blab in re nullest ruptatem rehendi ssint, volupta tinvenitis dolorestin nestionsed ma quid maximendus ea delit, quidiore, sam ium facerspis mi, odi volluptur?

- Ximenimendi tem velit is modit ma soluptatia vollorum susam, utent eum quas accus dollicid qui quunt odi quos rerrumque peribusaerum fugitas vidererum reperum quianimaio. Ovide delectem idit accum fugitas pelitatem nis prorese corro voluptatem everae volore custrum seditatem elesse nonsequis porrorem re sit debitaectem aut quam, volorecae laborro ipistiam conem quatiis sanducias volores trunti re ad ma eicatem. Ditis nes rehendias si dolum rere pre, nis nonsenitas que et officid eosanihil mint as plandio reperfe rsperis aut porerrorepro eum reptur? Qui voluptatiis ipsum fuga. Cum nulliquatur?

- Laccumquae nessunt quis eos sam, omnimin velento con ped et repel imendanim venditi orerchi citatio nseque elignis volum rerum,

CPSIA information can be obtained at www.ICGtesting.com
Printed in the USA
LVOW12s1605101014

408100LV00001BB/20/P